Douglas Sirk, Aesthetic Modernism and the Culture of Modernity

Douglas Sirk, Aesthetic Modernism and the Culture of Modernity

Victoria L. Evans

EDINBURGH
University Press

Edinburgh University Press is one of the leading university presses in
the UK. We publish academic books and journals in our selected subject
areas across the humanities and social sciences, combining cutting-
edge scholarship with high editorial and production values to produce
academic works of lasting importance. For more information visit our
website: edinburghuniversitypress.com

© Victoria L. Evans, 2017

Edinburgh University Press Ltd
The Tun – Holyrood Road
12 (2f) Jackson's Entry
Edinburgh EH8 8PJ

Typeset in Garamond MT Pro by
Servis Filmsetting Ltd, Stockport, Cheshire

A CIP record for this book is available from the British Library

ISBN 978 1 4744 0939 1 (hardback)
ISBN 978 1 4744 0940 7 (webready PDF)
ISBN 978 1 4744 0941 4 (epub)
ISBN 978 1 4744 5202 1 (paperback)

The right of Victoria L. Evans to be identified as author of this work has
been asserted in accordance with the Copyright, Designs and Patents
Act 1988 and the Copyright and Related Rights Regulations 2003
(SI No. 2498).

Contents

List of Figures	vi
Acknowledgements	vii
Introduction	1

PART ONE SIRK AND THE VISUAL ARTS
1. Thinking with the Heart: Sirk and Pictorial Reception — 13
2. Concerning the Spiritual in Art: *Magnificent Obsession* and the Influence of Modernist Painting — 34

PART TWO THE SHOCK OF THE NEW: TRACES OF MODERNITY
3. The Invasion of Machines and Machine Culture — 65
4. *Imitation of Life* and the Depiction of Suburban Space — 88

PART THREE TWO ARCHITECTURAL CASE STUDIES
5. *Final Chord* and '*Die Neue Welt*': The Mise-en-scène of *Aufbruch* — 115
6. Back to the Future: Modernist Architecture and *All That Heaven Allows* — 147

Bibliography	179
Index	191

Figures

I.1	Charles and Ray Eames, DCW Chair, 1947	2
I.2	Le Corbusier, Original Sketch, representing a view of Rio, for the book *La Maison des hommes*, c.1942	3
1.1	Naomi gazing at her family through the screen door in *All I Desire*	16
2.1	Edward Randolph painting in his studio in *Magnificent Obsession*	38
2.2	Picasso painting included in a John Stuart Inc. furniture advertisement	48
3.1	Roger and Laverne Schumann's reconciliation in *The Tarnished Angels*	68
4.1	Frankie's brutal beating of Sarah Jane in *Imitation of Life*	104
5.1	Willi Baumeister, *The Dwelling* (1927)	135
6.1	Illustration of Frank Lloyd Wright's Falling Water in *House Beautiful*	153
6.2	Looking through the window of the Old Mill in *All That Heaven Allows*	155
6.3	Drawing of the Old Mill before renovation	160
6.4	Drawing of the Old Mill during renovation	161
6.5	Drawing of the Old Mill after renovation	161

Acknowledgements

I am grateful to the many people who have provided me with intellectual or emotional support during the long process of bringing this highly interdisciplinary project to fruition. In particular, I would like to thank Stephanie Bröge, Catherine Fowler, Alistair Fox, David Gerstner, Ross Gibson, Gillian Leslie, Sally Milner, Hilary Radner, Bettina Senff and Erika Wolf. Since some of my insights have been grounded in the information that is contained in a number of unpublished documents, I would especially like to thank the two archivists who assisted me in finding them, Ned Comstock of the Doheny Library's Department of Special Collections (University of Southern California, Los Angeles) and the late Charles Silver (Museum of Modern Art, New York). My long-suffering partner, Michael Robertson, deserves a special mention for his unwavering faith in my ability to complete this project and his abiding love, which I have crossed two oceans to keep.

Finally, I would like to dedicate this book to the memory of three people who will always be important to me: Zdenka Volavka, who first sparked my interest in aesthetic Modernism at York University (Toronto), Joseph Camacho, a documentary maker who taught me that film could be an instrument for social good, and my mother, Betty Louise Evans.

Introduction

In a 1994 interview entitled 'Beyond Cinema', Peter Greenaway spoke of his growing frustration at having to work within the spatial and temporal constraints imposed by the two-hour-long narrative film. By erecting one hundred staircases topped with viewing platforms all across the city of Geneva for an art exhibition that was scheduled to last one hundred days, he was endeavouring to 'take the concept of the frame out of cinema and place it in a more public situation' allowing for the possibility of a '24-hour continual viewfinder'.[1] Greenaway's project has been read as a meditation on the death of cinema, but Laura Mulvey would subsequently contend that their later digital incarnation had brought many older films back to life.[2] She observes that this convergence of old and new technologies, which enables the 'pensive' viewer to suspend the moving image for further examination, inevitably fragments the 'traditionally linear structure of the narrative'.[3] During these moments of willed repose, the spectator may trace the many cultural referents that the film encodes beyond the frame, pursuing them through 'multiple possible channels' that include 'personal memory', 'textual analysis' and 'historical research'.[4] However, more than four decades before Greenaway's urban installation or the advent of the digital age, Douglas Sirk was already attempting to dissolve the limits of the cinematic medium by assimilating elements of avant-garde art, architecture and design into the mise-en-scène of many of his best-known films.

Sirk's importation of a high art aesthetic into the low genre of melodrama echoed the widespread European Modernist preoccupation with the creation of a synergistic *Gesamtkunstwerk* or 'total art work' during the period in which he intellectually came of age.[5] In fact, it was the fluidity of this cross-medium synchronisation and exchange that immediately struck me the first time I saw his 1953 'woman's weepie' *Magnificent Obsession*. Visible just behind Helen Phillips' head as a doctor in a Swiss neuropathology institute is telling her that she will probably never see again is the back panel of one of the most famous chairs to have been designed in the post-World War II era: a black version of Charles and Ray Eames' moulded plywood DCW (Dining Chair Wooden, Figure I.1).[6] For the full duration of this sequence, one or more of

Figure I.1 Charles and Ray Eames, DCW Chair, 1947.
Source: Photograph by the Eames Office, courtesy of the Herman Miller Archives

these skittish-looking mid-century Modernist masterpieces may be observed alongside the blind woman's face or body almost every time she appears in the frame. By the final scene of the film, when the ailing widow's health and sight have been miraculously restored in a white-walled room that was often suffused with a very non-naturalistic blue light, I was utterly intrigued. What is the meaning of these intimations of an extra-filmic artistic vanguard when they have been embedded within the mise-en-scène of a mass-marketed Hollywood film? Given the director's detailed knowledge of some of the most ground-breaking contemporary movements in the visual arts (something that Jon Halliday's interviews makes clear), the inclusion of such important Modernist objects, colours and settings in a work of such heightened artifice appeared to be no simple coincidence.

Moreover, the windows of the austere International Style hospital in which Helen Philips' life-saving operation takes place also reveal the rugged hills of the New Mexico desert that surround it (the home of such pioneering American abstract artists as Georgia O'Keeffe and the Transcendental Painting Group).[7] The planar 'pictures' of the landscape that we glimpse through this key building's gridiron glazing (along with the similar views of the New England countryside that may be seen from the interior of the Old Mill in *All That Heaven Allows*) recall a series of drawings that Le Corbusier

Figure I.2 Le Corbusier, Original Sketch, representing a view of Rio, for the book *La Maison des hommes*, c.1942.
Source: Fondation Le Corbusier archives B3(3)227 © FLC/DACS 2017

made for his 1942 publication *La Maison des hommes* (Figure I.2). Beginning with a gestural sketch of Rio de Janeiro's Sugar Loaf Mountain, the architect deepens our contemplation of this familiar landmark by first installing a surrogate spectator seated in an armchair in front of it, then further emphasising the selected perspective by enclosing it within the rigid geometry of a typical early twentieth-century European Modernist window. The rectangular pattern formed by the slender mullions operates as a focusing device that fixes and concentrates the viewer's attention in order to enhance his or her apprehension of the prospect under scrutiny.[8] Or as Le Corbusier noted in the caption that was attached to this drawing in the 1948 English translation of his book, 'the four obliques of a perspective' delineated by the large glass wall that has been placed 'before the site' not only make it more apparent but also manage to conduct 'the whole sea-landscape' into the adjacent room.[9] In other words, the framing of the selected vista channels the viewer's perception outward beyond the limits of this interior, before bringing the outside in due to the intensely empathetic connections that we have made.[10] While this moment of revelation does involve the projection of the observer's thoughts and feelings onto the external topography to some degree, it also implies a reciprocal willingness to open oneself up to the transcendent experiences and unknown geographies that lie beyond the borders of the depicted space. Although the separation provided by the window frame at least partially preserves the autonomy of the pre-existing terrain, this was not meant to provoke a sense of alienation in the viewer; rather, it encourages us to reorient ourselves in relation to this condensed image of a different reality that we now perceive with an even greater clarity. After having been prompted by the architecture to reflect upon a significant aspect of the exterior landscape, the spectator is irrevocably changed by this encounter too.

When they have been considered in this light, the apertures, grids, drapes, screens and vortices that are a prominent feature of Sirk's mise-en-scène also often seem to offer a spiritual or intellectual template for a deeper meditation on some sort of alternative world.[11] Moreover, the kind of concentration that these compositional schemas tend to induce generates a state of sympathetic attention in the observer that combines emotional engagement with more thoughtful deliberations. By framing a person or setting in a mirror or window or flooding them with a series of evocative non-objective colours, the director appears to be providing us with felt insights into his characters' motivations and dilemmas that we are then expected to apply to our own lives.[12] Like the German Expressionist paintings that had so inspired him at the beginning of his theatrical career, Sirk's best melodramas are almost always attempting to convey a political, moral or social transformation that would not necessarily remain confined to the screen. After viewing the mentally and emotionally charged scenes of these films through the intensifying lenses supplied by the director, the more sensitive members of the audience might well be persuaded to reflect upon and modify their own existing beliefs, ideas and communities too. As would have been the case with many of their original viewers, Sirk's melodramas have taken me on a journey to a number of destinations that I could never have imagined when I began to research this highly interdisciplinary study.

Douglas Sirk, Aesthetic Modernism and the Culture of Modernity has been based in an extensive investigation of nine of this director's most pivotal films, *Final Chord* (1936), *Has Anyone Seen My Gal?* (1951), *All I Desire* (1953), *Magnificent Obsession* (1953), *All That Heaven Allows* (1954), *There's Always Tomorrow* (1955), *Written on the Wind* (1956), *The Tarnished Angels* (1957) and *Imitation of Life* (1959), though other titles will be mentioned in passing. It is divided into three parts ('Sirk and the Visual Arts', 'The Shock of the New: Traces of Modernity' and 'Two Architectural Case Studies'), each of which contains two chapters that address interconnected themes or subject matter. Chapter 1 ('Thinking with the Heart: Sirk and Pictorial Reception') analyses some of the still moments of contemplation that have been built into the director's most striking *tableaux* in relation to three distinct models of pictorial reception (two of which were contributed by Michael Fried, one by Alois Riegl). These art-historical models of spectatorship will also be linked with current research on the film viewer's affective response to melodrama to some degree. A chapter that explores the influence of particular schools of painting on Sirk's mise-en-scène in greater detail follows this general discussion of the impact of the aesthetic object upon the observer. Chapter 2 ('Concerning the Spiritual in Art: *Magnificent Obsession* and the Language of Modernist Painting') begins with a reading of this film that has been partially guided by the theories of the pioneering German Expressionist artist Wassily Kandinsky. Sirk had deliberately tried to paint in this revolutionary style while he was still living in Germany, but his wide-ranging familiarity with Modernist art also extended to Surrealism. The latter aesthetic approach is actually adopted by two of the major characters in *Has Anybody Seen My Gal?*, a film that presents a vision of small-town American life during the 1920s in which an acceptance of avant-garde painting was already commonplace. This is not to say that the director has emptied these two radical artistic movements of their original rebellious intent; rather, the Expressionist or Surrealist inflections that are evinced in Sirk's mise-en-scène often underscore the anti-materialist critique of contemporary bourgeois society that runs through much of his work.[13]

Part Two of this book addresses the psychic ambivalence that is frequently elicited by the new technologies have had such a profound impact on Western culture during the twentieth century. Chapter 3 ('The Invasion of Machines and Machine Culture') builds upon Ben Singer's observation in *Melodrama and Modernity* that this genre makes manifest the spectator's growing fear of the machines that have increasingly infiltrated our space. It further expands upon this insight by moving beyond the widespread feelings of unease Singer identifies to address some of the more specific pathologies that arose from the mechanisation of war. This chapter culminates in an explication of *The Tarnished Angels* that is grounded in Ernst Jünger's paeans to the hard-bodied men who were forged in the furnace of battle, widely circulated writings that the German-born director would no doubt have known. After some discussion of the influence of the automobile on the shape of the twentieth-century American city, Chapter 4 ('*Imitation of Life* and the Depiction of Suburban Space') contrasts John Stahl's 1934 adaptation with Sirk's 1959 cinematic version of Fanny Hurst's best-selling 1933 novel. Among other things, this comparison shows how the director has inscribed the 'colour line' that divided African-Americans from whites after World War II into Lora Meredith's leafy suburb in the later remake. The historically informed interpretation of the built environment that supports this conclusion also establishes the unifying framework for Part Three, which consists of two architectural case studies that are each devoted to one crucial motion picture.

Chapter 5 ('*Final Chord* and "*Die Neue Welt*": The Mise-en-Scène of *Aufbruch*') examines the only film from Sirk's German period to depict twentieth-century urban life. In the prologue that the director added to the existing script, two antithetical aesthetics seem to reveal the philosophical and political disparities that distinguish a democratic New York from a Fascist Berlin. Because the architectural symbolism of these cities may be read from both a Modernist and a National Socialist point of view, after outlining several of the main arguments on either side I will then attempt to determine which metropolis offers the most desirable 'New World' of the future. Finally, since every stage of Ron Kirby and Carey Scott's relationship is marked by alterations in their domestic interiors, Chapter 6 ('Back to the Future: Modernist Architecture and *All That Heaven Allows*') explores some of the divergent social and cultural connotations that have been encoded into their respective homes. For instance, the final incarnation of the Old Mill evokes Le Corbusier's Machine Age villas of the 1920s, which dissents from the dominant mid-century view of the ideal home by suggesting a much less materialistic way of living. In an age where the rising tide of environmental degradation will only be stemmed if the wealthier nations can reduce their current preoccupation with mass production and consumption, we still have much to learn from this prescient director.

Notes

1. Torsten Beyer and Sabine Danek, 'Beyond Cinema', *Sight and Sound*, 4, No. 7 (July 1994, Special Supplement entitled *Art into Film*), 18.
2. Laura Mulvey, *Death 24x a Second: Stillness and the Moving Image* (London: Reaktion

Books, 2006), 21. According to Mulvey, the rebirth of historical cinema began in 1997 when the 'first marketing of film on digital format' took place (p. 18).
3. Mulvey, 186, 26.
4. Mulvey, 26.
5. The term '*Gesamtkunstwerk*'was originally associated with Wagnerian opera, but in an essay entitled 'On Stage Composition' [published in *The Blaue Reiter Almanac* (New York: Da Capo, 1974 English translation of the 1914 German edition), 195–7] Wassily Kandinsky argued that the libretto was still given too much prominence in the famous nineteenth-century composer's work. The revolutionary German Expressionist painter believed that the characters' inner experience would only be revealed if the director in charge of the staging emphasised colour, pictorial form and a less mimetic orchestral score to the same degree as the sung or spoken text, thus creating a truly synthetic, not to mention synaesthetic, 'total art work'. Since Kandinsky's writings were hugely influential (especially in Germany), Sirk would probably have been familiar with this essay as well as with the artist's highly abstract theatrical pieces, such as 'The Yellow Sound' (also included in *The Blaue Reiter Almanac*).

Of course, Sirk began his post-university career as a theatrical director during the 1920s and contemporary reviews of some of his *Bremen Schauspielhaus* productions seem to indicate that he had already achieved this kind of interdisciplinary fusion. One critic noted that the director had managed to bring out 'every suggestive modulation' of Strindberg's *Dreamplay* by translating it into 'colour, rhythm and tone, until from the string of successive scenes emerged the grand symbol of a spiritual line, which gave to the poet's visions the metaphysical expansiveness of the imagination' [quoted by Thomas Elsaesser in 'Documents on Sirk: With a Postscript by Thomas Elsaesser', *Screen*, 12, No. 2 (1971), 22]. In order to communicate the full extent of the playwright's commingling of fantasy and reality, Sirk made use of the combined attributes of drama, music, dance-like motion and painting (in coloured light) in his staging. Even after the director had taken refuge in the film world after the Nazis closed down his Leipzig production of Georg Kaiser and Kurt Weill's *The Silver Lake* in 1933, he continued to emphasise the fact that many different media contributed to the realisation of his cinematic projects. During one of his many interviews with Jon Halliday, Sirk insisted upon adopting the European definition of his preferred Hollywood genre, describing it as a combination of *melos* (music) and drama. See Elsaesser's 'Documents on Sirk' (pp. 19–20) and Jon Halliday's *Sirk on Sirk* (London: Faber & Faber, rev. 1997 edn), 27–30, 107–9.
6. Joseph Giovanni has credited Ray Eames (who studied with Hans Hoffman in New York and whose sculptures reflect the biomorphic shapes of Surrealism) with creating the sensitively sculpted contours of this innovative bent plywood chair. According to Giovanni, Charles Eames mainly provided the technical expertise that enabled its delicately curved profile to be realised. See his 'The Office of Charles Eames and Ray Kaiser: The Material Trail' in *The Work of Charles and Ray Eames: A Legacy of Invention*, ed. Diana Murphy (New York: Harry

Abrams, 1997), 45–71. In the July 1949 issue of the American design magazine *Interiors* [108, No. 12] George Nelson described the Eames chair as a 'total design package, integrating new techniques with modern art forms into a unified design that, perhaps more than any other, symbolizes "modern furniture"' (p. 99).

7. By contrast, this climactic operation takes place in a hospital in Rome in Lloyd C. Douglas's original book, after Helen has been injured in a train wreck while touring Italy. See his *Magnificent Obsession* (London: Allen & Unwin, 1952 repr. of the 1936 British edn), 295. While Georgia O' Keeffe's ineffable New Mexican desert landscapes are widely known, the Transcendental Painting Group (formed in 1938) also hoped to foster a 'more intense preoccupation with the life of the spirit' through the creation of completely non-objective works of art. Inspired by the writings of Wassily Kandinsky, they believed that 'painting that . . . [went] beyond the appearance of the physical world' would enable them to enter 'imaginative realms that are idealistic and spiritual'. See Gail Levin and Marianne Lorenz, *Theme and Improvisation: Kandinsky and the American Avant-garde 1912–1950* (Boston: Little, Brown, 1992), 88–9. I will later argue that this combination of European Modernist architecture with an unspoilt, spiritually charged American setting is highly significant.

8. In an essay that was published in 1933, Le Corbusier proclaimed that only by harnessing the revelatory potential of technically enhanced or expanded vision would 'The Spirit of Truth' be attained. He went on to attribute the superior perspicacity of the camera (*'this eye [that] sees differently from our own'*) to the fact that it is not 'deluged' by the 'the simultaneous presence of other [sensory] impressions intervening at the same moment'. See page 112 of 'The Spirit of Truth' in *French Film Theory and Criticism, Volume 2 – 1929–1939*, ed. Richard Abel (Princeton: Princeton University Press, 1988). Sirk expressed a similar belief in his 1977 interview with Michael Stern: 'Critics never see as much as the camera does. It is more perceptive than the human eye.' See 'Sirk Speaks'. Available at <http://www.brightlightsfilm.com/48/sirkinterview.htm> (last accessed 17 October 2005).

9. Le Corbusier and Françoise de Pierrefeu, *The Home of Man* (London: Architectural Press, 1948), 87.

10. The equality implied by the configuration of the window separating the inside from the outside in the final drawing suggests that nature is just as important a component in this equation as the stripped-down Modernist building from which it is being observed. The intellectual and emotional enrichment that might result from this respectful coexistence no doubt sparked Le Corbusier's desire to go 'where order is coming out of the natural dialogue between man and nature, out of the struggle for life, out of the enjoyment of leisure under the open sky, in the passing of the seasons, the song of the sea'. See page 6 of his *The Radiant City* (London: Faber & Faber), which is the English translation of the 1933 French text *La Ville Radieuse*.

11. I would like to thank Ross Gibson for helping me to clarify my thoughts on this matter.

12. As I discuss at greater length in the second chapter of this book, the pioneering German Expressionist painter Wassily Kandinsky believed that colour had a direct psychic effect on sensitive viewers that could 'communicate itself immediately to the soul'. See his *Concerning the Spiritual in Art* (New York: Dover, 1977), 25.
13. See, for example, *Final Chord* (1936), *La Habanera* (1937), *Has Anyone Seen My Gal?* (1951), *No Room for the Groom* (1952), *Magnificent Obsession* (1953), *All That Heaven Allows* (1954), *Written on the Wind* (1956) and *Imitation of Life* (1959).

Part One

Sirk and the Visual Arts

CHAPTER ONE

Thinking with the Heart: Sirk and Pictorial Reception

As one way of initiating the process of re-examining Sirk's cinematic corpus in terms of a broader examination of the relationship between art and film, I will briefly summarise Michael Fried's influential analysis of the two fundamentally different ways in which a pictorial object may attempt to address its 'beholder', since this seems to me to have some bearing on the current scholarship on melodrama. In particular, many '1950s family melodramas' have been portrayed as either totally incorporating the viewer's grief-stricken body (Fried's concept of 'absorption') or as precluding the viewer's psychological entry into the depicted space (the countervailing notion of 'theatricality'). Sirk's contributions to this genre have often been consigned to the latter category (due to the so-called 'Brechtian' alienation effect that is said to result from their formal stylisation). Yet neither of these polarities can fully encompass the complexity of the spectator's response to this director's best works, which more closely resembles a third model of aesthetic reception that was proposed by the Viennese art historian Alois Riegl during the late nineteenth century.[1]

Fried has traced the origin of the opposition between 'absorption' and 'theatricality' back to the eighteenth-century Salons of Denis Diderot. According to the prominent American scholar, Diderot claimed that if the figures within a contemporary picture 'seemed by virtue of the character of their actions and expressions to evince even a partial consciousness of being beheld', then their gestures would not be perceived as 'natural signs of intention or emotion, but merely as ... feignings' that were calculated to deceive the audience.[2] In other words, the viewer would only be convinced of the truth of the depicted events if each of the dramatis personae seemed 'engross[ed] or absorb[ed] in their actions and states of mind ... oblivious of everything but the object of his or her own absorption, as if to all intents and purposes there were nothing and no one else in the world'.[3] Paradoxically, this insistence upon 'an absolute discontinuity between actors and beholders, representation and audience' may actually heighten the spectator's response to the painting by transforming it into a quasi-corporeal experience.[4] In other words, by sealing these compositions off from the viewer's own physical surroundings, the artist is encouraging us to psychologically project ourselves into the depicted setting. Hence, Diderot described one of the landscapes he was reviewing in the Salon of 1765 as if he had suddenly materialised inside this fictitious terrain. At one point he remarked, 'I actually find myself there, [standing in the middle ground of Jean-Baptiste Le Prince's *Pastorale Russe*], [and] I shall remain leaning against this tree, between this old man and this young girl, as long as the boy plays [on his flute].'[5]

In a sharp contrast with this 'absorptive' strategy of seeking to neutralise the beholder by embedding him or her within the painting itself is the more modern understanding of 'theatricality', which Fried associates with the groundbreaking work of Edouard Manet. For example, in both *Le Déjeuner sur l'herbe* and *Olympia* a naked Parisian *cocotte* stares insolently out at the viewer in what appears to be a direct acknowledgement of the adjacent public space. Fried interprets this illusion breaking gaze as indicating that by the middle of the nineteenth century the spectator's existence could no longer be denied, which meant that his or her presence had to be established more abstractly by 'building into the [image] the separateness, distancedness, and mutual facing that had always characterised the painting–beholder relationship'.[6] The viewer soon recognises that we are not meant to psychologically enter into these pictures, since this pivotal figure's rather disconcerting look has mapped out a place for us that lies beyond their borders.

Nevertheless, Sirk's melodramas tend to dissolve the boundary between corporeal 'absorption' and the more detached 'theatricality' that Fried has attributed to certain quite specific historical epochs. Many of these films continue to forge a genuine connection with the viewer, even if their apparent stylisation prompts an immediate re-evaluation of this emotional appeal. Hence, I would argue that the sense of reflexivity that is generated by Sirk's non-naturalistic use of colour, highly mobile camerawork and complex compositions and framing evokes Alois Riegl's more humane notion of 'attentiveness' rather than the distanciation that Fried has ascribed to Manet. According to the Austrian art historian, when the characters commemorated in a seventeenth-century Dutch group portrait gaze outward at the viewer (or viewers, since the constituent figures often glance in different directions) the painter's intention was never to brutally unmask the beholder. Rather than simply shattering the reality effect, this reciprocal scrutiny suggests the empathetic mutual engagement that had been made possible by the development of a more egalitarian *communitas*. Within this circumambient space, neither the external onlooker nor the depicted civic guards ('made up of free citizens who enjoyed equal rights and joined the group of their own accord to support a common purpose') are portrayed as being subordinate to one another.[7] While this interrelationship might be charged with a greater or lesser emotional intensity (depending upon the historical period), it implied both a respectful regard for the spectator and an unwillingness to dominate one's environment through an exaggerated physical response.

It was for this reason that the Netherlands lacked a grand tradition of history painting, or so Riegl claimed in the introduction to this landmark contribution to reception aesthetics. In his carefully considered view, choosing to specialise in more quotidian artistic modalities such as portraiture, landscape or genre painting allowed for 'the complete suppression of any external action or at least the displacement of physical movement by certain psychological aspects of the action'.[8] Unlike 'the Italian work of art [in which] action is always the result of an act of will', even in the earliest Dutch group portraits Riegl almost always found a 'psychological interaction among the figures, so that emotion and attentiveness play a more important role than will'. He then went on to declare that 'these are qualities that become apparent after a process of reflection that we only associate with Northern Europeans'.[9]

This distinction between the contemplative stillness of Northern paintings and the action oriented compositions of their Italian equivalent is echoed in Sirk's description of the most salient trait that distinguishes melodrama from more typical Hollywood genres. In a 1978 interview with Jean-Claude Biette and Dominique Rabourdin, the director noted that American films were generally impelled by a series of dynamic events in which the Manichaean clash between good and evil is physically enacted. By contrast, he observed that melodrama was concerned with the production of emotion rather than action, although the dramatisation of this psychological struggle could almost be considered a kind of action 'that takes place inside the person'.[10] Sirk then pointed out that in *All I Desire*, a film that revolves around a middle-aged actress's return to her small town family home ten years after running away from a scandal, very little overt physical action actually occurs.[11]

After the director had suggested that this 1953 melodrama underscored the 'transition from theatre to cinema', Rabourdin rather astutely remarked, 'the house [in *All I Desire*] is filmed [just] like a theatre'. For example, when Naomi (played by Barbara Stanwyck) turns up the path and walks towards her husband's Colonial Revival home, the camera momentarily glides away in order to reveal the full expanse of the building's façade. From this perspective, in which the flatness of the front elevation has been aligned with the picture plane and virtually fills the screen, Henry's pristine dwelling recalls the painted backdrops that would have been a prominent feature of his wife's vaudeville career.[12] This fascination with theatricality is further underscored by Naomi's behaviour when she arrives at the main entrance of her husband's residence. Although the estranged mother soon discovers that a key was still being left for her in a nearby basket of flowers, she could not bring herself

Figure 1.1 Naomi gazing at her family through the screen door in *All I Desire*.

to cross the threshold of the family home after such a lengthy absence. Consequently, Naomi mimics the behaviour of the audience watching one of her performances, lingering on the veranda and gazing through the screen door as if it were a proscenium arch (Figure 1.1). Yet her view of Henry Murdoch and their three children from this position is much too remote, as well as being somewhat obstructed by the intricate framing that holds the wire mesh in place. The perspective from the adjacent window will prove to be even less satisfying, since the visual barrier formed by the wooden mullions occludes Naomi's vision of the interior even further.

The fact that the editing of this sequence forces the spectator to share the prodigal wife and mother's sense of unfulfilled yearning must also be stressed. As Naomi moves slowly towards the house in the grip of an almost trance-like reverie, the camera tracks backwards in tandem with this motion, sustaining a very telling close-up on her face for an additional several seconds. Despite the relative immobility of the actress's iconic countenance, Barbara Stanwyck (who Sirk once described as an 'astonishing' performer) manages to convey the paradoxical impression of being at once lost in reflection and stirred by powerful sentiments.[13] In the tradition of the seventeenth-century Dutch group portraits that Riegl so admired, Stanwyck's face discloses an 'amazing tragic stillness' that the director would later ascribe to her great 'depth as a person'.[14] To paraphrase one of Rainer Werner Fassbinder's most illuminating comments on his older mentor's work, the women who are enmeshed in Sirk's cinematic narratives (including Naomi) seem to both *think* and feel.[15] Moreover, this double appeal to cognition and passion also describes the viewer's complex reaction to many of the latter director's best-known melodramas.

To return to the homecoming scene of *All I Desire*, when the camera reacts to Naomi's motion by tracking back with her towards the house it appears to be revealing the reciprocal 'flow of inspiration between camera and people' that Sirk had deemed so essential in his 1977 interview with Michael Stern. In other words, in choosing to 'lay out' camera movements that were justified by the trajectory of the actors and vice versa, the director is communicating his belief that 'the good camera is curious' and that it shares the audience's interest in the plight of the protagonists.[16] When these mobile shots have been combined with a series of close-ups in which Naomi's pensive face stands out against a relatively indeterminate ground, the viewer can't help but be affected by the pathos of her situation. Not only do we immediately notice the tears glistening in the errant woman's eyes (which automatically elicits the spectator's compassion), but also our initial perception of the interior of the Murdoch residence is restricted to her subjective point of view. Therefore, when Naomi's urge to see her family has been thwarted by the limitations of her original vantage point, the spectator's desire for further information is frustrated too.

For the moment, the possibility of any implied physical intervention has been suspended, as both actress and audience adopt the attitude of 'selfless attentiveness' that Alois Riegl had associated with Northern painting.[17] Moreover, by obliging us to watch Naomi's husband and children through the frame within a frame provided by the architectural setting, Sirk encourages the onlooker to initially register the Murdochs as a strictly optical phenomenon. As a result, this group of characters and their domestic environment have been translated into opsigns, an abstract form of modern cinematic vision that stands for 'perceptible thought' (to borrow Gilles Deleuze's terminology).[18] Although Naomi retains a strong emotional bond with the inhabitants of this particular internal space, her (and our) purely specular apprehension converts their depiction into a conceptual rendering of a typical turn-of-the-century American 'family'. In other words, after quietly scrutinising this example of the broader social institution from the outside, the ageing actress must decide whether the values that it represents are worth relinquishing her fading theatrical career for.[19]

Only after Naomi has circled around to a more private door that opens directly onto the dining room will she/we finally obtain a clearer glimpse of her spouse's interactions with each of their very different offspring. While the outline of the door and the shot/reverse shot editing continues to separate the tentative mother's space from the interior that she is observing, these parallel worlds appear to be communicating vessels that may yet be conjoined by the sheer intensity of her regard. From this much closer perspective, where the warmth that suffuses Henry's mildly ironic exchanges with their children becomes palpable, his wife's dormant affection for her husband will be revived.[20] That Naomi's love is reciprocated soon becomes evident when the Swedish housekeeper looks up and glances out of the frame, her eyes brimming with tears. The reverse shot discloses what Lena (and the rest of the family) have finally noticed, her old mistress (and their wife and mother) staring back at them through the transparent aperture of the side door. At last, we witness the sympathetic communion between the beholder and the beheld that provided the cornerstone for Riegl's interpretation of the seventeenth-century Dutch group portrait. Both the audience and the players are seen to return each other's gaze, studying one another with a passionate attachment that belies Michael Fried's too narrow definition of 'theatricality'.

I FROM THE HAPTIC AND OPTIC TO THE AFFECTIVE AND BRECHTIAN

For the pioneering Viennese art historian, as Gilles Deleuze and Laura Marks have both emphasised, ocular perception was at once visual and physiological, cerebral and visceral. In contrast with the inorganic instrumentality of Le Corbusier's camera-eye, Deleuze contends that Riegl's conception of corporeal vision is predicated upon a 'touching which is specific to the gaze'.[21] Marks arrives at a similar conclusion, asserting that in Riegl's 'haptic visuality the eyes themselves function as organs of touch', which means 'it involves the body more than is the case with optical visuality'.[22] Of course, many directors (including Sirk) have combined shots with compositions that are 'haptic' ('appeal[ing] to tactile connections on the surface plane') with shots that are arranged in accordance with an 'optical' system ('giv[ing] up its nature as a physical object in order to invite a distant view that allows the viewer to organize him/herself as an all-perceiving subject') in any given production.[23] Nevertheless, Linda Williams argued more than two decades ago that the film genre that Sirk most favoured (melodrama) primarily targeted the body, since it stimulated such a strong emotional response in the viewer that he or she would actually be provoked into shedding tears.[24] More recently, this eminent scholar has further refined her understanding of the viewer's sensory reaction to the cinematic text by importing some of Jonathan Crary's discoveries about the nineteenth-century observer into a consideration of pornography. As Williams has pointed out, Crary asserts that this period constituted an important watershed because a new understanding of embodied vision began to supplant the decorporealised optical theories that had previously been extrapolated from the mechanics of the *camera obscura*.

According to this classical model of seeing (which dominated scientific discourse from 'the late 1500s until the end of the 1700s'), the eye's reception of external images occurred independently of the other senses since it 'was [thought to be] sundered from the physical body of the observer'.[25] In the wake of Kant's landmark speculations on the subjectivity of human perception, however, optical research started to take into account the way in which the 'human body in all its contingency and specificity' inflects the individual's visual experience.[26] Williams would go on to claim that if vision could no longer be separated from this 'carnal density', then Laura Mulvey's or Jean-Louis Baudry's calls for an end to the spectator's sensory imbrication in the images that pass before us must necessarily be futile.[27] Yet the almost exclusive emphasis on physical embodiment in this essay neglects the other side of the equation, which is the important contribution made by mental cognition to the observer's understanding of a cinematic text.

That Sirk's films were intended to elicit both a sensory and a cerebral response from the viewer is confirmed in the extended series of interviews that he gave to Jon Halliday in 1970. In this introspective director's opinion, one of the most crucial discoveries that shaped his cinematic style was the realisation that camera 'motion equals emotion'.[28] Even before he had arrived at this critical insight, Sirk had already concluded that camera 'angles are the director's thoughts [and] the lighting is his philosophy'.[29] Moreover, he remained convinced that ideas should primarily be transmitted through images for the full duration of his filmmaking career, confiding to Halliday, 'long before Wittengstein, I and my contemporaries had learned to distrust language as a true medium and interpreter of reality'.[30]

Even though Sirk's discussion of 'cinema values' was meant to illustrate the ways in which they diverged from 'literary (or stage) values', his earlier theatrical productions at the Bremen *Schauspielhaus* appear to have been imbued with a similar intellectual and emotional resonance.[31] Contemporary reports of his staging technique highlight the intense symbolic charge of the mise-en-scène, which exposed the 'inner truth' animating that particular drama (whether it was by William Shakespeare or Bertolt Brecht). These productions were also said to have 'trembled with feeling, like inaudible music flowing warmly through the soul', due to their director's 'ability to weld the ensemble together' through his delicate orchestration of the visual elements.[32] Yet in Sirk's later assessments of his American corpus, he sometimes claimed that the stylised form and the manifest content of his films deliberately contradict one another, which means that an intellectual subtext undercuts the reading that is present 'on the surface'.[33] Although this was not the director's position while he was engaged in the process of making these films (as my subsequent analysis of *The Tarnished Angels* should show), some of the comments that were recorded in *Sirk on Sirk* seemed to advise the spectator to adopt an attitude of ironic detachment to his work.

Given Sirk's inside knowledge of early twentieth-century German theatre, such remarks prompted an influential group of scholars to interpret his non-naturalistic formal style as a Brechtian alienation device, which was intended to distance the more sophisticated viewer from the apparent storyline. Paul Willemen had articulated this judgement as early as 1971, asserting that 'there appeared to be a discrepancy between the audience that the director was aiming at [those who understood the ideas of the European avant-garde] and the audience which he knows will come to see his films [those who allowed themselves to be carried away by their emotions in response to the depicted events]'.[34] He would ultimately conclude that 'Sirk makes his films on two levels by superimposing on to the cinematic mode of representation (i.e. the duplication of the pre-filmic world) a rhetoric informed by the theatrical concepts and theories developed at the beginning of this century in Russia and Germany . . . [to deflate] an extremely smug, self-righteous and *petit bourgeois* world view'.[35] Ten years later, in his book on Hollywood film genres, Thomas Schatz repeated the now-canonical assumption that Sirk's 'baroque' family melodramas construct a hierarchically organised two-tiered audience, although now the segment that is in the 'know' was said to consist of more recent viewers. Schatz went on to state quite unequivocally that while '[Sirk's] *All That Heaven Allows* appears to us today as an obvious indictment of America's repressive, sexist, and materialistic middle class, indications are that its contemporary audiences and critics read the film as a straightforward love story'.[36]

In the review that was published in *The Hollywood Reporter* just after the film's original release, however, Jack Moffitt managed to draw up a very similar list of the social concerns that were touched upon in *All That Heaven Allows*. Describing the basic story as a 'well-done study of suburban snobbery', Moffit also specifically mentioned the lonely widow's vulnerability to the 'pawings of a weary wolf in the country club set', her tree-farming lover's admirable disdain for her money, and her grown-up children's despicable efforts to persuade their mother to deny her sexuality.[37] While the studio's summary of the response cards that were filled in by those who attended the preview screening contained few comments on the broader issues that were raised by the film, more detailed information is available on the audience's reaction to *Magnificent Obsession*.[38] *All That Heaven Allows* had in fact reunited Jane Wyman with Rock Hudson in an attempt to duplicate their previous melodrama's enormous box office success.[39] Also directed by Douglas Sirk for Universal-International Pictures and released during the summer of 1954, *Magnificent Obsession* had provided Rock Hudson with his first major starring role.

In his initial project with Wyman, Hudson was cast as a spoilt playboy called Bob Merrick who is inadvertently responsible for both a self-sacrificing doctor's death and his widow's subsequent blindness. According to an anonymous member of the test screening audience, part of the Merrick character's process of redemption will entail learning that there are 'things which you cannot buy with a check'. This was one of the surprisingly abstract ethical observations that had been elicited by the routine studio question 'Which scenes did you like the most?'.[40] While other respondents favoured scenes that were more action oriented ('Speedboat, lake, colour and crash', 'Automobile accident') or more connected with the love story ('The two of them together in Europe', 'Fireworks and folkdancing scene'), a significant subset preferred the scenes that were associated with Bob Merrick's moral regeneration ('Bob's talk near the beginning with Randolph [his artist mentor]', 'Rock Hudson's return to reality – things which you cannot buy with a check'). Consequently, even though the film's romantic subplot is undoubtedly important, the comments that were recorded at its inaugural showing should make us realise just how multi-faceted the reception of the contemporary audience actually was. If nothing else, these brief critiques of *Magnificent Obsession* appear to confirm that the 1950s spectator exercised his or her emotional *and* cognitive faculties in order to make sense of this director's anti-mimetic approach to his material. Therefore, it seems clear that Sirk's films often elicit both aesthetic contemplation and empathy (in accordance with the theories of Alois Riegl) and reason and passion (as Sergei Eisenstein had also demanded).[41]

Quite aside from the contempt for a large portion of the predominantly female audience that Willemen's so-called 'Sirkian system' represents, it also suggests a covert condemnation of Eisenhower's America that does not appear to be consistent with the express content of the films themselves.[42] In her detailed explication of *All That I Desire*, Lucy Fischer has vehemently denied that two alternative readings inform the narrative. To her mind (and mine), the director serves this 'satirical vision' of the repressive conformity of a small Midwestern town 'straight up', in a manner that is 'devoid of camp'. She goes on to say, 'What this means is that there is no need for the audience to decode the secret messages of excessive moments, or to read conservative themes "against the grain".'[43] Likewise, in 'seek[ing] to demonstrate that Sirk was more than a parodist' Anne Morey asserts that *Imitation of Life* was unmistakably 'a woman's picture and a social problem film'.[44] Consequently, the personal difficulties experienced by Lora's Meredith's black maid were also political, since Annie's negative treatment (and that of her daughter,

Sarah Jane) was grounded in 'the racism inherent in 1950s society'.[45] While the falsity of the central protagonist (an actress played by Lana Turner) is acknowledged within both the plot and the dialogue, Morey points out that this does not mean that Sirk's relation to the depicted events is equally insincere. She will eventually decide that 'the film does not ... ridicule its audience's taste for "weepies" as much as it serves to explore a truth that the studio system has typically hidden from view – namely that success has its price' in the tears that are shed by those whose love the aspiring actress has neglected.[46] To some extent, I will be arguing in the final chapter of this book that *All that Heaven Allows* offers an equally straightforward indictment of the selfishness, acquisitiveness and sexual hypocrisy of an increasingly stratified American society.

This is not to say that the director's Hollywood melodramas aren't also operating on several different levels, which I later hope to demonstrate by investigating some of the art and architectural codings that are woven into their mise-en-scène; but while in Willeman and Schatz's discursive model a heightened formal structure usually negates the surface meaning, my own analysis of Sirk's cinematic corpus seems to reveal that these two aspects of his films generally reinforce one another. In other words, even though the director's self-conscious use of architecture, lighting, composition and colour often refers to an external high art aesthetic, these additional symbolic layers tend to deepen and reflect social observations that have already been made available to the viewer through the content of the narrative.[47] If, as Linda Williams contends, American melodramas 'share the common function of revealing moral good in a world where virtue has become hard to read', Sirk's most expressive visual flourishes serve to enhance rather than detract from this 'search for moral legibility'.[48]

Williams also asserted that melodramas almost always merge 'morality and feeling' in order to convey something of the typical victim-hero's 'felt good[ness]' to the viewer.[49] To my mind, many of Sirk's most important contributions to this genre still invoke the genuine pathos that is its most fundamental trait. Not even the most 'highbrow' spectator, whose intellect has been sparked by the director's sophisticated dialogue with the visual arts, could be expected to eschew every trace of sentiment as Brechtian interpretations of these works had once assumed. As Sirk told Peter Lehmann in 1980, 'you can't move masses by [appealing exclusively to the brain with] abstract thinking ... You have to move [the audience into becoming emotionally involved with politics by learning to] think with the heart.'[50] Consequently, in the director's view, it is precisely this ability to generate powerful feelings of outrage, pity or regret in the spectator that might actually inspire him or her to break free from an inequitable status quo. Who could fail to be moved by the terrible plight of Sarah Jane in *Imitation of Life*, whose desire for a viable entertainment career forces her to renounce her saintly African-American mother in order to pass for white? Far from resigning the viewer to despair or falsely resolving genuine social tensions through some fictitious catharsis, Sarah Jane and Annie's predicament should incite us to take action against racial injustice within our own political sphere.

II Going beyond Melodrama's Visual Metaphors

Melodrama has always brought to the spectator's awareness the most pressing social problems of the day, which in Sirk's case included a widening class divide, racial discrimination, the negative effects of sexual repression and promiscuity, alcoholism and a preoccupation with private pleasures or ambitions at the expense of others. Once these issues have been defamiliarised by the vividly non-naturalistic quality of the director's formal style (though this too is a generic trait), the audience is compelled to examine them anew. Rather than simply being estranged or alienated, the viewer remains a participant in the depicted events and can't avoid acknowledging some of the most unpleasant aspects of contemporary American society. Moreover, this thoughtful European director's manipulation of the mise-en-scène often highlights these ethical dilemmas rather than allowing them to simply fade into the background.

Sirk's adoption of this kind of pictorial punctuation may well have been triggered by what Jonathan Crary has described as the 'emergence of a social, urban, psychic, and industrial field [that is] increasingly saturated with sensory input'.[51] In the contingent, fragmented and distracting environment of the mid-twentieth-century United States, how could a Hollywood filmmaker hope to capture and fix his audience's attention, if only for an instant? According to Crary, Alois Riegl's valorisation of an 'unwavering' state of empathetic contemplation was already outmoded, because it represented a vain attempt to 'resolidify the unitary self that scientific psychology was in the process of dismantling'.[52] Yet human discernment, synthesis and judgement is still reliant upon a focused conscious awareness in order to select from, organise and interpret the plurality of raw data that surrounds us, even if this intensity of concentration can only be fleetingly sustained. As Crary's painstaking research also makes clear, a state of willed 'attentiveness' was the obvious adjunct to the 'long established critical characterisation of modernity in terms of experiences of distraction' that had been promulgated by 'Georg Simmel, Walter Benjamin, Siegfried Kracauer, Theodor Adorno and others'.[53] Given this explicit conviction, Crary's main deviation from Riegl's position (the belief that this sort of heightened perception is both harder to attain and much more transient than the latter had supposed) appears relatively minor.

Moreover, I would argue that the same 'tension between cohesion and disintegration' that Crary distilled from the paintings of Georges Seurat is also discernible in the films of Douglas Sirk. By employing comparable artistic techniques, the director channels the viewer's perception through the geometric framework of his settings or draws his or her eye to a particular portion of the screen with sharp contrasts in tonality or touches of pure, heavily saturated colour. Sirk's 'coherent constellation' of visual stimuli attracts and binds the spectator's regard to certain characters or events, although this artificially induced 'attentiveness' will soon wane unless it is re-synthesised in response to a subsequent configuration of optical signs.[54] Yet as Peter Brooks established more than thirty years ago, the melodramatic spectacle was derived from the frozen stage pictures of the *tableau vivant*, which not only provided temporarily arrested 'spots of time' in Crary's (or Wordsworth's) sense but were also intrinsically meaningful in themselves. Although the heroes, heroines and villains who populated this type of drama endlessly discussed their 'moral and emotional . . . conditions', the mute attitudes and gestures that they struck at the end of every scene revealed more about their inner turmoil or ultimate symbolism than words could ever say.[55]

For instance, in his visually arresting 1955 black-and-white melodrama *There's Always Tomorrow* the director utilises the extreme lightness or darkness of his leading lady's costumes to great emotional and symbolic effect.[56] Towards the end of the film, the two older children of a Los Angeles toy-factory owner confront the New York fashion designer with whom he has fallen in love and beg her not to take him away. Norma Vale had once been Clifford Groves' employee, so when she arrived in California to open a new shop she had decided to look him up. After his child-obsessed wife and self-absorbed offspring repeatedly ignore his needs, Cliff and his old friend end up spending a great deal more time alone together than they expected, including a chance meeting at a resort in Palm Valley that his son misconstrues. When Vinnie and Ellen come up to the designer's hotel room in order to find out if their suspicions are true, because of the strong visual emphasis provided by her clothing it is almost impossible to take our eyes off of Norma whenever she is in the frame. The powerfully graphic silhouette of the plain mat-black dress that covers her entire upper body from her neck to her wrists recalls some of Henri Toulouse-Lautrec's most striking images of the similarly clad Parisian dancer Jane Avril.[57] Whether she is glimpsed against the pastel-coloured wallpaper visible behind the bed or standing next to the white painted brick wall that surrounds the fireplace, this flat expanse of pure black fixes our attention on Norma even when all we see is a portion of her back. While Sirk also uses more cinematic means to highlight the visiting New Yorker's importance (for instance, in this scene she is the only character who moves in and out of the frame, and whom the camera pans to follow), the sight of the designer's pale cameo-like face floating above this inky black dress is almost impossible to forget.

Finally, too distressed to discuss the irreproachability of Cliff's behaviour, his great love for his children and their shameful neglect of their father any further, Norma asks Vinnie and his sister to leave, turns away from them and stands immobile looking out of the window. In the shallow space of this very planar composition, the rigid outline of the dark shape of her shoulders (set against white muslin curtains) and the frozen contours of her face are a testament to the poor woman's struggle to control her emotions. In fact, even before Ellen had implored her not break up their home, Norma had already resolved to abandon her own desires by renouncing Cliff's burgeoning love. At one point in this scene, the designer had said to his daughter 'the tragic thing about growing older is that you can't be quite as reckless anymore; you begin to understand what is important and what is not, and believe me the most important thing to [your father] is his family's happiness'. Yet even after Norma had begun to suppress any outward sign of her innermost feelings so as not to inflame Ellen's nascent hysteria, the director's non-naturalistic use of lighting still manages to communicate the full intensity of the devastated woman's grief. As she stands gazing out of the window at the conclusion of this tumultuous scene, the flickering shadows cast by the runnels of water flowing along the rain-streaked glass makes it seem as though tears are streaming down her face. In other words, Norma's subjective experience is being projected onto the external environment in the manner of the German Expressionist painters that the director had deliberately tried to emulate more than thirty years before.[58]

Thomas Elsaesser has noted that as the significance of speech lessened in Hollywood melodramas of the 1950s and early '60s, 'the semantic and syntactic contribution [of lighting, composition and décor increased until they became] ... functional and integral elements in the construction of meaning'.[59] He would eventually conclude that the mental conflicts that haunted the main protagonists of many of these films were almost always sublimated and displaced onto their surroundings.[60] While the artificial quality of Sirk's mise-en-scène does represent a sublimation of sorts, his stylised compositions and anti-illusionist use of colour and tonality appear to be attempting to transform these basic human emotions and situations into a more sophisticated form of 'art'. Consequently, on at least three occasions during the 1950s the Universal-International Pictures publicity department chose to emphasise the ties between this director's visually inventive melodramas and other related artistic disciplines. In a press release that began '[these prints provide] graphic proof that a camera is an instrument of artistic expression, instead of a mere mechanical device', an anonymous writer described the aesthetic beliefs and working processes of each of the five different photographers who had been asked to 'capture the mood of [*Magnificent Obsession*'s] highly dramatic tale' by taking their own distinctive stills of the two romantic leads.[61] Similarly, in order to publicise the forthcoming release of *All That Heaven Allows*, the studio commissioned a series of drawings that highlighted the architectural changes that were made during Ron Kirby's progressive renovation of the Old Mill.[62] Finally, several members of the New York Art Student's League were offered the opportunity to execute their 'concept of a "Tarnished Angel" as portrayed by Dorothy Malone' after attending a private screening of the director's latest film 'in the movie company's screening room'. The creator of the best painting (as judged by 'a nationally-known art figure') was to receive a one-hundred-dollar prize and the winning canvas would be 'toured in major cities throughout the nation in conjunction with local openings of "The Tarnished Angels"'.[63]

As we know from his interviews with Jon Halliday, Sirk studied at the University of Hamburg with the 'great art historian' Erwin Panofsky from 1920 until 1921. As 'one of the select' members of '[this distinguished scholar's] seminar', the director had written 'a large essay on the relations between medieval German painting and the miracle plays'.[64] Yet he would later declare that the tragedy of World War I marked the end of an era, which meant that art had to be reimagined along with everything else. In contrast to the nineteenth-century 'bourgeois' conception of an 'art without politics – an almost frozen understanding of beauty', in the chaos of the immediate post-war period 'art became political out of necessity'.[65] Sirk's pursuit of this new 'modern' ideal, which often produced images inflected with anguish and ugliness, may well have been at least partially prompted by his experiments with German Expressionist painting. Yet as early as 1923, when he worked briefly as a set designer in Berlin before being appointed the artistic director of the *Bremen Schauspielhaus*, what Sirk had begun to paint 'consisted mainly of sets, and sketches for the plays I was staging – and later the [motion] pictures'.[66] In other words, from this point onward the director had sought to move beyond the conventional boundaries of 'high art', while at the same time refusing to discard the nuanced awareness of composition and colour that he had already acquired. The more inclusive model of communication that he now aspired to 'was to be something populistic . . . something that the average man could understand, but with something additional – style'. Following in the footsteps of William Shakespeare, Erich von Stroheim and Josef von Sternberg (or so he claimed), Sirk would eventually decide that melodrama could epitomise this non-elitist form of exposition, again only if this inherited generic framework could be infused with some sort of readily perceptible aesthetic vision.[67]

For instance, according to the director, the striking chromatic palette of *Written on the Wind* was inspired by some of the most revolutionary artistic discoveries of the early twentieth century. In a 1977 interview with James Harvey, Sirk observed that because the film's main protagonists were 'heightened versions of reality' this seemed to require 'painting' the mise-en-scène 'in primary colours like [the German Expressionist artists Ernst Ludwig] Kirchner or [Emil] Nolde ... or ... [the Surrealist painter Joan] Miró'.[68] These Expressionist influences are especially apparent in the exterior views of the large Federal Style mansion that begin and end the sequence in which Kyle Hadley pulls into the driveway in his sports car, disappears inside and then staggers onto the outside porch and dies just after the opening credits. The instability implied by the rapid succession of shots that ricochet between Kyle's unsteady progress along the front of the house and the reactions of those inside looking out is often further exacerbated by the skewed framing, the unusually low vantage points, the restless tilting, panning or tracking of the camera, the wild thrashing of the tree branches and the dead leaves blowing in the wind. Once we have seen Kyle throw open the main door, stumble into the hallway and retreat into a nearby room, his sister glides down the stairs and vanishes into the same space, before the kaleidoscopic editing shifts our perspective back to a series of external views of the house. These constant changes in the spectator's perceived relation to the depicted events don't halt until the end of this scene, which means that our eyes aren't even allowed to linger on the crucial two shots in which a fatally injured man falls forward onto the driveway. Due to the unconventional framing and lighting of these shots (the first one cuts off the victim's head and the second one shows his darkened silhouette collapsing into the shadows cast by the columns) the identity of this character will remain hidden until much later in the narrative.

Yet the most intriguing remnant of Expressionism in this sequence isn't so much the general atmosphere of transience, uncertainty and psychological unease, but more specifically the highly subjective use of colour. While the glossy yellow hue of Kyle's sports car might have a plausible objective source, the red light that suffuses Marylee Hadley's face as she glances off-screen, or the blue light that illuminates the window behind her, clings to the shafts of the columns of the portico and collects on the surface of the driveway do not. These non-naturalistic traces of blue are even more evident when the same sequence is revisited towards the end of the film and we are finally shown the chain of events that leads to Kyle Hadley's death. In the lower level of the house, blue light streams through the window into the darkened bedroom of the frightened servants who have been awakened by the commotion made by their drunken employer searching for a gun upstairs. The same blue light irradiates the window of the study as Kyle and his sister struggle for possession of this weapon, after he threatens to kill Mitch in a jealous rage. Once the gun goes off and Kyle is accidentally shot, he seems to be irresistibly drawn towards the blue light that is visible through the open door of the Hadley family's home. While his face is initially bathed in a deep red light as he crosses the threshold and stumbles onto the porch outside, this momentary flush almost immediately gives way to a more subtle tincture of blue. In the final shot of this sequence, Kyle's body lies in a crumpled black heap at one end of the driveway while a blue light washes over the other, offsetting the yellow diagonal formed by the gleaming body of his car.

Nevertheless, although many of the colours that have been included in the mise-en-scène of both versions of this scene are subjective, I would argue that they are far from arbitrary. According to the aesthetic codings that Wassily Kandinsky had already established in *Concerning the Spiritual in Art*, the yellow of Kyle's car signifies not only a preoccupation with earth-bound gratifications but also a predisposition to 'violent raving lunacy', which is an apt description of his psychological condition by this stage in the film.[69] While red has many connotations depending upon the shade, the pioneering Expressionist painter claimed that it always contained some hint of corporeal vigour and therefore 'glows within itself' to a greater or a lesser degree.[70] In the context of *Written on the Wind*, the red light that periodically floods the faces of both Hadley siblings represents not just the strength of their passions but also the life force that is rapidly draining from Kyle's critically wounded flesh. Finally, since in Kandinsky's system blue 'is the most heavenly colour', the otherworldly tinges of blue that pervade much of the external landscape during this scene imply that Kyle (whose soul has almost left his body) is on the verge of entering a more spiritual state. In other words, by deploying an interdisciplinary fusion of dramatic narrative and German Expressionist aesthetics, Sirk manages to suggest not only 'emotions beyond the reach of words' but also the more metaphysical realms that are revealed by the true artist's '"inner need" to create'.[71] In my next chapter, I will explore some of the transcendental implications of Sirk's allusions to Kandinsky's early twentieth-century theories even further, as part of a detailed rereading of his slightly earlier Hollywood melodrama *Magnificent Obsession*.

Notes

1. From 1920 until 1921, Sirk studied Art History at the University of Hamburg under the auspices of Erwin Panofsky [Halliday, 11]. During those years,

Panofsky published two papers that explored key aspects of Alois Riegl's ideas: 'The Concept of the *Kunstwollen*' and 'The History of Human Proportions as a Reflection of the History of Styles' [Margaret Iversen, *Alois Riegl: Art History and Theory* (Cambridge, MA: MIT Press, 1993), 149]. This means that Panofsky's students (including Sirk) might well have learnt something about Riegl's theories from their eminent professor.

2. Michael Fried, *Courbet's Realism* (Chicago: University of Chicago Press, 1990), 7.
3. Fried, 7.
4. Fried, 7.
5. Michael Fried, *Absorption and Theatricality: Painting and Beholder in the Age of Diderot* (Berkeley: University of California Press, 1980), 121.
6. Fried, *Courbet's Realism*, 200.
7. Alois Riegl, *The Group Portraiture of Holland* (Los Angeles: The Getty Research Institute, 1999), 173.
8. Riegl, 63–4.
9. Riegl, 74.
10. Jean-Claude Biette and Dominique Rabourdin, 'Entretien avec Douglas Sirk', *Cinema*, No. 238 (1978), 14.
11. Biette and Rabourdin, 14. Sirk also thought that, both formally and thematically, *All I Desire* emphasised the 'transition from theatre to cinema'.
12. The spectator never actually sees Naomi acting in a professional engagement on the stage, although we do observe an important exchange that takes place in the dressing room of the Bijou Theatre at the beginning of the film. Due to the demands of the narrative, we watch the ageing actress 'perform' mainly within the domestic setting of the Murdoch family home. Most notably, her moving recitation of Elizabeth Barrett Browning's poem 'How Do I Love Thee' at her daughter's post-production party rekindles Henry's dormant passion.
13. Biette and Rabourdin, 14.
14. James Harvey, undated typewritten essay entitled 'Interview with Douglas Sirk: Lugano, July 1977', 15. This draft manuscript is preserved in the Museum of Modern Art's 'Sirk, Douglas' clipping file in New York. The final version was published under the title of 'Sirkumstantial Evidence' in *Film Comment*, 14, No. 4 (1978), 52–9.
15. In his analysis of Sirk's 1956 film *All That Heaven Allows*, Fassbinder remarked: 'Usually women are always reacting, doing what women are supposed to do, but in Sirk they think.' See his 'Six Films by Douglas Sirk' in *The Marriage of Maria Braun*, ed. Joyce Rheuban (New Brunswick, NJ: Rutgers University Press, 1986), 199.
16. Michael Stern, 'Sirk Speaks'. Available at <www.brightlightsfilm.com/48/sirkinterview.htm>, 10 (last accessed 17 October 2005).
17. Riegl, 158.
18. Gilles Deleuze, *Cinema 2: The Time-Image* (Minneapolis: University of Minnesota Press, 1989), 6–9, 16–18.
19. Characters in Sirk's films are often shown gazing through the panes of

strategically placed windows, a position that enables them to contemplate the dreamlike landscape behind the glass with a certain amount of intellectual detachment. See my analysis of the director's use of the window motif in *All That Heaven Allows* in the final chapter of this book.

20. In an interview conducted for an early television show called *Hollywood Spotlight*, Alexander Golitzen (the art director of *All I Desire*) confirmed that the Murdoch family's domestic setting was meant to reinforce the actress's renascent feelings of 'warmth and security' by radiating a welcoming 'hominess'. See the undated document entitled 'Excerpt from a 15 minute TV show called *Hollywood Spotlight* – 2nd episode featuring All I Desire. Erskine Johnson interviews various members of the technical staff' in Box 391, File 04404 of the Universal-International Pictures Archives, Cinema-Television Library of the University of Southern California, Los Angeles.
21. See Le Corbusier's 'The Spirit of Truth' in *French Film Theory and Criticism, Volume 2, 1929–39*, ed. Richard Abel (Princeton: Princeton University Press), 112, and Deleuze, 13.
22. Laura U. Marks, *The Skin of Film: Intercultural Cinema, Embodiment and the Senses* (Durham, NC and London: Duke University Press, 2000), 162–3.
23. Marks, 162.
24. Linda Williams, 'Film Bodies: Gender, Genre and Excess', *Film Quarterly*, 44, No. 4 (Summer 1991), 3–4.
25. Linda Williams, 'Corporealized Observers: Visual Pornographies and the "Carnal Density of Vision"' in *Fugitive Images: From Photography to Video*, ed. Patrice Petro (Bloomington: Indiana University Press, 1995), 6–7. In the second quotation, Williams is reproducing Crary's words, which may be found on page 39 of *Techniques of the Observer: On Vision and Modernity in the Nineteenth-Century* (Cambridge, MA: MIT Press, 1991).
26. Crary, 68–9.
27. Williams, 'Corporealized Observers', 8–11.
28. Halliday, 44.
29. Halliday, 40.
30. Halliday, 40.
31. Halliday, 166–9.
32. 'Documents on Sirk', trans. Thomas Elsaesser, *Screen*, 12, No. 2 (1971), 22.
33. Halliday, 109–10, 140, 151–2, Stern, 10–11 and Biette and Rabourdin, 20–2. See also James Harvey's typewritten essay entitled 'Interview with Douglas Sirk: Lugano, July 1977', 8–10.
34. Paul Willemen, 'Distanciation and Douglas Sirk, in *Imitation of Life*, ed. Lucy Fischer (New Brunswick, NJ: Rutgers University Press, 1991), 270.
35. Willemen, 272.
36. Thomas Schatz, *Hollywood Genres: Formulas, Filmmaking and the Studio System* (Boston: McGraw-Hill, 1981), 252.
37. Jack Moffitt, 'All That Heaven Allows Strong in Popular Appeal', *The Hollywood*

Reporter, 25 October 1955. See Box 440, File 13494 of the Universal-International Pictures archives.
38. The studio's analysis of the 'Preview Reaction Cards' that were returned for *All That Heaven Allows* may be found in Box 508, File 14513 of the Universal-International Pictures archives.
39. Halliday, 109.
40. See 'Reports picked up from the theatre after the first sneak preview, held Monday, January 11, 1954 at the Encino Theatre, Encino California' in Box 690, File 22500 of the Universal-International Pictures Archives.
41. Sergei Eisenstein, 'Montage 1938' in *Eisenstein, Volume 2: Towards a Theory of Montage*, ed. Michael Glenny and Richard Taylor (London: British Film Institute, 1991), 296.
42. Paul Willeman, 'Towards an Analysis of the Sirkian System' in *Imitation of Life*, ed. Lucy Fischer (New Brunswick, NJ: Rutgers University Press, 1991), 273–8.
43. Lucy Fischer, 'Sirk and the Figure of the Actress: *All I Desire*', *Film Criticism*, 23, No. 2/3 (Winter/Spring 1999), 139.
44. Anne Morey, 'A Star Has Died: Affect and Stardom in Domestic Melodrama', *Quarterly Review of Film and Video*, 21 (2004), 95, 102.
45. Morey, 102.
46. Morey, 104.
47. In Eckhardt Schmidt's 1991 documentary *From UFA to Hollywood: Douglas Sirk Remembers* (the edited version of a 1980 filmed interview with the director), Sirk appeared to concur with this opinion. At one point he states that 'the surface isn't really the surface, but rather a manifestation of the depths', and that 'It's better to read the meaning or allegory or symbol on the surface than to dig down to dark depths [in the German way, where there's 'a contempt for the surface']'.
48. Linda Williams, 'Melodrama Revised' in *Refiguring American Film Genres*, ed. Nick Browne (Los Angeles: University of California Press, 1998), 54–5.
49. Williams, 'Melodrama Revised', 55.
50. Peter Lehman, 'Thinking With the Heart: An Interview with Douglas Sirk', *Wide Angle*, 3, No. 4 (1980), 47.
51. Jonathan Crary, *Suspension of Perception: Attention, Spectacle and Modern Culture* (Cambridge, MA: MIT Press, 1999), 13.
52. Crary, *Suspension of Perception*, 51.
53. Crary, *Suspension of Perception*, 48.
54. Crary, *Suspension of Perception*, 176.
55. Peter Brooks, *The Melodramatic Imagination: Balzac, Henry James, Melodrama, and the Mode of Excess* (New Haven: Yale University Press, 1976), 48, 56–9.
56. Because Barbara Stanwyck was playing a fashion designer in this film, Jay Morley, Jr. decided that the clothes he designed for this character needed to reflect a 'high fashion' rather than 'movie star' persona. As a result, 'the entire collection of twelve outfits – from bathing to evening gown' that Morley envisioned was entirely 'done in black and white'. According to 'Miss Stanwyck', by choosing to emphasise 'line rather than color, Jay has produced an effect that is

far more striking than any combination of colors could be'. See the press release credited to Thompson dated 14/04/55 in Box 444, File 13185 of the Universal-International Pictures archives.

57. Sirk once described the visual approach he adopted in *Written on the Wind* as a 'poster style', 'with a flat, simple lighting that concentrates the effects', including the strong, unmodulated blocks of colour that characterised late nineteenth-century and early twentieth-century poster design. When Mitch Wayne first meets Lucy Moore (the executive secretary who would later become Kyle Hadley's wife), she is placing a series of advertising posters on easels in the head office of the Hadley Oil Company in New York. These posters highlight some of the same symbols of modernity (airplanes and motorcars) that appeared in Le Corbusier's *Towards a New Architecture* during the 1920s, and the dynamic simplicity of the lithographic design is more reminiscent of that period. The sophistication of the Hadley Company's New York office (versus the vulgarity of their small town home) is further accentuated by the abstract geometric painting that has been placed on the wall directly beside the doorway, the top portion of which we see in close-up as Mitch enters this space.

Given Sirk's detailed knowledge of modern art, I have no doubt that he was familiar with Toulouse-Lautrec's many striking images of Jane Avril clothed entirely in black, such as the *Divan Japonais*. Moreover, Lisa mimics Avril's mode of dress and dancing style in *An American in Paris*, a Vincente Minnelli musical that we know Sirk admired. Finally, the main focus of the Modernist painting glimpsed hanging on the wall beside the vanity in Norma's hotel room is a woman's stark white face that has been illuminated from below, which again recalls Toulouse-Lautrec's vivid portraits of the bohemians who frequented the Moulin Rouge.

58. Lehman, 46. Although *There's Always Tomorrow* was shot in black and white, colour indirectly imbues the final shot of this scene when we hear non-diegetic snatches of 'Blue Moon' (the song that Norma shares with Cliff) being played by a cello and a violin over the image of Norma looking out of the window. The colour blue had enormous significance for the influential German Expressionist painter Wassily Kandinsky and to his synaesthetic sensibilities the sound of the cello produces the impression of a 'darker blue'. According to Kandinsky's theories, a darker colour of blue 'echoes a grief that is hardly human', and black (the colour of Norma's clothing) would also have represented 'grief and death'. See pages 38–9 of his *Concerning the Spiritual in Art*. In other words, the fact that Norma is dressed entirely in black in the scene in which she decides to give up the only man that she has ever loved is extremely telling, from an Expressionist point of view.

59. Thomas Elsaesser, 'Tales of Sound and Fury: Observations on the Family Melodrama' in *Imitations of Life: A Reader on Film, Television and Melodrama*, ed. Marcia Landry (Detroit: Wayne State University Press, 1991), 76.

60. Elsaesser, 81–7.

61. See the press release dated 7/4/54 in Box 547, File 17479 of the Universal-

International Pictures archives. The five 'renowned' photographers were William Hortensen, Tom Kelley, Ray Jones, T. Estabrook and William Walling.
62. I will discuss these drawings at greater length in the last chapter of this book.
63. See the article dated 22/12/57 entitled 'Universal-International Offers Award for Best Angel' that was published in the *New York Journal-American*. A copy of this article may be found in Box 461, File 00275 of the Universal-International Pictures archives.
64. Halliday, 11.
65. Stern, 4.
66. Halliday, 9, 14.
67. Stern, 5.
68. Lehman, 55–6.
69. Kandinsky, 38.
70. Kandinsky, 40–1. The deeper shade of red that suffuses Kyle's face shortly before he dies increases this self-contained 'inward glow', which is the visual equivalent of the 'sad, middle tones of the cello'.
71. Kandinsky, 2, 33–6, 55.

CHAPTER TWO

Concerning the Spiritual in Art: Magnificent Obsession *and the Influence of Modernist Painting*

The exaggerated artifice of Douglas Sirk's best-known melodramas has often been remarked upon, but it has yet to be interpreted in the light of his detailed cognisance of the major art and architectural movements of the period. Despite the fact that this director's ongoing fascination with Modernist painting was first disclosed in a series of interviews that took place more than three decades ago, the influence of the theories of the German Expressionists upon his non-mimetic use of colour and composition has yet to be explored. When a sophisticated German expatriate reveals that in his university days he was '½ literary, ½ a painter', then perhaps it is time for the second portion of this statement to be taken more seriously.[1] To my mind, there seems little doubt that this director's non-naturalistic formal approach has been at least partially inspired by contemporary experiments in the visual arts. In other words, I would argue that Sirk rarely chose to manipulate his rich palette of intensely saturated colours simply to estrange the audience from the storyline or just for decorative effect. Rather, he tended to use particular hues that were already freighted with a pre-existing symbolic meaning in order to underscore the central themes of the narrative. Since in Sirk's version of *Magnificent Obsession* it is an Expressionist painter who initiates Bob Merrick into the cryptic philosophy that will change the course of his life, in this chapter I will attempt to re-examine this infamous film through the prism of the writings of Wassily Kandinsky.[2]

In the first of the director's two projects starring Jane Wyman, Rock Hudson was cast as the reckless playboy (Bob Merrick) whose irresponsible actions cause a saintly doctor to die and his widow to go blind. These thoughtless deeds will eventually be redeemed once Merrick has completed his medical training and performed the operation that restores Helen Phillips' sight. It is important to note, however, that this character's whole moral regeneration turns upon what he has learned in a chance encounter with an enigmatic painter called Edward Randolph. Merrick chooses to follow Randolph's advice, and only then discovers that an unwavering dedication to helping others also enables him to tap into some powerful transcendental force. Moreover, the glimmerings of spirituality that this rather mystical artist reveals are so fundamental to the meaning of the film that they were explicitly acknowledged in several of the studio's publicity department memos just before its release. According to the anonymous author of one of these documents, the removal of the 'stilted comedy situations' that had been included in John Stahl's previous adaptation of the Lloyd C. Douglas novel shifts the focus of the 1953 remake back to the central drama, thus rendering Merrick's spiritual journey more credible.[3] In an additional unpublished typescript, David Weiss predicts that the new version of *Magnificent Obsession* will prove to be as 'phenomenally successful' as *The Robe* (a slightly earlier film based on a Lloyd C. Douglas book), due to the 'great revival of religious feeling in the United States today'.[4] Nevertheless, the kind of ineffable spirituality that this fascinating melodrama implies bears little resemblance to the orthodox Christianity that Weiss claims many Americans share, starting with 'Eisenhower and going down into the hearts of millions'. Hence, it is my belief that Sirk's 'exalted' film is drawing upon the same sort of non-traditional religious sources that inspired some of the most groundbreaking innovations in early twentieth-century European art.[5]

As the best-selling novel that *Magnificent Obsession* was adapted from makes clear, the mystical convictions that pervade this popular melodrama were loosely based upon theosophy (a late nineteenth-century attempt to create a universal religion that borrowed its most fundamental precepts from both East and West).[6] The main teachings of Christianity are not excluded from this alternative metaphysical system (as Randolph says in the film, 'one of the first men to [adopt this way of life] went to the cross at the age of thirty-three'), but they have been supplemented by a series of ideas that were taken from Buddhism and Brahmanism. Among these was the notion of karma ('the sum of a person's bodily, mental and spiritual growth, often accumulated during numerous incarnations'), which assumes that the benevolent acts that a person carries out in one lifetime will enable him or her to evolve into a more spiritually enlightened being in the next.[7] Within the context of *Magnificent Obsession*, Doctor Wayne Phillip's mysterious compulsion to assist anyone in need and to refuse any form of material recompense because he had already been 'paid' in full makes sense, when it is viewed from this perspective. Edward Randolph's warning to Merrick that 'investing one's life in [helping] others' means aligning 'one's self' with the cosmic 'forces [that are] leading [the soul] up and on' is also consistent with this occult model of a gradually ascending progress. Moreover, theosophists believe that everything that exists in the material world is conjoined by a single transcendent current flowing through us all (so that in essence, every living being is animated by a portion of the same Divine *pneuma*). Again, in perhaps the most pivotal scene in Sirk's cinematic realisation of Lloyd C. Douglas's original story, Edward

Randolph describes this celestial emanation as a sort of 'electricity' being emitted by an inexhaustible 'powerhouse' that anyone can choose to tap into, a conception that is totally in keeping with this much less sectarian religious faith.

Therefore, when Jean-Loup Bourget lists a few of the many instances in which the 'gaudy mysticism' of *Magnificent Obsession* deviates from traditional Christianity, I would argue that most of these observations are beside the point.[8] Within this film's theosophical framework, the physical and temporal distinctions that separate Doctor Phillips (the eminent surgeon) from Bob Merrick (the reformed playboy) from Edward Randolph (the visionary painter) from Jesus Christ (the murdered prophet) are utterly inconsequential.[9] If 'Christ was only "one" among several who achieved infinite power through philanthropy', then this is because a spark of God's eternal light illuminates the soul of every living creature, a soul that may be so perfected by performing acts of kindness that it eventually merges with the Absolute. Bob Merrick will become 'everything that Wayne Phillips was' only after he has learned how to harness the Divine afflatus that they both encapsulate and that connects them to the rest of humanity.[10] Moreover, as Bourget and Sirk have both noted, when Randolph hovers overhead during the climactic operation in which Bob Merrick restores his beloved's sight, the painter appears to be acting in a much greater capacity than just a spiritual adviser and moral conscience.[11] As a celestial choir intones a cascading series of notes that wordlessly evoke Beethoven's 'Song of Joy', the iconography of this sequence almost seems to align the artist's elevated figure with God himself. Yet given the boundlessness of the cosmology that has already been sketched out, I would argue that Randolph's image should not be read as a straightforward personification of the Almighty in the manner of a baroque painting as Jean-Loup Bourget has suggested.[12]

In keeping with the repeated mention of electricity as a metaphor for the sacred in this film, theosophists no longer conceived of the Supreme Being as an imposing grey-haired man with a beard, but rather as an infinite, supra-natural force that courses through the whole of Creation.[13] Madame Blavatsky, the Russian co-founder of the Theosophical Society, had in fact specifically criticised the Judaeo-Christian tendency to anthropomorphise this undifferentiated 'Universal Soul' into the figure of Jehovah.[14] In her opinion, the indeterminacy of the supernal world can only be represented by a more incorporeal substance that is capable of penetrating everywhere, such as 'breath' or 'light', which in Sirk's film has coalesced into the notion of electrical flow.[15] Hence, during the shot/reverse shot exchange in which Randolph looks down onto the operating room from above, he should not be interpreted as a straightforward 'symbolic substitute' for this genuinely 'incognizable Deity', to adopt Madame Blavatsky's terminology.[16] Instead, the artist should be viewed as simply providing a conduit for channelling more of this ineffable energy towards his friend. Since Randolph walks out of the frame almost as soon as Helen's operation has begun, it only succeeds in the end because Bob Merrick has learned how to draw additional spiritual voltage from the same transcendent source as his mentor.[17] In other words, making 'contact' with the divine has 'unlocked' the frivolous playboy's latent abilities and enabled him to fulfil his true 'destiny' of becoming an accomplished surgeon.

As *Magnificent Obsession* reveals, anyone can benefit from an additional influx of this generative force, which may be used to fuel scientific invention (as in this instance) or artistic creation (in the case of Edward Randolph). While this theosophical doctrine may seem 'crazy' from a rational point of view, it is no more so than the major tenets of many other religions (including Christianity). Indeed, the director used the same pejorative adjective to describe Shakespeare's *Hamlet* and Elizabethan drama in a 1977 interview with Michael Stern, since these canonical works were just as riddled with *ad hoc* coincidences and constrained by external commercial and social concerns as his best-known films.[18] Yet if their non-naturalistic qualities did not prevent these plays from being considered enduring masterpieces, why should *Magnificent Obsession* be treated any differently? Again according to the director, even the most popular genre can be transformed into art when it has been infused with 'style . . . signs and meaning', and his version of Lloyd C. Douglas's story does manage to capture something of the novel's numinous faith. Unlike many of his subsequent critics, in this interview Sirk urges us to take the film's melodramatic denouement completely seriously, asserting that 'down there on the operating table, a miracle really is happening'.[19]

Indeed, according to Edward Randolph's account of his own halting aesthetic development, it is precisely this kernel of spirituality that legitimises certain strands of contemporary art. He would soon discover that 'making fairly adequate copies of the Masters' was not enough, nor was engaging in empty formal innovation for its own sake. In order to become a real artist, Randolph (guided by Wayne Phillips) had to learn to create new works that were suffused with the same transcendent force as those of his most illustrious predecessors. Hence, Sirk's presiding visionary is no longer the sculptor who appears in the book and in the first film adaptation of this narrative but a painter, whose attenuated images are more in keeping with Theosophy's de-materialised conception of the Divine. The formlessness of this suprasensible realm (apprehended by clairvoyants as a fluctuating field of coloured light and musical tones) is echoed in the turbulent background of Randolph's canvases, although he has not yet dispensed with physical matter entirely.[20]

Figure 2.1 Edward Randolph painting in his studio in *Magnificent Obsession*.

In fact, what the two most clearly observable pictures in the artist's studio seem to represent is the moment when the soul trembles on the verge of leaving the body, before returning to a state of pure energy (Figure 2.1).

According to the theories of Madame Blavatsky, Randolph's painting of a gaunt, crucified Christ would have signified the destruction of 'the man of flesh and his passions' that preceded being 'reborn as an Immortal'.[21] The other composition, featuring a group of flickering, angular figures moving towards a brilliant white vortex of light, also suggests an incipient passage to a more spiritual plane. To a theosophist, this striking iconography would no doubt have evoked the 'one white ray' that symbolised the eternal truth of the 'Universal Mind', which was said to unite 'the seven prismatic aspects of color', the earth with the heavens, and the principal religions of East and West.[22] Yet these figurative images are emblems of transition rather than resolution, because no mortal being (however sensitive) can advance beyond this threshold without first discarding the 'enwrapping veil' of his or her corporeality.[23] Although artists could show others 'the way ... to the newly awakened spiritual life' by illustrating its intangible surroundings, even their perception of this supernal realm was incomplete and the heightened level of consciousness that it required could only be sustained intermittently.[24]

As Jean-Loup Bourget has already emphasised, *Magnificent Obsession*'s hazy mysticism places its audience in the uneasy position of struggling to see 'through the glass darkly'. Given the theosophical cosmology that the film has already established, however, I would dispute his conclusion that the spectator's faint, somewhat distorted perception of the Absolute should be read as an indication that 'God is Dead'.[25] To my mind, it simply means that the imperfections of the flesh inevitably impair our ability to grasp the true nature of what is essentially a purely spiritual phenomenon. In other words, the blindness that results from Helen Phillip's tragic accident is symptomatic of a much more generalised human condition. By the end of Sirk's version of Lloyd C. Douglas's story, raising the spectator's awareness of his or her limited capacity to see and to understand this higher reality seems to have become the main objective of the mise-en-scène, despite the accompanying narrative of love and redemption.

In particular, the audience is only allowed to observe Sirk's 'miracle' taking place indirectly, by watching the mirror image of Helen's life-saving operation that is visible on the overhead window. After showing us the surgeon's first few decisive gestures, the camera then tracks forward past the actors, tilts up and focuses exclusively on this translucent screen. At first, the spectral reflection of the doctors at work on their patient frames the upper portion of Edward Randolph's equally insubstantial form (since he monitors their progress from behind the same layer of glass). Even after the artist has gone, our view of the surgical procedure that restores the widow's health is still refracted through this gleaming apparition. Hence, the white-clad figures of the medical team appear to be so weightless that they almost look like the astral projections that had been described at great length by two well-known theosophists. As the art historian Sixten Ringbom has pointed out, in *Thought-Forms* (1901) and *Man Visible and Invisible* (1902) Annie Besant and C. W. Leadbeater assigned fixed meanings to the different colours that are apparent in the aura that surrounds the human body. Of these various mental and spiritual emanations, the most rarefied (those that are closest to the Universal Mind) were associated with an incandescent light that was not tinted with any hue, much like Sirk's unusual presentation of Helen Phillips's operation.[26] In effect, the director's luminous two-dimensional image of this critical event reveals the intersection of heaven and earth in a manner that is analogous to Edward Randolph's paintings. While the viewer cannot yet pass through the portal that it discloses and completely fuse with the Divine, we are still part of a cosmic circuit that links us to the empyrean. Whatever is transpiring down below (and there is no doubt that Merrick's medical training also plays a vital role), the injured widow's recovery could not have been achieved without invoking a loftier power.

This is not to say that that Sirk was necessarily familiar with the writings of Madame Blavatsky, Annie Besant, Charles Leadbeater, Rudolf Steiner or any of the other major exponents of this syncretistic religion. Since the director once stated that he 'worked during the Expressionist period as a stage director [and also] painted in an Expressionist manner', however, it is probably safe to assume that he would at least have been acquainted with the best-known publications of Wassily Kandinsky, who was one of the major progenitors of this pioneering early twentieth-century aesthetic movement.[27] As many scholars have already pointed out, Kandinsky's *Über das Geistige der Kunst* or *Concerning the Spiritual in Art* was steeped in theosophy, and the artist specifically placed the adherents of this religious faith among those enlightened groups 'who seek to approach the problem of the spirit through inner knowledge'.[28] According to Sixten Ringbom, the Munich-based Russian painter was acquainted with many of the key theosophical texts that would have provided him with a template for a transcendental realm 'where freely floating colours and forms . . . reveal the . . . ideas and thoughts of spiritual beings [and] . . . the observer feels himself in the midst of the creative laws of the Cosmos'.[29] In seeking to describe how certain pictorial elements manage to convey the celestial infinity that lies just beyond material reality in *Concerning the Spiritual in Art*, this revolutionary artist also laid the groundwork for many subsequent mystically-inclined Modernist painters all around the world.

It is important to note that Kandinsky believed colours and shapes could still be manipulated to produce the desired psychic effect (eliciting vibrations from the onlooker's mind and soul) even if an image was not strictly non-objective.[30] Since in 1912 'the revolt from nature was just beginning', he would eventually concede 'purely abstract forms are beyond the artist at present', going on to say that 'to limit [the painter] to the purely indefinite would be to rob him . . . of possibilities [by] exclud[ing] the human element and therefore weaken[ing] his expression'.[31] By the time *Concerning the Spiritual in Art* was finally published, however, Kandinsky had begun to experiment with wholly abstract compositions, relying upon the 'the language of form and colour' that he had already codified to suggest the ineffable space of the Divine. Nevertheless, it seems clear that the symbolic associations the artist had attributed to a select group of hues, tonalities and shapes in his pioneering Expressionist treatise would continue to be apparent even when they are being utilised within a more figurative context. While Sirk's use of colour would become even more groundbreaking in *All That Heaven Allows*, the palette that he has chosen for *Magnificent Obsession* is still extremely significant from a Kandinskian point of view. In particular, spots or swathes of the revolutionary painter's most mystical colours are immediately discernible in many of the latter film's most pivotal sequences.

Perhaps because its coolness makes this tint appear to be receding from the viewer's gaze, Kandinsky classified blue as the primary hue that appeals to the spirit rather than the body, crediting it with an ability to transport the viewer to new levels of understanding. As we have seen, after observing that the 'power of profound meaning is found in blue' he would eventually proclaim it 'the typical heavenly colour'.[32] Similarly, the artist associated white with the upper reaches of this celestial sphere, while also listing its more traditional connotations of 'joy and spotless purity'. Although the world that it represents (one 'from which all colour has disappeared') might seem too remote 'to touch our souls', white continues to be 'pregnant with possibilities' that include the spectator's potential spiritual rebirth.[33] Perhaps in deference to this anti-materialistic painter's metaphysical ranking, Sirk adds touches of blue and/or white to every scene in *Magnificent Obsession* that has been infused with a similar cosmic consciousness or is important to Bob Merrick's moral regeneration.

A Kandinskian interpretation of the most prominent colours that appear in the scene in which the handsome protagonist first meets Edward Randolph would go something like this. Late one evening, after drinking too much in the limbo of a dark grey bar ('composed of two inactive colours'), Merrick breaks free from his decadent friends and begins his life-changing journey by driving off in a blue car, an especially spiritual colour that is also endowed with 'an active coolness'.[34] He soon fails to negotiate a right-hand turn and crashes into a ditch in front of the mysterious painter's house. The director then cuts to an American shot that is held for a relatively long period, which forces the camera to track alongside Merrick as he performs a whole string of separate activities. As the drunken playboy climbs out of his convertible, stumbles along the length of its body, drops to his knees to examine a damaged front wheel, straightens up, reaches down to pick up a piece of a broken barricade, and stands and gazes off into space (towards the painter's residence), the background continues to be dominated by the shadowy blue bulk of his car. It should also be noted that the wooden barrier that his automobile destroys (which includes the plank inscribed with the word 'danger' that he carries up to the artist's house) has been painted yellow, a colour that Kandinsky associates with a shallow, self-serving materialism.[35] Hence, this shattered structure appears to offer an obvious warning against continuing along his current path, a conclusion that Merrick's fateful encounter with Edward Randolph will subsequently confirm.

The hapless motorist then staggers up the hill towards the artist's studio, where he will find himself surrounded by white painted walls, gazing upon a group of equally luminous canvasses that are largely coloured blue and white, all of which Kandinsky would suggest points to a more celestial sphere. Moreover, Randolph himself is dressed in similar hues, wearing a deep blue cravat, a white shirt and a long white smock, since he had been engaged in working on a painting before hearing a knock on his door. Despite joking 'As far as I'm concerned, Art is just a man's name', Merrick appears genuinely shaken by the force of Randolph's latest image as soon as he realises that it is a portrait of Doctor Wayne Phillips. The tipsy intruder immediately turns the face of this canvas away from himself in a spontaneous gesture of shame, an action that also denies the viewer any glimpse of the saintly physician's material form. During the shot/reverse shot sequence in which Merrick lists the series of strange connections that has left him feeling 'haunted' by Phillips' spectral presence, we are never allowed to see anything more than the inchoate whorl of colour (again dominated by blue) that forms the lower corner of Randolph's portrait of his friend. Hence, this disembodied figure comes to represent the cosmic energy that flows from the Universal Mind, which has the power to trigger corresponding vibrations within our souls. Only after Merrick's conscience has been stirred by this blue-tinted and rather ghostly depiction of his self-sacrificing predecessor will he begin to be redeemed. Nevertheless, this wayward character's spiritual awakening has already been foreshadowed by the blue light that suffused his clothing whenever he mentioned his affinity with the dead philanthropist whose life and work he would eventually carry on. Merrick then passes out, and it is while they are having breakfast the next day that Randolph discusses Wayne Phillip's altruistic philosophy (his 'magnificent obsession' was to 'be of real service' to those in need) as well as the transcendental source of his own art. In the shot/reverse shot exchange that occurs near the end of this scene (in which the two men are seated across from one another at the dining room table), the painter is glimpsed against an empty expanse of white wall flanked by a side table occupied by a lamp.

In my opinion, everything about Randolph's presentation in this sequence alludes to the higher plane that he is speaking of, both the 'heavenly' colour scheme (the white background and his blue ascot and shirt) and the lamp that he turns on and off in order to illustrate his description of the flow of this celestial energy. Although Merrick's clothing looks very different after the sun has risen, his half light (a white shirt and tie 'pregnant with possibilities') and half dark (a black suit implying 'no possibilities') attire still seems to indicate that he has arrived at a significant moral crossroads.[36] From this point onward, the wealthy malingerer must choose either to go forward into the 'great period of the spiritual' or to remain enmeshed in the ongoing 'nightmare of materialism'.[37] Merrick elects to pursue the former course, which is signalled as much by his subsequent emulation of the artist's fondness for blue and white as by his growing devotion to the welfare of others. For instance, on the afternoon that he begins his tender friendship with Helen Phillips, concludes the secret arrangements for her financial support, and tells Edward Randolph that he has decided to return to medical school, he is wearing a white shirt, a dark blue sweater and a dark blue and white ascot. As we have already seen, during the surgery in which Helen Phillip's sight is miraculously restored, Bob Merrick and the rest of the medical team are dressed completely in white. Even after this procedure has been completed, and we finally see the doctors wheeling their patient out of the white-walled operating room, their radiant spiritual doubles still flicker on the darkened window overhead. This ethereal image seems to suggest that by this time the souls of Wayne Phillips and Bob Merrick have finally converged, as the younger man continues to observe the late doctor's directive to 'Go out of your way to do good for others, accept[ing] no payment or acclaim'.

Perhaps Kandinsky's most radical discovery was the realisation that non-objective painting had an affective power that could directly influence the viewer's inner psyche. In the last chapter of *Concerning the Spiritual in Art*, he declared: 'Colour is the keyboard, the eyes are the hammers, the soul is the piano with many strings', and 'the artist is the hand which plays, touching one key or another [in order] to cause vibrations in the soul'.[38] But according to this philosophy, the true artist wasn't seeking to evoke a particular spiritual sensation for its own sake, but rather to galvanise the onlooker into pursuing a less self-serving and acquisitive way of life. I would argue that Sirk's nuanced use of colour in *Magnificent Obsession* produces a similar effect, heightening the spectator's awareness of an alternative reality that calls into question the widespread materialism of the current age.

I Some Popular Mid-century American Responses to Modernist Art

Yet the link that this cultivated German director makes between Modernist painting and transcendent spirituality is at odds with more typical Hollywood representations, at least according to Diane Waldman. Her detailed analysis of five 'Gothic romances [released between 1940 and 1948] which centre around a female protagonist and her ambivalent relationship with her husband' apparently yielded 'frequent hostile allusions to modern art and occasionally to high art in general'.[39] Waldman supports the conclusions she drew from this rather small sampling of films with the supplementary evidence provided by several opinion pieces that appeared in a number of widely circulated general-interest publications during the same period.[40] For instance, in a 1943 *Harper's Magazine* article entitled 'The Victory and Defeat of Modernism', George Biddle had accused Pablo Picasso of indulging in formalist 'escapism' at the expense of comprehensibility in the mural that the latter had created in response to the German bombing of the small Spanish town of Guernica.

Given the fact that the world was still embroiled in a bloody war against Fascism, shouldn't it be possible to question a European artist's rather mythic depiction of a horrific civilian slaughter without being branded an isolationist reactionary? In the excerpt from this essay that Waldman quotes as an example of a 'mass' cultural denunciation of aesthetic Modernism (though its author was a trained painter and not a layman), Biddle makes the source of his reservations about Picasso's chosen surrealist idiom perfectly clear: 'In semi-abstract symbols he attempted to describe his horror of the Nazi brutality in Spain [but] I would venture to say that these symbols would have a hundred different meanings to a hundred different people.' He went on to state with even greater clarity: 'If one speaks to be understood one must speak in a common language.'[41] Unlike Waldman, I wouldn't read this passage as being symptomatic of a more general atmosphere of 'anti-intellectualism, xenophobia and redbaiting' or even of a pervasive 'nostalgia for the past'.[42] Since Biddle was a committed leftist, whose proposal for a federally funded mural project had persuaded President Franklin Delano Roosevelt to establish the Public Works of Art scheme that had sustained many American painters during the Depression, it would be quite unfair to attribute such malignant traits to what is essentially a straightforward condemnation of aesthetic obfuscation.[43] In other words, Biddle's attack on *Guernica* did not issue from a position of entrenched political conservatism; on the contrary, the American painter had decided that Picasso's mural was not revolutionary enough, since its ambiguous content and avant-garde style would only appeal to the 'small, intellectual bourgeoisie of the metropolitan cities of Europe and the New World'.[44]

Out of Biddle's friendship with Diego Rivera and his familiarity with the 'Mexican mural renascence' of 'the early twenties' had arisen the conviction that the arts should 'play a more integrated role in the social life of the community'.[45] If the films of Walt Disney fascinated the average man far more than the Modernist distortions of the School of Paris, wasn't this simply because more 'highbrow' forms of artistic articulation no longer transmitted a set of readily intelligible, widely shared beliefs to the viewer?[46] While acknowledging that artistic realism had been hijacked into promoting totalitarian causes in the Soviet Union, Nazi Germany and Fascist Italy, Biddle thought that the solution to this problem was simply to utilise the same efficacious vehicle to disseminate a countervailing democratic 'social faith'.[47] Just six months later, however, *Harper's* printed a refutation of the well-known 'American Scene' painter's original article under the rather provocative heading 'What about Modern Art and Democracy?'. Written by the self-described 'colonial cubist' Stuart Davis, this essay already contains the germ of the argument that would later be promulgated by the Museum of Modern Art in the exhibitions of contemporary American painting that it toured overseas throughout the 1950s.[48]

Davis contends that the continuance of artistic abstraction in the United States indicated a political climate of increased individuality and liberty, since many repressive single-party governments had actually banned non-objective modes of painting. Consequently, censoring any particular type of art on the basis of 'local racial, national and cultural prejudices' must be construed as anti-American, since 'democracy in culture is dependent upon the free exchange of ideas'.[49] If the majority of the nation's population favours the 'familiar, the literal or the 'folksy' . . . to the exclusion of [a] new vision and [a] new synthesis', then this is only because it has not yet been educated to understand some of the more recent innovations in the visual arts.[50] Although Waldman's article does reproduce the passage from this essay in which Davis claims that 'Modern Art . . . will become part of the common art language of the masses as [soon as an] opportunity for participation in [an] authentic art experience is made available to them', she chose to place much greater weight upon the artist's account of the institutional barriers and entrenched attitudes that might militate against this ever happening.

Waldman's shift in emphasis suppresses the fundamental optimism of Davis's contribution to the current debate on the social functions being performed by more non-naturalistic forms of painting in the United States. Not only did the pioneering American painter accept that 'Modern art brings to its subject matter the new spatial concepts of our epoch'; he also thought that 'there is no innate barrier between public understanding of modern and technological concepts and their spiritual equation in the advanced forms of Modern Art'.[51] While Davis also believed that progressive artists would continue to require government support (due to the business community's tendency to exploit 'traditional and provincial ideology'), he still hoped that 'opportunity will . . . clarify and extend the scope of the [public's] present understanding . . . [of even] the most advanced forms of contemporary Modernism as well as the art forms of past epochs'.[52]

Similarly, in her fleeting mention of the broad-ranging exchange that was published in 1948 under the heading 'A *Life* Round Table on Modern Art', Waldman cites only the single paragraph in which the moderator summarises Aldous Huxley's brief analysis of a seventeenth-century French Classical painting by Nicolas Poussin. Yet the influential magazine had flown the British author from California to Manhattan primarily in order to request his opinion on a series of much more contemporary works, since he had already voiced his objections to non-representational painting in a widely circulated essay entitled 'Art and the Obvious'. In the penthouse atop the Museum of Modern Art Huxley, along with a number of other writers, curators, art historians and philosophers from London, Paris, St. Louis, New Haven and New York, was invited to address the following questions: '*Is modern art, considered as a whole a good or a bad development? That is to say, is it something that responsible people can support, or may they neglect it as a minor and impermanent phase of culture?*'[53]

Although this discussion group included several high-profile opponents of the twentieth-century artistic avant-garde, their criticism of many of the works that they were asked to examine was surprisingly mild. Of Jackson Pollock's rather attenuated vertical dripped painting *Cathedral*, for instance, Huxley remarked that 'It raises a question of why it stops when it does ... [since] it seems to me like a panel for a wallpaper which is repeated indefinitely around the wall'.[54] Similarly, Theodore Greene (a professor of philosophy at Yale) commented that the pattern that had been created by Pollock's gestural palimpsest would make 'a pleasant necktie'. These opinions were more than offset by the laudatory judgements that were expressed by the New York critic Clement Greenberg and the Paris-based editor Charles Duthoit in response to this composition; both had concluded that this 'exquisite' image was extremely powerful, though the latter had never been exposed to Pollock's paintings before. Even Francis Henry Taylor (the director of the Metropolitan Museum of Art), who had recently proclaimed that 'the intelligentsia of today' have 'divorced [art] from ... common human experience and made it a form of private communication', considered this particular abstract piece to be 'very lovely'.[55]

Whether they were strong proponents of the School of Paris (Meyer Shapiro's magisterial reading of Picasso's *Girl Before a Mirror* took up almost a whole page), of the emerging New York School, or of more traditional modes of painting, all fifteen participants agreed that the viewer must be prepared to 'look devotedly' at any picture (ancient or modern) with a completely open mind.[56] 'Author and lecturer' James J. Sweeney described the ideal viewer's almost Riegl-like state of sympathetic attentiveness in the following way:

> There are first-level artists and second-level artists ... first-level observers and second-level observers ... What we have been urging is that the observer on the lower level make what effort he can to come to a fuller enjoyment, a deeper appreciation of modern art – and in that way enrich his psychological, his spiritual world.[57]

Consequently, if the viewer did not understand what a non-naturalistic painting was attempting to convey (and after admitting that the fault might lie in his or her own limitations), he or she must still be prepared to accord its creator the regard that is due to someone who is engaged in an 'honest search' for 'genuine' meaning in an epoch marred by transience and uncertainty. As Clement Greenberg unexpectedly affirmed, 'It is one of the *tragedies* of our time ... that great painting has to do without a recognisable subject matter.'[58] Now that the contemporary painter 'has been stripped ... of the useful standards that sustained the artists of the past and helped to make them comprehensible – religious beliefs, moral codes, esthetic dogmas', the spectator must trust him or her to conduct us on a spiritual and intellectual journey even if we are not yet capable of recognising our final destination.[59]

Sirk actually underscored the transformative potential of this nascent relationship between the Modernist painter and those viewers who were broad-minded enough to be receptive to his or her most challenging work in his 1951 musical comedy *Has Anyone Seen My Gal?*. The central protagonist of this film is only pretending to be an artist ('John Smith' is in fact Samuel Fulton, a self-made millionaire trying to decide whether he should leave his money to the family of his former sweetheart), but the abstract image that he creates the day after arriving in the Blaisdell household has an immediate effect on the adolescent girl who would become one of his closest friends. While they have both been engaged in painting the barn that may be glimpsed from the balcony located just outside the elderly lodger's room, Roberta is clearly puzzled by the non-representational nature of the image that Smith ultimately produces. As she carefully studies the looping skeins of red, blue, black, yellow and green her companion has daubed onto the canvas, the bemused teenager is told that 'it's [a] Surrealist [work]' inspired by a 'new school of painting founded in Paris', which means 'instead of painting what you see, you paint what is inside you'. Although, as a result of this explanation, Roberta deduces from the swirling vortex of his composition that Smith is 'all mixed up', she never doubts the veracity of the older artist's perception of his small town setting and winds up destroying her own much more naturalistic sketch of the barn and the surrounding landscape instead. The impressionable young girl's admiration for this particular abstraction culminates in her mentor winning first prize in a local painting competition, after she has entered this picture without his knowledge. Roberta will later demonstrate her own mastery of avant-garde art by drawing a moustache and goatee on one of the Rococo statues that her social-climbing mother had placed in the foyer of their pretentious new home; a gesture of rebellion that is reminiscent of Marcel Duchamp's Mona Lisa parody L.H.O.O.Q.

The *Life* Round Table group of critics' widely disseminated call for a universal deference to any artist (abstract or figurative, European or American) who was embroiled in the 'tremendous, individualistic struggle . . . to discover . . . and to express him*self*' in the name of 'freedom' is far from the attitude towards modern painting that Waldman claims to have detected in the popular press of the period. In fact, over the next decade *Life* magazine would publish a whole series of even-handed and generally respectful articles on contemporary artists that included the controversial 1949 profile of Jackson Pollock that made him a household name.[60] While there was always the possibility that a non-naturalistic painting would remain unintelligible to the viewer, most of the writers who raised this issue in *Life* and *Harper's Magazine*

48 *Douglas Sirk, Aesthetic Modernism and the Culture of Modernity*

during the 1940s and '50s were prepared to give the artists responsible the benefit of the doubt. At worst, these non-objective images were consigned to the category of the merely decorative, rather than being denounced as the product of a deranged, childlike or politically subversive mind as Waldman has maintained.[61] For instance, the Jackson Pollock canvasses used as the backdrop for a fashion shoot that appeared in a 1951 issue of *Vogue* or the Picasso painting that was included in a room filled with contemporary

Figure 2.2 Picasso painting included in a John Stuart Inc. furniture advertisement.
Source: *Interiors*, July 1954, p. 3.

furniture in a 1954 advertisement published in *Interiors* (Figure 2.2) risk being perceived as strictly ornamental.[62] In this respect, a motion picture director has at least one advantage over the Modernist painter in that he can clarify the significance of his non-mimetic use of colour by linking certain combinations of hues with specific narrative events.

In other words, when watching Douglas Sirk's *Magnificent Obsession*, Sweeney's second-level viewer does not need to know that the director's mise-en-scène might have been influenced by the theories of Wassily Kandinsky. As we have seen, the pioneering Expressionist painter had associated blue with a state of transcendent spirituality, and this colour often tinges Sirk's images when his characters are engaged in introspection or immersed in faintly mystical situations. Yet because *Magnificent Obsession*'s 'exalted' subject matter is also disclosed through the plot and dialogue, the exaggerated intensity of the director's non-naturalistic formal aesthetic is less likely to be misunderstood.[63] Moreover, even George Biddle allowed that 'abstract colour and design offer a stronger stimulant to the viewer, and one to which there is a more immediate response, than does traditional art', though he (not unlike Sirk) wanted to harness this affective quality to 'a restatement, reflection, reaction, criticism or experience of life'.[64]

Waldman's consideration of art in her chosen films revolved around the 'use of the presence of a realistic portrait as an occasion to valorize an illusionist over a modernist aesthetic'.[65] By contrast, the only 'realistic portrait' that features prominently in Sirk's cinematic oeuvre (a painting of Texas tycoon Jasper Hadley grasping a model of the oil derrick that is the symbol of his corporate success in *Written on the Wind*) turns out to be as just as 'fake' or misleading as the most enigmatic Modernist abstraction. This painting appears to show a man with a strong, forceful personality who dominates everything he surveys, which the spectator knows is far from the truth. Despite his undeniable business acumen and ability to hire others to do his bidding, Hadley is actually a small, impotent character who can't control the destructive impulses of either of his children, an alcoholic son and a promiscuous daughter. Moreover, when Marylee Hadley becomes the head of the family company after her father's death, she sits at the desk that has been placed beneath this looming image wearing a similar tailored suit, fondling the same miniature oil derrick, and weeps inconsolably. At the very moment that she has acceded to a position of great wealth and authority (at least within a commercial sphere), the heartbroken woman also loses the only man she has ever loved. For both the father (whose offer to donate a million dollars to a hospital could not prevent his wife from dying on the operating table) and his daughter, a life without passion will ultimately prove to be empty and deeply unsatisfying.

By contrast, the only other portrait that plays a significant role in Sirk's best-known melodramas (Randolph's painting of Doctor Wayne Phillips in *Magnificent Obsession*) is never fully revealed, and the small fragment that we do manage to glimpse consists of nothing more than a few abstract swirls of pure colour. Hence, in this director's cinematic corpus at least, modern art is associated with psychological revelation or spiritual rebirth rather than with madness, where it has eclipsed the realistic portrait as a means of disclosing hidden truths. This tendency is even evident in *Has Anyone Seen My Gal?* (Sirk's first film shot in colour), since a highly revealing Expressionist painting is visible on a nearby wall for the entire sequence in which Charles Blaisdell confesses to his elder daughter's wealthy prospective father-in-law that he has lost what remained of the $100,000 that his family had been given by an unknown benefactor (namely Smith/Fulton) on the stock exchange. In this disturbing piece of art, which combines the brooding intensity of a Max Beckmann self-portrait with the drifting instability of the fiddlers of Marc Chagall, an older male figure's ghostly-looking head hovers above his grotesquely distorted body as he struggles to play a violin. The jagged lines formed by this anxious-looking musician's limbs, the violent clash between the patches of orange, yellow and blue that divide the background, and the tight compression of the depicted space, all seem to offer the viewer some insight into Blaisdell's current psychological state. His growing sense of entrapment in the upper-class milieu his wife was forcing him to inhabit and his increasing agitation at having lost the wherewithal to sustain it are clearly echoed in this rather unsettling image. Of course, Lester Pennock will refuse to lend the former 'shopkeeper' the money he needs to cover his debts and will immediately proceed to call off his son's wedding, now that he knows that Milli's family is no longer rich. Her father will subsequently be obliged to admit that he and his wife behaved just as badly when they dissolved their daughter's previous engagement to a poor but honest soda jerk after receiving this mysterious bequest. Perhaps not unexpectedly, given Sirk's intimate knowledge of Expressionist art, Blaisdell's illuminating confession takes place in front of a set of plain floor-length drapes that have been tinted a very Kandinskian blue.[66]

Finally, I would argue that Waldman's exclusive focus on the importance of the individual paintings that appear in a handful of 'Gothic romances' is quite a limited method of investigating the interrelationship of art and cinema. What if the director's use of boldly non-naturalistic colour or ambiguous post-Cubist space is no longer confined to the parameters of discrete objects but instead spills across the entire frame? In *All That Heaven Allows*, for instance, where Sirk had begun to flood his mise-en-scène with washes of pure colour that have been detached from any particular entity or source of illumination, he repeatedly introduced a very Expressionist collision between large areas of yellow and blue. For instance, when Cary opens her front door to admit Ron just before his first encounter with her children, he is bathed in a free-floating blue light that appears to symbolise his non-materialistic way of life. On the other side of the hallway, Ned and Kay have been immersed in a diffuse yellow hue that signals their contrary preoccupation with money, status and possessions.[67]

Mary Beth Haralovich has interpreted the same meeting in Cary's foyer somewhat differently in a reading that draws upon genre criticism and the conventions that were codified by 'Natalie Kalmus for the Color Advisory Service of the Technicolor Company'. In '*All That Heaven Allows*: Color, Narrative Space and Melodrama' she observes that the 'deep blue from the night and the yellow from the hallway compete for the viewer's attention'.[68] Pools of the same two 'visually contentious' hues are also discernible when Howard assaults Cary on the terrace of the country club, a juxtaposition that Haralovich would eventually conclude underscores the 'ideological[ly] problematic' nature of the widow's burgeoning sexuality.[69] But if this striking colour contrast was meant to simply provide additional visual emphasis, why is the night sky in *All That Heaven Allows* so intensely blue (and not purple or black) and the light in its interior sequences generally so yellow (and not orange or white)? When Ned tells Cary that he doesn't approve of her impending marriage or Kay bursts into tears because of the malicious rumours being spread about her mother and Ron, why do the same two antithetical hues suffuse the room? Many other possible combinations of colour or tonality are 'neither especially harmonious nor restful to the eye', so why does this clash between yellow and blue recur with such unusual frequency?[70] Again, given this director's specific intellectual and cultural background, his decision to deploy two of Kandinsky's most symbolically resonant colours at certain key points in the narrative seems to evoke many of the associations that were codified in *Concerning the Spiritual in Art*. Hence, the struggle between yellow and blue that is manifested in *All That Heaven Allows* also serves to highlight the major conflict in the storyline, which pits an ethos of modest frugality against the much more mercenary concerns of the suburban commuter.

II CINEMA AND PAINTING: COMPOSING OTHER MODELS

In his introduction to a collection of essays entitled *Picture This: Media Representations of Visual Art and Artists*, Philip Hayward declared that film directors 'have often attempted to recreate the visual and/or lighting styles of particular painters (with varying degrees of success)'.[71] Although Hayward's brief discussion of these cinematic 'recreations of the . . . visual environment(s) suggested by the mise-en-scène of particular painters' . . . work' only refers to a few examples that were shot by relatively recent art house filmmakers such as Derek Jarman and Terence Malick, this kind of artistic allusion is not a new phenomenon.[72] The settings of many of the most dazzling Hollywood musicals of the late 1940s and 1950s were obviously affected by some of the most radical experiments of twentieth-century art, especially in terms of the anti-mimetic use of colour, vibrant graphic patterns and the commingling of fantasy and reality. According to Gilles Deleuze, during the integrated musical's fluid passage 'from the narrative to the spectacular', 'flat views' of 'landscapes, towns and silhouettes' were often permitted to 'show through', like 'postcards or snapshots' or Modernist paintings, 'where colour takes on a fundamental value' of its own.[73] In this way, the spectator enters a dream-like state, which in the hands of a brilliant director like Vincente Minnelli enables us to experience a 'plurality of worlds' that vacillate between the actual and the imaginary, as well as the past, present and future.[74]

After having already mentioned that for much of that decade the best films were being made in the United States rather than in Europe, Sirk spoke of his lasting admiration for Vincente Minnelli's 1944 musical *Meet Me in St. Louis* as well as for certain sequences of *An American in Paris* in a *Cahiers du Cinéma* interview that was published in 1967.[75] Just like his expatriate German admirer, Minnelli had initially tried painting before becoming a theatrical set and costume designer and later a stage director in New York.[76] The talented Broadway recruit came to Hollywood for the second time in 1940, and many of his subsequent films exhibit the dual fascination with American popular culture and high art that continued to shape his career.[77] In both *Meet Me in St. Louis* and *An American in Paris* (1951), artistic renderings (whether they resembled Currier and Ives or Raoul Dufy) are brought to life and fill the screen, so that the realm of art bleeds inexorably into the characters' everyday existence, which becomes just as stylised and suffused with colour. This self-conscious 'artistry' is equally evident in those elements that these motion pictures do not share with painting: the nuanced use of figure and camera movement, the rhythmic editing construction and the music that communicates the characters' overwhelming outpouring of feeling. Again, many of these qualities are also characteristic of Douglas Sirk's most successful melodramas, a genre that was expected to be just as artificial and showy.

Given Minnelli's enduring interest in the visual arts, it isn't surprising that Angela Dalle Vacche devotes the first section of *Cinema and Painting: How Art is Used in Film* to an analysis of *An American in Paris*, the work that contains the most explicit references to Modernist painting. Because this conspicuously 'artistic' musical was released at the beginning of the 1950s, Dalle Vacche detects the playing out of a rivalry between a virile American 'action painting' and a refined and therefore effeminate French Modernism that has become part of the fabled chronicles of Abstract Expressionism. Her thesis is somewhat undermined by the fact that *An American in Paris* was released in 1951, which means that it was already in production before the first photographs of Jackson Pollock throwing paint at an empty canvas had even been published or the first definitive public statement of this myth (by Harold Rosenberg) had actually appeared in print.[78] Despite the face-off between French and American art and civilisation that Dalle Vacche has ascribed to Minnelli's film, during this period most New York School painters would have assumed that modern artists working in both countries were part of the same aesthetic continuum. For instance, in the answers to a questionnaire he filled out for *California Arts and Architecture* in 1944, Jackson Pollock declared, 'I accept the fact that the important painting of the past one hundred years was done in France.' He also stressed the significance of the fact that a large proportion of the European artistic vanguard had fled the terror and devastation of World War II and were currently living in the United States.[79] Although the continental painters who had most directly affected his stylistic approach (Picasso and Miró) remained overseas, Pollock confessed that the exiles in New York had taught him that 'the source of art is the unconscious'.[80]

Dalle Vacche herself acknowledges this patrimony in statements such as: 'Although no direct evidence of Pollock's influence on Minnelli can be found, both these artists were deeply interested in the way Surrealism linked artistic creativity to the unconscious.'[81] As I have already noted, this ground-breaking European artistic movement was explicitly mentioned in Sirk's 1951 evocation of small-town America *Has Anybody Seen My Gal?*, though Smith's description would have been just as applicable to German Expression. Surrealism had, of course, originated in France and its correlation of 'pure psychic automatism' with a condition of heightened creative invention had no doubt inspired many of the subsequent American experiments with automatic painting.[82] Moreover, the 'future resolution of . . . dream and reality' that was at the core of André Breton's definition of the 'absolute reality' of *surréalité* is also evident in Minnelli's enduring preoccupation with liminal states. For instance, the extended dance sequence that concludes *An American in Paris* begins with Jerry's (and the viewer's) psychological entry into his delicate drawing of an idealised French park whose threshold is marked by the tracery of a wrought iron gate. An extreme close-up on the artist's face, followed by a double exposure that projects his body into this chimerical space, alerts us to the fact that we are at the same time infiltrating his subconscious mind. The resultant chain of interconnected fantasies (where Jerry's athletic execution of a succession of tap, jazz and ballet movements carries him through a series of tableaux that imitate works by specific Impressionist and Post-Impressionist painters) is tinged with both Eros and Thanatos, just as one would expect from a good Surrealist.

At first, the American painter seems to feel threatened by a French gendarme and several gyrating women, but the sudden appearance of his youthful paramour draws him deeper into this world of dreams. As Lisa takes on a variety of guises, becoming in turn '[Pierre-Auguste] Renoir's *femme-fleur* ... Henri Rousseau's gypsy girl' and [Henri] Toulouse-Lautrec's Jane Avril', her various personae reinforce 'the association of art with femininity' (according to Dalle Vacche).[83] Yet as this sequence progresses, the so-called 'masculine' principle of Gene Kelly's energetic and often American-style dancing (his vaudeville hoofing countering her French classical ballet) will finally merge with the iridescent vision of Toulouse-Lautrec. Even before this artistic and choreographic climax, where Lisa/Jane Avril's vivacious can-can matches Jerry/Chocolat's African-American-inflected prancing step for step, the director had begun to seamlessly integrate these received images into his psychic landscape.

Just before the transition to Toulouse-Lautrec's bohemian *demi-monde*, the two lovers had executed a gracefully romantic pas de deux around the Neo-classical statues that surround the park's central fountain. Throughout this sequence, Minnelli had created an emotionally charged atmosphere by painting an amorphous background with successive washes of undiluted colour, light and shadow. Here we are shown that both the director and Jerry are capable of applying the lessons that they have learned from early French Modernism in order to generate a more abstract and introspective environment of their own. Yet, as Dalle Vacche has suggested, the most utopian moment of the film occurs when 'Chocolat's raised hand poignantly conveys the attainment of that blissful state that the musical's integration of painting, dance and music always strives for'.[84] In other words, the temporary formation of a community perfected by 'art' was made possible (however briefly) by a confluence of the choreography of Gene Kelly with the sinuous calligraphy of Henri Toulouse-Lautrec. Long before Jackson Pollock had developed his 'method of dripping paint over the canvas', the French artist's gestural drawings had captured the 'values of fusion, creativity and spontaneity' that Dalle Vacche attributes solely to the United States.[85] Nevertheless, I would argue that what makes this scene from *An American in Paris* so powerful is rather its complex cultural syncretism: African-American jazz music and dance blend with French popular culture; nineteenth-century high art combines with the industrial aesthetic of twentieth-century motion pictures. Just like the Surrealists, Minnelli believed that only by being open to the prospect of losing oneself could one attain a state of genuine creative transcendence, a conviction he would again demonstrate in *Lust for Life* (an adaptation of Irving Stone's biography of Vincent Van Gogh).

Sirk's sophisticated fusion of music, moving images and drama represents an equally synergistic synthesis of European and American culture, which also embraces both high and low art. Yet although *Magnificent Obsession* and *All That Heaven Allows* do offer some glimmerings of utopia, their director pulls back from the brink of Minnelli's sense of an embodied plenitude. Both of these films end with a very planar 'picture' of an idyllic vista that we must view through the rigorous geometry of an International Style window. In each case, the framing of the landscape precludes the spectator's psychological entry to some degree, although it also helps to deepen the act of contemplation by enabling us to focus our gaze. Perhaps achieving a state of sympathetic attention now requires a 'machine' to correct the audience's vision in order to prevent this paradisaical 'garden' from being overlooked. Or even more likely, the beauty of nature and the artistic creations of man may be equally imperfect reflections of an ideal world, which together they can only approximate.[86] Yet despite his 'acute awareness of pain, failure and death', Sirk continued to subscribe to a philosophy of hope to some degree.[87] The many different art forms that the director deploys all serve to heighten the audience's awareness of human suffering, in an attempt to persuade us to address the contemporary social problems that were their main cause.

Nevertheless, random events still regularly shatter the synthetic perspective of even the most carefully composed panoramas in many of Sirk's films. Although this director's images often meet James Lastra's definition of the staged 'Albertian' composition that has been arranged within a delimiting frame, the sudden irruption of a speedboat, car, plane or shooting accident also lends them some of the characteristics of the critic's second type of depiction. When viewing this alternative category of picture (again as described by Lastra), we are meant to continue to consider the larger world that exists outside the frame, which remains both oblivious to our presence and beyond our control.[88] In other words, the great fear that Brigitte Peucker ascribes to 'the fragmentation imposed upon the body by cinema' is often quite palpable in Sirk's cinematic corpus, but I would argue that it reflects more generalised cultural anxieties rather than a sense of unease arising from the structure of the medium itself.[89] As this director's contemporary viewers well knew, any industrialised society now had the capacity to mutilate and destroy human bodies on an almost unimaginable scale, something that had been quite graphically demonstrated over the course of two World Wars. By revealing a deep-seated suspicion of even the most quotidian machines, Sirk's films are also disclosing the fear of the new technology that was another crucial aspect of the experience of modernity, something that I will examine at greater length in the next chapter of this book.

Notes

1. Stern, 4.
2. In John Stahl's 1935 adaptation of Lloyd C. Douglas's best-selling book, the artist who transmits the late doctor's spiritual message to the wealthy playboy is a sculptor rather than a painter, carving much more concretely realised angels out of marble in a highly traditional Christian style. Sirk's divergent depiction of this key scene is amenable to a very different interpretation of spirituality, as we shall see.
3. See the document entitled '"Magnificent Obsession" – Campaign Ideas – A. Movies are Growing Up' in Box 414, File 12352 of the Universal-International Pictures archives.
4. David Weiss's 'Magazine and Newspaper Ideas for Magnificent Obsession' in Box 414, File 12352 of the Universal-International Pictures archives.
5. Jim O'Connor's review (published in the *New York Journal-American*, 5 August 1954) was entitled '"Magnificent Obsession": Dramatic, Exalted Film'. See the Douglas Sirk Clipping File in the Museum of Modern Art, New York.
6. While discussing Doctor Hudson's personal convictions in the novel, one of his medical colleagues remarks: 'You would think, to hear his prattle, that he was a wealthy and neurotic old lady trying to graduate from theosophy to Bahaism.' See page 5 of Lloyd C. Douglas's *Magnificent Obsession* (London: Allen & Unwin, 1952 repr. of the 1936 edn). Dr Hudson's surname was changed to Phillips in Sirk's film version of this novel because Rock Hudson had been cast in the part of Bob Merrick.
7. Dennis Reid, *Atma Buddhi Manas: The Later Works of Lawren S. Harris* (Toronto: The Art Gallery of Ontario, 1985), 12.
8. Jean-Loup Bourget, 'God is Dead, or Through a Glass Darkly'. Available at <www.brightlightsfilm.com/48/sirkgodis.htm, 2–4> (last accessed 17 October 2005).
9. According to theosophists, Christ did represent just one of a whole brotherhood of spiritual Adepts who have guided the upward ascending evolution of humanity. Others include Buddha, Confucius, Lao-tzu, Solomon and many others. See Bruce F. Campbell's *Ancient Wisdom Revived: A History of the Theosophy Movement* (Berkeley: University of California Press, 1980), 54.
10. Bourget, 2.
11. Bourget, 4–5, Stern 10.
12. Bourget, 5.
13. Reid, 12.
14. H.P. Blavatsky, *Collected Writings 1888: The Secret Doctrine* (Adyar: The Theosophical Publishing House, 1979), II, 507–9.
15. Blavatsky, 492, 511–12.
16. Blavatsky, 472.
17. The prominently placed lighting fixtures are perhaps the most important mystical motifs in this scene, since they are readily apparent throughout and seem

to indicate some sort of divine effulgence. When Merrick struggles to find the courage to try out his former professor's new surgical technique, he is standing directly below the light that extends outward from the wall on the far side of the room. This juxtaposition is just as significant as the reverse shot of the artist, whose unwavering gaze seems to be willing his friend to go on. After Randolph has left, Merrick will complete this complex medical procedure beneath the large circular lamp that is suspended over the operating table.

18. While developing a parallel between William Shakespeare and the Hollywood director, Sirk pretends to be a producer pitching a 'crazy story' featuring 'ghosts, murder, tearing the hair', wittily concluding with the statement 'It's called Magnificent Ob . . . no, Hamlet'. See page 5 of Stern's 'Sirk Speaks'.
19. Stern, 10.
20. Sixten Ringbom, '"The Epoch of the Great Spiritual"': Occult Elements in the Early Theory of Abstract Painting', *Journal of the Warburg and Courtald Institutes*, 29 (1966), 402–6.
21. Blavatsky, 561–2.
22. Blavatsky, 492 and Ringbom, 396.
23. Annie Besant, *A Study in Consciousness* (Adyar: The Theosophical Publishing House, 1967 reprint of the 1904 edition), 26, 31.
24. Kandinsky, 9, 46–7.
25. After asserting that Dr Wayne Phillips = God (which means that God is dead), Bourget then proposes that the figure of the artist is presented as a God-substitute, and that the director himself performs a similar function (page 4). As I have already pointed out, within a theosophical system all of these individuals would have been expected to share a portion of this divine afflatus and to remain linked to God to some degree. Even though as long as we remain within our fleshly bodies we can neither completely fuse with nor fully comprehend this originary Oversoul, it is never entirely absent.
26. Ringbom 397–8.
27. Lehman, 46.
28. Kandinsky, 13.
29. Ringbom, 404.
30. Kandinsky, 24–6.
31. Kandinsky, 47, 30.
32. Kandinsky, 38.
33. Kandinsky, 39.
34. Kandinsky 39, 38.
35. Kandinsky, 37–8. On page 38 of *Concerning the Spiritual in Art* Kandinsky describes yellow as the least spiritual and most earthbound of colours, a hue that 'can never have profound meaning'.
36. To Kandinsky, black represented 'A totally dead silence . . . a silence with no possibilities . . . the silence of death'. See page 39 of *Concerning the Spiritual in Art*. While Merrick's suit is technically a dark, charcoal grey, the way in which it has been lit during this metaphysical discussion makes it appear to be black.

37. Kandinsky, 'Reminiscences/Three Pictures' in *Kandinsky: Complete Writings on Art*, Volume I, ed. Kenneth C. Lindsay and Peter Vergo (London: Faber & Faber), 377, and *Concerning the Spiritual in Art*, 2.
38. Kandinsky, 25.
39. Diane Waldman, 'The Childish, the Insane, and the Ugly: Modern Art in Popular Film and Fiction of the Forties', in *Picture This: Media Representations of Visual Art and Artists*, ed. Philip Hayward (London: John Libbey, 1988), 130–1.
40. Waldman, 128.
41. Waldman, 130.
42. Waldman, 128.
43. Fred R. Kline Gallery, Santa Fe, New Mexico, 'George Biddle', 15 November 2005. Available at <http://www.klinegallery.com/Biddle01_Bio.html> (last accessed 15 November 2005).
44. George Biddle, 'The Victory and Defeat of Modernism: Art in a New World', *Harper's Magazine*, 187, No. 1,117 (1943), 34.
45. Biddle, 35.
46. Biddle, 35.
47. Biddle, 35–7.
48. David and Cecile Shapiro, 'Abstract Expressionism: The Politics of Apolitical Painting', in *Pollock and After: The Critical Debate*, ed. Francis Frascina (New York: Harper & Row, 1985), 146–7.
49. Stuart Davis, 'What About Modern Art and Democracy?', *Harper's Magazine*, 188, No. 1123 (1943–4), 19.
50. Davis, 19, 17.
51. Davis, 18.
52. Davis, 22, 19, 17.
53. Russell W. Davenport, 'A *Life* Round Table on Modern Art: Fifteen Distinguished Critics and Connoisseurs Undertake to Clarify the Strange Art of Today', *Life*, 25, No. 15 (11 October 1948), 56. In 'The Victory and Defeat of Modernism', George Biddle commented on the role that was increasingly being played by mass circulation magazines in developing the American people's taste for art. 'It is estimated that *Life* magazine has fifteen million readers a week and *Esquire* about five million a month (figuring several readers per copy). If we include *Coronet* and other semi-quality magazines, and the Sunday rotogravure papers, it is safe to estimate that expensive colored or black-and-white reproductions of classic and the best current American art are enjoyed by a weekly audience of over twenty million people.' See Biddle, page 36.
54. Davenport, 62.
55. Francis Henry Taylor, 'Modern Art and the Dignity of Man', *Atlantic Monthly*, 182, No. 6 (1948), 30.
56. Davenport, 68.
57. Davenport, 67.
58. Davenport, 78.
59. Davenport, 79.

60. Dorothy Seiberling, 'Jackson Pollock: Is He the Greatest Living Painter in the United States?', *Life* 27 (8 August 1949), 42–3, 45.
61. Waldman, 128. On page 48 of an article entitled 'The State of Modern Painting' that was published in *Harper's Magazine* [197, No. 1,181 (1948)] Lincoln Kirstein asserts: 'The influential artist of our time . . . is not concerned with what artists see or how they see, but with how they paint . . . [which means that] the contemporary Academy of Abstract Painting is primarily decorative.'
62. See 'Spring Ball Gowns', *Vogue* (1 March 1951), 156–9.
63. In an article that was published on page 13 of the 5 August 1954 issue of the *New York Journal-American*, *Magnificent Obsession* was described as a 'Dramatic, Exalted Film'. This headline was taken from a sentence in the second paragraph, where the writer (Jim O'Connor) states: 'The dramatic, exalted story it tells is that God moves in a mysterious way His wonders to perform.' Similarly, the review of the film that appeared in *Boxoffice* (8 May 1954), *Variety* (12 May 1954) and *Motion Picture Daily* (11 May 1954) also emphasised the message of 'faith, hope and charity' (without 'heavy-handed preachment') that Sirk's version of this story manages to communicate to his viewers. There is no doubt that the spiritual overtones of this narrative would have been difficult to miss.
64. George Biddle, 'Modern Art and Muddled Thinking', *Atlantic Monthly*, 180, No. 6 (1947), 59–60.
65. Waldman, 131.
66. The equally self-centred mother in Sirk's next small town comedy (*No Room for the Groom*, 1952) tries to have her daughter's unconsummated marriage to the man she loves annulled so she can be wed to someone who is much wealthier. The anti-materialistic message of *Has Anyone Seen My Gal?* (and of the director's later film *All That Heaven Allows*) is even more obvious in *No Room for the Groom*. When his young wife's relatives try to pressure him into selling his family vineyard to Herman Strouple (the rich owner of the Strouple Cement Company, and Lee's prospective suitor), Alvah Morrell accuses them of translating everything into a 'dollar and cents value'. From this perspective, 'Moral values, principles [and] sentiment' don't 'count anymore', which means that they will inevitably be 'chucked out' for 'a quick buck'. Needless to say, Alvah and Lee are finally reconciled and don't sell the vineyard in the end.
67. Kandinsky described yellow as the least spiritual and most earthbound of colours, a hue that 'can never have profound meaning'. See *Concerning the Spiritual in Art*, 38.
68. In *Close-Viewings: An Anthology of New Film Criticism*, ed. Peter Lehman (Tallahassee: Florida State University Press, 1990).
69. Haralovich, caption for Figure 4-10 and pages 68–9.
70. See Haralovich, 68.
71 Philip Hayward, 'Echoes and Reflections: The Representation of Representations', in *Picture This: Media Representations of Visual Art and Artists*, ed. Philip Hayward (London: John Libbey, 1988), 5.
72. Hayward, 5.

73. Deleuze, 62.
74. Deleuze, 62.
75. Serge Daney and Jean-Louis Noames, 'Entretien avec Douglas Sirk', *Cahiers du Cinéma*, 189 (1967), 20, 23. In *Magnificent Obsession* the transition from the United States to Switzerland is effected by animating the still picture of a postcard that Helen has sent Bob Merrick from Lucerne. This might be a *hommage* to *Meet Me in St. Louis*, a film in which every 'chapter' of the narrative begins by bringing a picture of the small town to life and drawing the viewer into this space.
76. Angela Dalle Vacche, *Cinema and Painting: How Art Is Used in Film* (Austin: University of Texas Press, 1996), 14. Beth Genné, 'Vincent Minnelli's Style in Microcosm: the Establishing Sequence in "Meet Me in St. Louis"', *Art Journal*, 43 (1983), 247.
77. Joe McElhaney, 'Vincent Minnelli', *Senses of the Cinema* 2004, 7 April 2005. Available at <http://www. senses of the cinema.com/contents/directors /04/minnelli.html>, 4–5 (last accessed 7 April 2005).
78. A selection of Hans Namuth's photographs of 'Pollock Painting' (taken at his Long Island studio in 1950) would not be published until a year later, when they accompanied an article written by Robert Goodnough entitled 'Pollock Paints a Picture' [*Art News*, 50 (May 1951), 38–41]. New York critic Harold Rosenberg coined the term 'action painting' (a method of creation for which Pollock was the most obvious model) in an article that was published in 1952. See his 'The American Action Painters', *Art News*, 51 (December 1952), 22–3, 48–50.
79. As a prelude to the Chicago Art Institute's 1947 exhibition of 'abstraction and surrealism in America', two of its curators were sent out to determine just 'how widespread these movements were' within the United States. Frederick A. Sweet and Katharine Kuh 'traveled over 25,000 miles' and found 'hundreds of men and women working vigorously with abstract means'. Moreover, they found that 'at least three out of every four painters working in these modes were native-born Americans, contradicting the often repeated statement that art of this sort is the work of "foreigners"'. See page 47 of Daniel Catton Rich's 'Freedom of the Brush', which was published in the February 1948 issue of *The Atlantic Monthly* [181, No. 2].

Rich also noted that the 'arrival of practically a boatload of famous European modernists before the war ... vastly stimulated the non-representationalists', while observing that these exiled artists were influenced in turn by their new American environment (p. 49). In other words, the result was a 'crossing of styles' rather than any perception of opposition (p. 48).
80. 'Jackson Pollock', *Arts and Architecture*, 61, No. 2 (February 1944), 14.
81. Dalle Vacche, 15.
82. In 1924, André Breton defined Surrealism in the Surrealist Manifesto as 'Pure psychic automatism, by which one intends to express verbally, in writing or in any other method, the real functioning of the mind. Dictation by thought, in the absence of any control exercised by reason, and beyond any aesthetic or moral preoccupation'. See William S. Rubin, *Dada, Surrealism and Their Heritage* (New York: The Museum of Modern Art, 1968), 64.

83. Dalle Vacche, 20.
84. Dalle Vacche, 35.
85. Dalle Vacche, 30.
86. Another factor that militates against a completely utopian interpretation of this final image is the presence of an invalid in the same room. In the case of *Magnificent Obsession*, Helen Phillips is lying on a nearby bed swathed in bandages. Although her operation has been successful, she has not yet recovered from her difficult surgery. Similarly, in *All That Heaven Allows* the injured body of Ron Kirby has been laid out on a couch directly beneath this window. The tree-farmer does regain consciousness by the end of the film, but has yet to be nursed back to health by the woman he loves.
87. Robert E. Smith, 'Love Affairs That Always Fade'. Available at www.brightlightsfilm.com/48/sirkloveaffairs.htm, p. 1 (last accessed 17 October 2005).
88. James Lastra, 'From the Captured Moment to the Cinematic Image: A Transformation in Pictorial Order', in *The Image in Dispute: Art and Cinema in the Age of Dispute*, ed. Dudley Andrew (Austin: University of Texas Press, 1997), 268–9. Lastra borrows this binary opposition from art historian Svetlana Alpers. Alpers initially developed this model in order to explain the differences between Renaissance Italian and seventeenth-century Dutch painting. In the *Art of Describing*, she declared that '"northern painting" . . . is constructed "as if the world came first"'[quoted by Lastra, p. 268].
89. Peucker, 10.

Part Two

The Shock of the New: Traces of Modernity

CHAPTER THREE

The Invasion of Machines and Machine Culture

According to Ben Singer, a widespread fear of increasing social chaos, of the inevitable uncertainties of fate and of exposing ourselves to unknown dangers has been a staple of the melodramatic form since at least the turn of the twentieth century. In particular, Singer has meticulously documented an all-pervading fear of the machines that have come to symbolise the accelerated pace and bodily perils of modern life. While many previous scholars have built upon Georg Simmel, Siegfried Kracauer and Walter Benjamin's 'neurological conception of modernity', the notion that the metropolitan environment is constantly bombarding us with perceptual stimuli that subject our senses to a 'barrage of shocks, impressions and jolts', Singer also highlights the increased possibility of experiencing actual physical maiming and death.[1] In my view, many of Sirk's most accomplished works exhibit a similar sense of anxiety, a dread that would have been further exacerbated by the almost unimaginable carnage of World War I. Nevertheless, many of these films also contain traces of the early twentieth-century avant-garde's 'machine euphoria', the concomitant belief that the new technology might enable us to change society for the better as well as for the worse.

Singer based his fascinating conclusions upon a detailed investigation of a wide range of middlebrow commentaries published between the late 1880s and 1920 that included 'cartoons [appearing] in the illustrated press (both in comic magazines such as *Puck*, *Punch*, *Judge* and *Life* and lowbrow sensational newspapers such as New York's *World* and *Journal*)'. Apparently, his scrutiny of this broad cross-section of popular periodicals yielded innumerable accounts of the wholesale slaughter that was supposed to be taking place on the city streets. For instance, in 1905 Henry Adams observed that '[against the metropolis] Nature violently revolted, causing so called accidents with enormous destruction of property and life . . . The railways alone approached the carnage of war'.[2] Singer would go on to persuasively link this obsession with the 'horrific' side effects of mass transportation and production with a 'cultural uneasiness surrounding the onset of urban modernity'.[3] Fifty years later, the same atmosphere of violence and danger continued to enfold the speedboats, fast cars and airplanes that are a prominent feature of *Magnificent Obsession*, *Written on the Wind* and *The Tarnished Angels*.

Yet as both a participant in the heavily industrialised First World War and a refugee from the increasingly mechanised threats of the Second, Sirk had even more reason to distrust recent advances in technology than Singer's turn-of-the-century metropolitan pedestrian.[4] One well-known military historian has estimated that 'by 1914 a single regiment of field guns could deliver in one hour more firepower than had been unleashed by all the adversary powers in the Napoleonic wars'.[5] As a result, during the 'futile year-long effort on the part of the Germans to take the fortress city of Verdun in 1916' the 'combined German–French losses … may have reached as high as 420,000 dead and 800,000 gassed or wounded'.[6] Sirk, who had been drafted into the German navy and had spent the last year of World War I stationed in Turkey, returned home in 1918 deeply scarred by 'five years of mass slaughter for nothing'.[7]

This is not to say that a certain subset of the German population didn't continue to revel in the transformative properties of the battlefield. Some survivors of World War I would later long to return to the close-knit camaraderie of the trenches. Throughout the Weimar Republic and the Third Reich, the shared memory of the '*Kriegserlebnis* (war experience) presented … [the nation's more reactionary inhabitants] with a fully up-to-date masculine alternative to bourgeois society, one preferable to the effeminate and escapist fantasies of previous generations of less daring conservatives'.[8] In the opinion of the influential right-wing writer Ernst Jünger, the body of the ideal soldier-worker had to be tempered by the technological equivalent of World War I's 'storm of iron' before it would be 'hammered, chiselled and hardened' into the 'steel form' of the new man.[9] The glossy metallic shell that remains after all 'bourgeois and feminine refinements' have been burned away resembles nothing more or less than a precisely calibrated 'machine', which places it 'beyond pleasure, pain, and emotion', a quality that was not universally admired, as we shall soon see.[10]

I Softening the Armoured Heart: Douglas Sirk's *The Tarnished Angels*

The pilot highlighted in Sirk's 1958 film *The Tarnished Angels* represents the American analogue of one of Ernst Jünger's war-hardened robotic beings, but in the democratic setting of the United States Roger Schumann's indifference to the well-being of his wife and son is not considered to be a virtue. At various points within the narrative, the other protagonists condemn Roger's heartless disregard for Laverne's feelings, while at the same time recognising that a far crueller mistress holds him in thrall. According to Burke Devlin (a newspaper reporter played by Rock Hudson), the World War I hero was a 'child of the twentieth-century' 'who had outgrown ... motor bikes and ... motor cars ... [by developing] a hunger for the flying machine'. As his mechanic was frantically attempting to repair a defective engine in time for the following day's race, Roger had confided to Devlin 'my first love was airplanes, my [first] flirtation with death'. In order to gain access to a second aircraft (after his own plane had been destroyed in a mid-air collision), the pilot had tacitly pressured his wife into agreeing to offer herself to the wealthy manufacturer who owned it. Jiggs (the mechanic) and Devlin were suitably outraged by this proposal, and not only because they were both in love with the beautiful parachute jumper themselves. Although even Roger is too embarrassed to meet his wife's gaze throughout much of this sequence, he underscores the force of his compulsion by telling her 'I need this plane, like an alcoholic needs his drink'.

In the end, Devlin protects Laverne from sexual compromise by persuading Matt Ord to let Roger Schumann fly his plane in return for free publicity. Yet the aggrieved woman chose not to reveal this to her husband until just before his final competition, hoping to make him feel guilty for what he had asked her to do.[11] Until that moment, Roger's desire to fuse with his aircraft was so strong that he had been transformed into a sort of man–machine hybrid, to whom all normal human emotions and conventions seemed inconsequential. Devlin had tried to explain this 'alien' quality to his editor soon after his first encounter with 'the flying Schumanns' at a fairground airshow. In particular, the reporter argued that the pilot and his rivals:

> couldn't turn ... [the] pylons [that mark the race course] the way they do if they had ... any human brains. Burn them and they don't even holler. Scratch one and that's not even blood that they bleed. They are a strange race of people without any blood in their veins at all, just crankcase oil.

This speech is a greatly condensed version of the tirade that the reporter delivers to his fellow journalists in *Pylon*, the William Faulkner novel that the script was based on.[12] Yet the 'steely' endurance that it confers upon this itinerant group of flyers might have seemed too cold and remote to an American audience, who had largely escaped the infernal discipline of World War I. Consequently, the writer of the script of *The Tarnished Angels* layers an additional metamorphosis onto Faulkner's mechanical body metaphor that does not appear in the original book.

In the cinematic version of this story, the pilot's machine-like detachment is finally undone when he declares his love for his wife and son from the cockpit of Matt Ord's plane, just before taking off. Until now Roger and Laverne have exchanged few words or glances directly, but within the

Figure 3.1 Roger and Laverne Schumann's reconciliation in *The Tarnished Angels*.

intimate space of a two shot that remains focused upon their profiles, the couple finally do really seem to connect. Moreover, the lingering close-up that shows them staring into each other's eyes also accentuates the rapture of their subsequent kiss (Figure 3.1). As a result of this passionate coming together (which does not occur in the novel), a sea change has taken place that will ultimately precipitate Roger's fatal crash. Burke Devlin actually points this out in his closing peroration, which is again addressed to his colleagues in the office of the New Orleans *Picayune*:

> The night before [Roger Schumann] fell into the lake, he fell so far and so hard for the sake of the flying machine that the crankcase oil burst from his veins and a heart heavy with shame pumped blood back into them. When he turned the last pylon he was something that he thought he'd never be again, a human being. And he died only because he was thinking of the human beings that he might kill if he tried to land on the field. For among them was a woman and a boy whose love he had finally accepted. A wife and son for whom he was going to forsake his flying machines, [which] in the end forsook him.

Like Devlin, most viewers would probably have interpreted the rebirth of Roger's humanity and his renewed ability to reciprocate his family's feelings as a victory. It was, however, a pyrrhic one. Paradoxically, the softening of the pilot's armoured heart had also made him vulnerable to the lethal tendencies of the machine, and the sudden failure of Matt Ord's engine would soon afterwards lead to his downfall.[13] Nevertheless, this scene was a favourite of many of those who attended the film's September 1957 preview, presumably because it contained both the primary romantic climax and the dramatic flying sequence that ends in Roger's death.[14]

Just before *The Tarnished Angels* went into production, Sirk was still concerned that the audience might not understand the character of Roger Schumann, despite his last-minute transformation into a devoted husband and father. In a letter dated 19 August 1956 that he sent to Albert Zugsmith (the film's producer) from Zurich, the director remarked that although 'the story itself is excellent', at this stage he 'didn't feel drawn into . . . [the narrative], [and] remain[ed] detached, cold'. Sirk attributed the distancing effect of the current script to the way in which several of the protagonists 'act or – rather – don't act'. At this point, he considered Jiggs and Matt Ord to be too passive and 'nice' to provide sufficient dramatic conflict, a shortcoming that would subsequently be corrected. With regard to the figure of Roger Schumann, Sirk noted:

> His motivations are, at least to me – not clear. I don't know why he is obsessed with flying, the deeper reason for this – the mainspring of the picture – remains vague. It is *stated* in the script but not *dramatized*. The deep rift in his character: his obsession with a life that makes him and Laverne almost outcasts of society, gypsies, aimless floaters – and his ultimately emerging love for Laverne and his longing to retire and return with her to a more orderly, sheltered and bourgeois life – are not dramatically demonstrated or contrasted.[15]

Although I didn't manage to locate a copy of the screenplay that Sirk was referring to, the main element that appears to be missing from the director's brief description of the pilot's motivation is any mention of his military service. Again, Faulkner never stated that the original character had been a World War I flying ace, but this aspect of Roger Schumann's past would dominate his persona throughout the film that was released at the end of the following year.

To Sirk, and anyone else who was acquainted with this catastrophic conflict, the pilot's involvement in a series of murderous skirmishes would probably have explained why he had developed such a callous personality. If, on a daily basis, you were forced to risk your own annihilation in an attempt to kill an often equally accomplished enemy, then your survival would to some extent depend upon anaesthetising your fear. Moreover, a combat-ready pilot could not allow himself to be overcome with grief as he toasted the friends who didn't come back after returning from a mission. In Roger's reminiscences of wartime France, he recalls not only that 'every night was Saturday night' but also that the guests of honour who were fêted at these endless parties were always dead. Consequently, when a grateful restaurant owner arranges an elaborate banquet to commemorate the ex-Air Force captain's visit to New Orleans, this gesture inevitably foreshadows the latter's imminent destruction. On the evening of this dinner, as Claude Moulet and the remaining flyers raise their glasses to the 'hero who came to the rescue of my beloved native land in its darkest hour', the body of the World War I flying ace is lying at the bottom of a nearby lake. Even before his sudden demise, Roger Schumann had been haunted by premonitions of doom. Laverne may remember her husband's portrait on a Liberty Bonds poster, and Jack recites the number of German planes that his father shot down with pride, but the pilot still had nightmares about falling from the sky after losing an aerial duel with Baron von Richthofen.[16]

According to Ernst Jünger's World War I memoir, those fighters who were best adapted to modern mechanised combat were the steel helmeted 'denizens of a new and harsher world' who had 'nothing left [in their voice] but equanimity [or] apathy [because] fire had burned everything else out . . .'[17] This is not to say that even the most obdurate techno-warrior felt no emotion whatsoever. *Storm of Steel* also records the extreme euphoria that arises from the unashamed slaughter of your enemy, an elation that becomes even more pronounced once the initial skirmish is over and you realise you are still alive. As his platoon attacked the English trenches that were located near Vraucourt in Belgium in 1918, Jünger recollects that the 'immense desire to destroy that overhung the battlefield precipitated a red mist in our brains'. He would go on to say 'an impartial observer might have concluded that we were all ecstatically happy' after listening to the 'sobbing and stammering fragments of sentences [that we called out] to one another'.[18] Moreover, this influential author's later writings make it equally plain that nothing in the veteran's post-war experience would ever provoke such an acute state of mental transport again.

The best that the returning soldier, sailor or pilot could do in an attempt to simulate the shared exaltation of the battlefield was to drive a fast car or an airplane at increasingly hazardous speeds, or so Jünger claimed. Only by reintroducing an element of jeopardy into everyday life would the veteran (and everyone else) be shaken out of the enervating stasis that is the product of bourgeois complacency and an over-reliance upon reason.[19] In fact, Jünger remained convinced that the whole Enlightenment campaign to eliminate misfortune, unpredictability and risk from the world was founded upon an illusion. From this perspective, the truism that scientific 'inventions like the automobile engine have already resulted in greater losses than any war' seems to indicate that in modern twentieth-century societies 'order and [explosive] danger' are inextricably intertwined.[20] In other words, when the best-selling writer observes that 'the history of inventions also raises ever more clearly the question of whether a space of absolute comfort or a space of absolute danger is the final aim of technology', we are left in no doubt as to which answer he would choose.[21]

Throughout the 1920s and early '30s (while Sirk was still living in Germany), Jünger continued to insist that only a 'total mobilisation' of 'the economy, civic life and individual morale' offered any real protection in a world that was so saturated with menace.[22] What this notion essentially entailed was ensuring the nation's perpetual readiness for war by reconfiguring civilian institutions to more closely resemble their military counterparts. According to this philosophy, an individual will only be able to cope with the utter chaos of modern life if he or she has been absorbed into the carefully regulated hierarchy of an authoritarian regime. In other words, the reintegration of the returned serviceman into society no longer meant requiring him to put aside his combat training in order to adopt the more peaceful pursuits of a democratic state. Instead, the civilian population must be drilled into the hardened equivalent of worker-soldiers, whose bodies have been conditioned to automatically obey the pared-down leadership of an armed technocracy.[23]

For much of *The Tarnished Angels*, Roger Schumann appears to epitomise Jünger's proto-fascist ideal of the eternal warrior. Although only Matt Ord speaks openly of the thrill that he gets from watching his pilot's dangerous manoeuvres, the ex-World War I flying ace never seems to be truly energised unless he is hurtling through the air. Whether this is because the velocity of flight triggers something akin to the exhilaration of battle or because flying represents 'the living expression of a powerful life force' (in Jünger's words) isn't immediately apparent.[24] What the film does make clear is Roger's longstanding inability to accept the very different responsibilities of civilian life, which he largely repudiates by continuing to perfect the same skills that he had acquired during the war. According to a studio press release dated 12 December 1957 and credited to 'nicholas', this was typical of many of the pilots who had managed to eke out a precarious existence on the 'barnstorming' racing circuit during the early 1930s. They knew 'that they face death each time they take their frail . . . craft up to scrape the pylons [marking the parameters of the official course] but this [was] their life, a life they [had] learned in the skies above France a few years before'.[25]

The unrelenting 'air mindedness' of this combat-hardened group of fliers almost made it seem as if the Armistice had never been declared.[26] In the case of *The Tarnished Angels*, Roger's perception of the entire first race (viewed from the cockpit of the same plane that he had flown into battle) closely resembles the standard Hollywood representation of an aerial conflict. A series of point-of-view shots reveals the trained fighter chasing down his rival with an unyielding determination, a quality that is further reinforced by the reverse shots of his mask-like face. Again according to the author of the same studio publicity piece, '[*The Tarnished Angels*] . . . [was expected to] find a worthy niche beside . . . [such] aviation films of the past . . . [as] *Hell's*

Angels (1931), *Men With Wings* (middle 30s) . . . *Dawn Patrol, Only Angels have Wings* [and] *Spitfire*'. Needless to say, the majority of these films were fictitious depictions of war.

Roger Schumann's superior flying ability and reckless courage bring him to the verge of winning, even though the pilot that he holds in his sights throughout this sequence (Frank Burnham) is operating a more technologically advanced plane. In the end, the tightness of the ex-war ace's turns around the pylons forces him to clip his competitor's wings, which causes the body of Burnham's aircraft to suddenly break apart. Until this juncture, the spectator has never glimpsed a reverse shot from the latter's point of view, despite the fact that several medium close-ups showing him looking into space have been juxtaposed with similar shots of Roger Schumann. A shift to Burnham's perspective only occurs after he, as the designated 'enemy', has begun his precipitous fall from the sky. The last image that the viewer witnesses through the condemned man's eyes is his plane smashing into the ground (followed by an external shot of his limp body being flung into the air), leaving us in no doubt as to the outcome of this contest. The 'daring' captain had notched up yet another corpse, while at the same time irreparably damaging his own beloved machine. After Roger landed on the field in a cloud of smoke, his wife and mechanic had to forcibly prevent him from rushing back towards his aircraft once it had burst into flames. At that moment, we hear the ghostly strains of the popular World War I song 'Mademoiselle from Armentières' playing on the sound track, which seems to indicate that the pilot's attachment to this fragment of military technology is still stronger than his loyalty to his family and friends. While Jünger would have applauded Captain Schumann's deep-seated unwillingness to demobilise, Sirk implies that his fixation with aviation is a sickness that has been exacerbated by the trauma of battle.

By contrast, during the racing sequence that takes place after Roger has pledged to dedicate himself to his family, he no longer seems so inured to suffering and is consequently much more sensitive to the welfare of those around him. Far fewer of the pilot's point-of-view shots are allocated to sizing up the opposition and he no longer appears to overtake his competitors in such a distinctly predatory way, hunting down key individuals in an imitation of combat. While in one over-the-shoulder shot the viewer does notice Roger passing two other planes at a distance, most of what we witness from his perspective during this scene unfolds only after his engine has begun to fail. Over and over again, the spectator shares the pilot's perception of the terrified onlookers in the path of his low-flying plane who are scrambling to get away. To avoid injuring any of these unknown bystanders (which did not include his wife and son, as Devlin's later account would suggest), Roger slams his aircraft into the adjacent lake and thereby brings about his own destruction. It seems clear that after breaching his psychic defences in order to return the love of his wife and son, the pilot could no longer avoid empathising with the potential victims of his impending crash. In other words, his (and our) compassionate view from above is the antithesis of the abstracted, forensic vision that Ernst Jünger had previously ascribed to aerial surveillance in 'War and Photography'.[27]

With his newly receptive attention sharpened and concentrated by the framing of the windscreen, Roger had finally acknowledged his common humanity with the frightened onlookers scattered across the field below. Soon afterwards, the myth of the techno-warrior's invincibility will vanish completely, once we realise that the pilot has sacrificed himself in an attempt to avoid any further casualties. Although this altruistic gesture must be accorded the respect that it deserves, I would argue that the source of Roger's redemption lies in his renascent fellow feeling rather than in his later, somewhat pointless immolation. Indeed, most spectators would probably agree that the aviator's continued willingness to risk mutilation or death for a reward 'as big as birdseed' was evidence of a lingering psychopathology.[28] This is not to say that *The Tarnished Angels* endorses a strictly pacifist ideology, since many of its protagonists speak of Roger Schumann's heroic war record with great admiration. While the goal of freeing occupied France might be worth the price of a pilot's life, the meagre prizes available for winning a fairground air race are probably not, at least according to any rational calculus.

Yet once you have become ensconced in Ernst Jünger's resolutely martial mode of being, wielding a body that has been disciplined to function as a highly efficient fighting machine, then the practice of combat becomes an end in itself. If, in the well-known author's words, '[w]hat is important is not what we fight for, but how we fight', then the strategic objectives that your officers have in mind soon pale into insignificance.[29] Instead, the true warrior is galvanised by 'vital feelings of [an] unknown force' as well as by the pleasure of skilfully executing the aggressive rituals that he has been taught to perform without necessarily fathoming their meaning.[30] As we have already seen, the seasoned soldier, sailor or aviator's addiction to the heightened excitement of battle may never recede, regardless of whether or not a ceasefire has been declared. Therefore, it is somewhat ironic that Roger succumbs to the dangerous side-effects of this disturbing condition only after he has agreed to renounce flying for the love of his family.

Of course, Jünger would have dismissed Captain Schumann's embryonic willingness to open himself up to subjective emotional attachments as a feminine weakness.[31] Indeed, there is no doubt that empathy for ordinary human beings tends to impede the efficient functioning of the male body as weapon. Consequently, in celebrating the dissolution of the battle-hardened pilot's resistance to non-military preoccupations and sympathies, Sirk is also repudiating the crypto-fascist notion of the 'total mobilisation' of the civilian population. Instead of adopting a semi-feudal model of an ideal community that is grounded in 'an ontology of combat and war'[32] the director appears to be advocating (at least in peacetime) an adherence to more democratic precepts, which includes a mutual respect for one's fellow citizens regardless of their gender, class or place of origin. As Walter Benjamin once pointed out in a review of a collection of essays edited by Jünger that was published in 1930, the associated goals of combat readiness and military supremacy need not be the central objectives of a modern industrialised society. Scientific, engineering and manufacturing resources may also be deployed much more constructively, enabling a free people to devise socially useful solutions to the everyday problems of contemporary life. Benjamin would eventually conclude that the fascist 'habitues [*sic*] of the chthonic forces of terror ... will not learn one-tenth of what nature promises its less idly curious, but more sober children, who possess in technology not a fetish of doom but a key to happiness'.[33] Nevertheless, as this prescient critic well knew, technical innovations will only result in a more beneficent future if we are capable of imagining its outline.

II TWO CONFLICTING VIEWS OF MODERN TECHNOLOGY

Six years later, Benjamin would write that contemporary armed conflicts represented the ultimate perversion of the creative possibilities that are inherent in the inexhaustible forces of mechanisation. Where the uneven distribution of private property hinders the most 'natural utilization' of this colossal power, 'the increase in technical devices, in speed, and in the sources of energy will press for an unnatural utilization, and this is found in war'. He went on to say that 'instead of draining rivers, society directs a human stream into a bed of trenches; instead of dropping seeds from airplanes, it drops incendiary bombs over cities'.[34] While only a few of Sirk's films actually portray combat situations (most notably, *Hitler's Madman*, *Battle Hymn* and *A Time to Love and a Time To Die*), the vulnerability of human flesh to the onslaught of modern technology is still apparent in many of his best-known melodramas. In *Magnificent Obsession*, for instance, a prominent surgeon dies because his life-saving inhalator had already been taken elsewhere in order to revive the irresponsible victim of a speedboat crash; somewhat later, the dead man's widow is inadvertently blinded after she falls into the path of an oncoming car.[35]

A similar convergence of machinery, acceleration and danger occurs at the beginning of *Written on the Wind*, where we observe a bright yellow roadster careering through the deserted streets of a small Texas town. These menacing overtones are even evident in the brief summary of this sequence that was included in the studio's relatively neutral shot-by-shot continuity breakdown. The constant repetition of the word 'racing', which is virtually the only verb used to describe the motion of Kyle Hadley's high-powered vehicle in this text ('sportscar racing past refinery', 'sportscar racing into town', 'sportscar racing down driveway'), produces an obvious *frisson*.[36] Moreover, at the time of *Written on the Wind*'s original 1956 release, even the mere appearance of such an automobile would have excited a vicarious thrill in the minds of many viewers. According to an article that was published in *Better Homes and Gardens* the following year, owning a sports car (defined as a small, streamlined, extremely fast European vehicle that is as 'responsive as a good horse', but 'must be *driven*, not just steered' lest it run away with you) was still a fairly exclusive phenomenon that was so far restricted to the very rich.[37] Of course as the first scene of *Written on the Wind* unfolds, almost as soon as the reckless driver has parked his low-slung machine beside the Hadley mansion and stumbled inside, an unknown assailant with a gun will fatally wound him. Finally, as we have already seen, two pilots (including war hero Roger Schumann) are killed outright in *The Tarnished Angels* as a result of the abrupt failure of their planes. The lesser casualties in this film include Colonel T. J. Fineman, the wealthy sponsor of the air race, who still walks with the aid of crutches due to the injuries he sustained in a previous flying accident.

In addition to this physical impairment, Sirk's characters also often appear to be stymied or held captive by the circular revolutions of some vaguely sinister machine. For instance, in *Final Chord*, two close-ups of the spinning phonograph record playing the jazz music that is leading her into temptation have been inserted into the sequence that begins with a shot of Charlotte Garvenberg's rather trance-like dancing at an elegant soirée. Charlotte's subjection to the music's sensual syncopation is further underscored by the tiny clockwork couple who are shown twirling incessantly around the centre of this revolving disc, offering a succinct visual illustration of Sirk's understanding of the notion of '*échec*'.[38] While he was discussing the inherent fatalism of *Written on the Wind* (a film that begins with its ending, so the audience knows that Kyle Hadley is doomed from the start), the director defined a number of the richly nuanced connotations of this word for Jon Halliday. After declaring that *Written on the Wind* and *The Tarnished Angels* are both studies of 'failure', he went on to say: 'in French *échec* means much more than that: it [also] means no exit, being blocked.'[39] Along with the doomed circling of the pilots flying around the pylons that mark their course, the latter film contains another striking example of a gyrating machine signalling the fact that there is no way out of a hopeless situation. After Roger Schumann has begun his hazardous descent midway through the second race, his son struggles to get off the carnival ride that continues to whirl him inexorably around. Instead of running alongside his mother towards the scene of his father's crash, Jack is forced to remain in this miniature aircraft high above the ground, held prisoner for the full duration of its automatic motion.

This equation of the motif of a turning wheel with a key character's entrapment by an ineluctable fate is perhaps most evident in *Imitation of Life*. Unlike Lora Meredith, Sarah Jane Johnson will probably never move beyond low-level exploitation in the entertainment business because of her African-American ancestry (even if she attempts to 'pass' for white). Yet this experience of perpetual subordination was also more broadly typical of the twentieth-century working class; throughout this period, a high proportion of manufacturing jobs had become increasingly de-skilled, standardised and repetitive due to the imposition of certain widely accepted principles of scientific management that had been passed down from above. This so called 'Americanist' system of modern industrial organisation, which combined procedural and spatial rationalisation with greater mechanisation in order to enhance productivity, was largely based upon the discoveries of Frederick Winslow Taylor (an efficiency expert employed by Bethlehem Steel) and Henry Ford (the famous automobile magnate). Whether a factory hand's gestures were prescribed by a Taylorist timing 'of his basic work actions' and 'programmed task instruction cards' or by a Fordist division of labour and the tempo set by a moving assembly line, the result was the same.[40] In either case, a large group of underlings was supposed to cede all personal agency to a small cadre of specialised technocrats who regulated every aspect of their working life. Many historians have noted that Taylor's application of engineering principles to the management of human beings would have unfortunate ideological repercussions, particularly once his endorsement of a more coercive corporate hierarchy had filtered outward into the larger political sphere.[41] When *Imitation of Life* has been examined in this light, Sarah Jane's final theatrical routine (staged on a slowly rotating conveyor belt that dictates the pace of her actions) may be read as a critique of the longstanding American quest for total control over the workforce.

At the beginning of this performance (which occurs just before her mother's death), the aspiring actress appears to be nothing more than a standard component of a row of showgirls that is being displayed for the pleasure of the patrons of a West Coast nightclub called 'Moulin Rouge'. When compared with her previous solo engagement in New York, Sarah Jane's disciplined participation in one of the massive production numbers that were a major specialty of this actual Hollywood location seems far less individual and much more objectifying, despite her continuing ability to pass as white.[42]

Within the more intimate space of 'Harry's Club', the sultry chanteuse could address her suggestive song ('an empty purse can make a good girl go bad . . . fill my life brim-full of charm') to the members of the audience who were seated right next to her tiny stage. Over the course of this sequence, Sarah Jane gazes into the eyes, touches the hair and reclines on the table of a succession of middle-aged men (each of these glancing encounters taking place within the same frame). Although the budding performer's delivery of this bluesy musical number is undoubtedly highly sexualised (as Marina Heung and Michael Selig have both pointed out), it also showcases her talents in a way that her later mute re-enactment of feminine allure would not.[43] In New York, Sarah Jane remains the main focus of our attention for the full duration of the song that was written expressly for this film.[44] Moreover, during the four extended American shots that make up this sequence, the singer's sinuous movements provide the sole motivation for the gliding motion of the camera.

By contrast, in the 'Moulin Rouge' revue the various functions that Sarah Jane had once fulfilled (looking appealing in a revealing costume, establishing an emotional bond with the spectator through her ability to sing and dance) have been divided into more limited tasks that have been distributed to several distinct categories of chorines. In deference to the overriding vision of their unseen choreographer-manager, some girls simply stand beneath a giant proscenium arch arrayed in elaborate pseudo-Rococo costumes that evoke the glittering decadence of pre-Revolutionary France. At the same time, another group of women, wearing clothing that exposes more of their legs, files past the audience on a catwalk that will eventually merge with the stage. In the midst of this dense constellation of elements, a single female dancer executes a softshoe pas de deux along with the only man who is visible behind the footlights. This blue-clad couple stands out against the sea of yellow-hued showgirls who have not been allowed to exhibit such a complex series of physical skills. Yet none of these players contributes anything to this production number's musical accompaniment or attempts to break out of its solipsistic structure by interacting with the audience. In this sequence, the editing construction vacillates between fixed long shots that emphasise the separation of the performers from their patrons and equally static American shots, in which the two blue dancers stare only at each other.

This introverted pair is finally swept away by the arrival of a moving assembly line carrying a series of identically attired women (dressed in golden evening gowns and jewels) that includes Sarah Jane. Each of these figures executes the same sequence of actions in complete unison with the rest, remaining fixed to her assigned position on the conveyor belt that slowly rotates around the outer rim of the stage. The machine-like quality of this group simulation of the pleasures of the leisure class renders even Sarah Jane's proficient performance strangely non-erotic. It seems clear that every member of this Fordist corps of dancers has had to learn to suppress her own initiative, creativity and intelligence in exchange for whatever wages she is being paid. As these interchangeable beauties kick their legs in the air with a robotic precision and mime drinking a glass of champagne, the spectator can't help but be reminded of Siegfried Kracauer's 1927 description of a celebrated English precision dancing troupe called the Tiller Girls. According to the influential Weimar critic, the women who were subsumed into this enormous chorus line 'are no longer individual girls, but indissoluble girl clusters whose movements are demonstrations of mathematics'.[45] In his view, 'the hands in the factory correspond to the legs of [these anonymous chorines]', and he would eventually conclude that the prescribed gestures of both groups represent 'the aesthetic reflex of the rationality toward which the prevailing economic system aspires'.[46]

Although the de-natured rhythms that have been drilled into the worker by the increased rationalisation of modern life were to some extent impelled by reason, Kracauer notes that they are the product of a 'murky reason' that '*does not encompass man*'. Therefore, he can only conclude that 'the regulation of the production process is not regulated according to man's needs, and man does not serve as the foundation for the structure of the socioeconomic organisation'.[47] In anticipation of Langford Winner's later conception of 'autonomous technology', Kracauer appears to be implying that mechanisation (in the service of capitalist thinking) has somehow 'gotten out of control and follows its own course independent of human direction'.[48] In other words, unless society chooses to harness the tremendous energies that have been released by modern mass production by diverting them into achieving more worthy collective aims, they may instead be used to brutalise and enslave us. Walter Benjamin would later compare the mindless tedium of an assembly line job, which was said to be suffused with 'emptiness' due to the worker's 'inability to complete something' in a manufacturing process that has been divided into discrete parts, with the equally sterile, involuntary compulsions of the addicted gambler. In an illuminating analysis of a lithograph of a gambling club, he observes that 'the figures presented show us how the mechanism to which the participants in a game of chance entrust themselves seizes them body and soul, so that even in their private sphere, and no matter how agitated they may be, they are capable only of reflex action'.[49]

Nevertheless, a few years earlier Benjamin had also suggested that the widespread diffusion of a standardised 'machine' culture could lead to equally radical social advances. Hence, a tone of cautious optimism dominates one of his most groundbreaking philosophical contributions from this period, 'The

Work of Art in the Age of Mechanical Reproduction'. This is despite the fact that it concludes with a passionate warning against the imminent menace of Fascism (which threatened to extinguish the revolutionary promise of the 'growing proletarianization of modern man and the increasing formation of [the] masses' by deflecting these powerful forces towards the wrong objectives).[50] Earlier in this essay, Benjamin had declared that a widely disseminated, mass-produced art form (such as photography or film, for which there was no 'original' in the conventional sense) could elicit a 'direct, intimate fusion of visual and emotional enjoyment with the orientation of the expert', thus stimulating a response from the public that was no longer limited to the connoisseur.[51] As we have seen, this notion recalls Douglas Sirk's understanding of the efficacy of certain Hollywood genres (especially melodrama), which are able to attract a broad cross-section of viewers because they engage the audience on many different levels. Again much like the director, Benjamin credited the filmic medium with dissolving the sense of distanciation that German philosophers had associated with aesthetic contemplation since at least the eighteenth century.[52] Through the judicious use of close-ups, carefully plotted travelling shots, editing between distinct vantage points and so on, a motion picture may shock the spectator out of any semblance of detachment and compel us to reassess our surroundings from a completely divergent perspective.[53] Even more importantly, the German critic insisted that the cinema not only 'extend[s] our comprehension of the necessities that rule our lives' but also 'manages to assure us of an immense and unexpected field of action'.[54] While Sirk was less dismissive of older artistic traditions than Benjamin, choosing to combine certain aspects of painting and architecture with the advantages of more recent technologies, he too thought that the best films should prompt the audience into considering some sort of self-transcendent purpose. By directing the viewer's attention back into the public arena, a good melodrama might actually inspire us to take part in the ongoing struggle against social injustice.

Of course, the far-reaching technical innovations of the twentieth century did not alter the capitalist 'property structures which the masses strive to eliminate' in either Henry Ford's America or Walter Benjamin's Germany, as many social critics had once envisaged.[55] This was not the fault of the process of mechanisation, however, since it is those who are responsible for programming the machines who decide what goals the new technology will set out to achieve. Hence, a number of Sirk's most important cinematic works still contain some glimmering of the utopian vision of the Machine Age that was so prevalent in Germany during the 1920s and early 1930s. At that moment, a significant portion of the artistic *avant-garde* had hoped that increases in industrial productivity might be put to more constructive uses than simply enriching a small group of private individuals.[56] From this alternative point of view, the new technology promised to mechanically or cybernetically enhance human agency rather than negate it.

In Andreas Huyssen's very lucid examination of the cultural environment that shaped Fritz Lang's (and by extension, Douglas Sirk's) intellectual development, these polarised views of modern industrialisation were attributed to two successive artistic movements, German Expressionism and the *Neue Sachlichkeit* or New Objectivity. According to Huyssen, the first perspective 'emphasizes technology's oppressive and destructive potential and is clearly rooted in the experiences and irrepressible memories of the mechanized battlefields of World War I'. He then went on to state: 'during the stabilisation phase of the Weimar Republic this . . . view was slowly replaced by the technology cult of the *Neue Sachlichkeit* and its unbridled confidence in technical progress and social engineering.'[57] While Lang's *Metropolis* may be seen to ricochet between these two opposing perspectives, R. L. Rutsky would later maintain that both polarities represent an equally reductive response to the instrumental rationality that is a major feature of contemporary industrial capitalism. As Rutsky makes clear, Joh Frederson performs the specialised role of the 'superhuman (or inhuman)' 'brain of Metropolis', designing a civic order where 'workers must adapt themselves to a functional, technological rationality . . . function[ing] like machines in lockstep and geometric formation, their individual identities lost'.[58] Of course, the obverse face of the inorganic logic of the machine is the extreme irrationality of the good Maria's disembodied spirituality as well as the false Maria's demonic sensuality. Rutsky concludes that nothing less than the 'reconciliation of [the brain and the heart, rationality and emotion, the scientific and the magico-spiritual] is the true ideological project' of Lang's prophetic 1927 film.[59] In other words Lang, like Sirk and Eisenstein, sought to appeal to the spectator's reason and passion, by suggesting a less restrictive conception of society in which scientific construction and biological creation could be successfully combined.

Rutsky went on to align the ostensible 'wholeness' that *Metropolis* achieves in the end with the *Heimat* or home that the Nazi Party would subsequently provide, in which the 'leader-mediator offers . . . a restoration of [the 'eternal' spirit of Germany] . . . a "re-enchantment", that will "reanimate" a "dead", technologically modern world'.[60] By contrast, Sirk's films usually place this faint hope of a symbiotic co-operation between nature, humanity and technology in an American landscape that has been corrected by (an often European) art. Even in *Final Chord* (a 1936 German melodrama that I will analyse at greater length in the last section of this book), a despondent widow's failing will to live is resurrected within the Functionalist space of her New York apartment and not in Berlin. Similarly, in *Magnificent Obsession*, the doctors attached to a Swiss research clinic located in the heart of historic Lucerne are unable to cure Helen Phillips's blindness, despite the up-to-date technology that is implied by their Bauhaus-style office building and Charles Eames chairs. Her sight and health will only be restored in a tiny International Style hospital located in the vast expanse of the New Mexico desert, where Bob Merrick must himself perform this critical operation on the woman that he loves. Even in *The Tarnished Angels*, one of Sirk's most despairing Hollywood narratives, the relatively downbeat ending is mitigated by the fact that a talismanic emblem of modernity (an airplane) will carry Laverne and her son back to the cornfields of Iowa to begin their lives over again.

By the 1950s, the progressive symbolism that had once been encoded into this kind of European Modernist architecture seemed to have lost its meaning, unless it was situated in a new land that might actually be receptive to social change. In this respect, many of Sirk's films recall the particular variation on the Virgilian pastoral that critic Leo Marx has traced through two centuries of American literature. After studying the bucolic writings of Hawthorne, Melville, Emerson, Thoreau, Whitman and many other authors, he concluded that in the bulk of these works technology and nature quite happily coexist within the cultivated middle ground of the garden.[61] This was true, of course, only if the occupants of such a landscape also adhered to the classical conventions, which stipulated that rustic characters must renounce urban luxuries in favour of a less materialistic way of life.[62] Within this powerfully regenerative space, where industrial waste and despoliation are held in check by the very moderation of the common citizen's desires, Old World attitudes may be converted into the values that befit a contemporary democracy.

For instance, Ron Kirby's Old Mill in *All That Heaven Allows* could be said to represent the confluence of the 'Two Kingdoms of Force' that Marx has distilled from this peculiarly American Arcadian myth: 'The Machine' (manifested in the echoes of International Style architecture that are heightened by its progressive renovation) and 'The Garden' (an apt description of the building's rural Connecticut setting). Moreover, the abstemiousness of this unpretentious structure's owner (who neither craves affluence nor feels compelled to 'keep up with the Joneses', in Alida's words) makes him the modern counterpart of the 'noble husbandman' that Thomas Jefferson had hoped would help to preserve the American continent's classless state, for white men at least.[63] Even in *All That Heaven Allows*, however, the dream of constructing a more egalitarian society is often deferred or thwarted, since this utopian ideal was never universally endorsed, even within the United States. Indeed, much of Sirk's Hollywood corpus appears to suggest that wealthier or more established American communities (such as Cary Scott's privileged New England enclave, the Texas oil town of *Written on the Wind* and the decaying New Orleans of *The Tarnished Angels*) were already exhibiting signs of the conservatism, class stratification and decadence that were endemic in older European municipalities. These invidious distinctions were especially evident in the suburbs that began to spring up all across the United States after World War II, where segregation by income and race posed a singular problem for anyone who subscribed to the nation's founding myth that 'all men are created equal'. This is one of the dilemmas that I intend to address in my next chapter, as part of a broader discussion of Sirk's depiction of contemporary urban and suburban space.

Notes

1. Ben Singer, 'Modernity, Hyperstimulus, and the Rise of Popular Sensationalism', in *Cinema and the Invention of Modern Life*, ed. Leo Charney and Vanessa Schwartz (Berkeley: University of California Press, 1995), 72–84. In the fourth chapter of the book that contains a slightly revised version of this essay [*Melodrama and Modernity* (New York: Columbia University Press, 2001)] Singer discusses the so-called 'modernity thesis' that has been promulgated by other scholars, which 'stresses key formal and spectatorial similarities between cinema – as a medium of strong impressions, spatiotemporal fragmentation, abruptness, mobility – and the nature of the metropolitan experience' [p. 102].
2. Singer, 'Modernity', 74–5.
3. Singer, *Melodrama and Modernity*, 89–90.
4. Sirk told Peter Lehman that he served as a German naval officer during World War I ['Thinking with the Heart: An Interview with Douglas Sirk', p. 15]. The director left Germany in 1937 accompanied by his Jewish second wife and hence avoided being drafted into the armed forces again. See Halliday, 31–2, 55–6.
5. Michael Howard, quoted by Michael Adas in *Machines as the Measure of Men: Science, Technology and the Ideology of Western Domination* (Ithaca: Cornell University Press, 1989), 367.
6. Adas, 373.
7. Harvey, 'Sirkumstantial Evidence', 59 and Halliday, 27, 165.
8. Jeffrey Herf, *Reactionary Modernism: Technology, Culture, and Politics in Weimar and the Third Reich* (Cambridge: Cambridge University Press, 1984), 24.
9. Herf, 72, 73, 75.
10. Herf, 75, 78.
11. The reason Laverne gives for this deception in the film is similar to the one that was suggested by Geoffrey Shurlock, the representative of the Motion Picture Association of America who analysed the screenplay of *The Tarnished Angels* for any Production Code violations. His first objection to the revised script in a letter dated 8 November 1956 was 'its excessive sordidness and over-all low tone' [p. 1]. Among the more specific objections raised was 'the reaction of Laverne

to Burke's having saved her from giving herself to Matt'. He 'objected to her line, "I want him to believe I went to Matt Ord" [because] ... what she should say at this point is that she *does* want Roger to squirm, and to suffer a bit for the lowness of his suggestion to her' [p. 2]. See Box 188, File 0587 of the Universal-International Pictures archives. In the final film Laverne does say that she wants Roger to squirm, after having confessed to Devlin that she minds 'each and every sin' that she committed on her husband's behalf.

12. William Faulkner, *Pylon* (London: Chatto & Windus, 1955), 34. Sirk once told Jon Halliday he had always been 'fascinated by flying' and that he 'flew in a plane searching the Baltic for mines' as part of his naval service during World War I. Since Faulkner's 1934 novel revolves around an itinerant group consisting of a barnstorming pilot, two parachute jumpers and a mechanic, the director had wanted to shoot a cinematic version ever since he first read a German translation shortly after its original publication. Sirk wrote a screenplay for UFA while he was still living in Berlin, but nothing came of it. In 1957, the Hollywood writer George Zuckerman wrote a script based on this novel independently of the director, though fortunately the latter was asked to shoot it after the success of *Written on the Wind*. See Halliday, 136; and 'George Zuckerman on Sirk', available at <www.brightlightsfilm.com/48/sirkzuckzug.htm, 1–2 (last accessed 17 October 2005).

13. *The Tarnished Angels* was set in the early 1930s, a period during which the technological limitations of the existing aircraft made flying planes a very hazardous way to make a living. See page 264 of Modris Ekstein's *Rites of Spring: The Great War and the Birth of the Modern Age* (London: Bantam, 1989) for a whole host of specific examples of pilots being killed in air displays. Hence, the fatalistic atmosphere of Sirk's film was no exaggeration.

14. In answer to the question 'Which scenes did you like the most?' several respondents mentioned 'the crash scene in the lake', which one person specifically mentioned made them cry. Another stated that they preferred all of the 'ones with honest dialogue and emotions', which would have included Roger's reconciliation with Laverne at the beginning of this scene. See 'Report on Preview comments "Pylon"' dated 11/9/57 in Box 510, File 14985 of the Universal-International Pictures archives.

15. Unpublished letter by Douglas Sirk sent to Albert Zugsmith from Zurich, dated 19 August 1956, located in Box 188, File 05787 of the Universal-International Pictures archives. This letter clearly contradicts the thesis that Sirk was attempting to employ Brechtian alienation techniques in order to distance the spectator from the depicted events. In the director's opinion, the fact that this version of the script of *The Tarnished Angels* prevented the spectator from getting close to the characters because 'everything appears to take place on a very distant stage, very far removed from where we are' was not a desirable outcome.

16. Near the end of World War I Jünger was hospitalised with a young fighter pilot under von Richtofen's command who lived up to the squadron motto 'Hard – and crazy with it'. As Sirk well knew, this group of aviators would have brooked

no mercy, so their enemies would have been obliged to be just as 'hard' and 'crazy'. See Jünger's *Storm of Steel* (London: Allen Lane, 2003), 288–9.
17. Jünger, 92. According to Andreas Huyssen, '14 editions [of this book had been] published by 1934 with a total of about a quarter million copies sold'. See his 'Fortifying the Heart: Ernst Jünger's Armoured Texts' in *New German Critique*, No. 39 (Spring–Summer 1993), 8.
18. Ernst Jünger, 232.
19. Ernst Jünger, 'On Danger', *New German Critique*, No. 59 (Spring–Summer 1993), 27–9.
20. Ernst Jünger, 'On Danger', 30.
21. Jünger, 'On Danger', 30. In this essay, Jünger bluntly states that 'scarcely a machine, scarcely a science has ever existed which did not fulfil, directly or indirectly, dangerous functions in . . . war' [p. 30].
22. Peter Fritsche, 'Machine Dreams: Airmindedness and the Reinvention of Germany', *The American Historical Review*, 98, No. 3 (June 1993), 688.
23. Herf, 90–1, 100–5.
24. Quoted by Jeffrey Herf, 85.
25. Box 483, File 14195, Universal-International Pictures archives.
26. Peter Fritsche has described the postwar 'airmindedness' that Sirk would have been familiar with from his youth in Germany in the following terms: '[According to this view], the horrors of total war did not eliminate the rationale of armed engagement but instead called for a more thorough organization of civil society and promised to secure the military advantages and political unity that Germany lacked in World War One. Airmindedness provided postwar Germany with the technological means to reinvent itself. Airmindedness was not a utilitarian code of conduct that derived logically from the frightening realities of air war. Rather, it added up to an ideologically inflected diagnosis of danger and opportunity by which the Nazis could build a national community.' See page 688 of his 'Machine Dreams: Airmindedness and the Reinvention of Germany'.
27. Ernst Jünger, 'War and Photography', *New German Critique*, No. 59 (Spring–Summer 1993), 25.
28. After Laverne has completed the parachute act that is a key part of a 'Flying Schumanns' performance she tries to minimise the risk by telling Devlin that this kind of jumping is as easy as 'falling out of bed'. The journalist highlights the danger of the stunt by asking Laverne what would happen if she blacked out, which prompts the unhappy woman to increase her efforts to de-romanticise what they do for a living. She retorts (in a very disparaging tone of voice, and often glancing backwards at her husband who is preparing for his next race): 'You miss the point of our act. I'm just the girl assistant with the exposed legs. Roger, he's the big magician. A little tape and he turns himself into a bird, a crazy bird, chasing after prizes as big as birdseed.' The pilot then tacitly confirms that his desire to fly is not fuelled by the prospect of financial gain by saying to the reporter, 'Are you in the newspaper business for the money?'
29. Quoted by Huyssen, 10.

30. Jünger, quoted by Huyssen, 20.
31. This fear of women, and of the softening effect their influence might induce, was something that Jünger apparently shared with the rest of the German warrior caste during the period between the two World Wars. Klaus Theweleit's disconcerting analysis of some of the writings published by members of the *Freikorps* concludes that their fear of engulfment was so strong they channelled their sexual energies into creating the masculine community of the army, choosing to brutally murder their female enemies rather than rape them. See book one of Theweleit's *Male Fantasies* (Minneapolis: University of Minnesota Press, 1987), 3–204.
32. Huyssen, 8.
33. Walter Benjamin, 'Theories of German Fascism: On the Collection of Essays War and Warrior, edited by Ernst Jünger', *New German Critique*, No. 17 (Spring 1979), 128.
34. Walter Benjamin, 'The Work of Art in the Age of Mechanical Reproduction' in *Illuminations* (New York: Schocken Books,1969), 242.
35. In 'Look Out, Here I Come!', an article that was published in the December 1946 issue of *The Atlantic Monthly* [178, No. 6], Bergen Evans bases his assertion that 'about half of [the 25 million cars in use in the United States] seem to be operated by temporary paranoiacs' in a very alarming series of statistics. He notes: 'In the past twenty-five years more than seven hundred thousand people have been killed by automobiles in the United States. This is almost twice as many as have been killed in all the wars in which this country has ever been engaged. Some fifteen to twenty million others have been injured, more than a million of them permanently disabled' [p. 119].
36. Box 175, File 05459, Universal-International Pictures archives.
37. Ken W. Purdy, 'Why All the Interest in Sport Cars?', *Better Homes and Gardens*, 35, No. 5 (May 1957), 228, 230. Purdy claims that prior to World War II, there were no more than 100 genuine sports cars in the United States, 'nearly all of them in Boston and New York'. Because American servicemen 'stationed in Europe immediately after the war' had been intrigued by their 'nimbleness, speed and braking power', 'the first wave of foreign-built sports cars docked in New York' in 1946 [p. 227]. Nevertheless, these vehicles would remain the sole preserve of the wealthiest stratum of American society for quite some time. As Purdy points out, the 'man who owns a Mercedes-Benz 300SL will tell you he likes it because it will do 160 miles an hour, but really more important to him is the fact that only 1,000 are made every year for the entire world market, and he has one of them' [p. 228].
38. In Sirk's 1946 thriller *Lured*, the skipping of a spinning record shown in close-up playing on a phonograph with the needle traversing the same circular groove over and over again sends a mentally unstable fashion designer into a rage, since the sudden interruption of the music breaks the illusion that he is showing his latest creation to a princess and her aristocratic friends.
39. Halliday, 135–6.

40. Charles S. Maier, 'Between Taylorism and Technocracy: European Ideologies and the Vision of Industrial Productivity in the 1920s', *Journal of Contemporary History*, Vol. 5, No. 2 (1970), 29, 55.
41. See Maier, 28–9, 35–45, Herf, 152–88 and Mary Nolan 'Imagining America, Modernizing Germany', in *Dancing on the Volcano: Essays on the Culture of the Weimar Republic*, ed. Thomas W. Kniesche et al. (Columbia, SC: Camden House, 1994), 83–4.
42. According to the uncredited production notes, the 'famous Moulin Rouge in Hollywood makes a rare appearance in a true-life role for "Imitation of Life" in a sequence in which Susan Kohner [who plays Sarah Jane] earns her living as a showgirl'. One of the major attractions of 'the musical sequence is the "Rockin' Chair Blues" number, a featured production number in the Donna Arden revue at the famous nightspot, with Miss Kohner joining the regular show members in presenting the number'. See Box 696, File 23704 of the Universal-International Pictures archives.
43. Marina Heung, 'What's the Matter with Sarah Jane? Daughters and Mothers in Sirk's *Imitation of Life*', in *Imitation of Life*, ed. Lucy Fischer (New Brunswick, NJ: Rutgers University Press, 1991), 315 and Michael Selig, 'Contradiction and Reading: Social Class and Sex Class in Imitation of Life', *Wide Angle*, 10, No. 4, 21.
44. For a brief discussion of the music used in this film, see 'Mahalia Jackson and Earl Jackson Both Sing in New Film Classic' on page 4 of the combined *Showman's Manual* that was prepared by the studio to promote *Flower Drum Song* and *Imitation of Life* [Universal-International Pictures archives].
45. Siegfried Kracauer, 'The Mass Ornament', in *The Mass Ornament: Weimar Essays* (Cambridge, MA: Harvard University Press, 1995), 75–6.
46. Kracauer, 79.
47. Kracauer, 81.
48. Langdon Winner, *Autonomous Technology: Technics-out-of-Control as a Theme in Political Thought* (Cambridge, MA: MIT Press, 1977), 13.
49. 'On Some Motifs in Baudelaire', in *Illuminations* (New York: Schocken Books, 1968), 177–8.
50. 'The Work of Art in the Age of Mechanical Reproduction', 241.
51. 'The Work of Art in the Age of Mechanical Reproduction', 234.
52. See, for instance, Immanuel Kant's *Critique of Judgement* (New York: Hafner, 1951), 43–5.
53. 'The Work of Art in the Age of Mechanical Reproduction', 236–7, 240.
54. 'The Work of Art in the Age of Mechanical Reproduction', 236.
55. 'The Work of Art in the Age of Mechanical Reproduction', 241.
56. As Hilde Heynen has noted, critics frequently overlook the ambiguous nature of the Modernist project. Along with its emphasis on 'silences, empty signs, fragmentation and necessary incompleteness, dissonances and fragility' was a concomitant joy. In other words, modernity not only gave rise to a sense of 'loss and bereavement' but also created 'opportunities for progress and development'.

See her *Architecture and Modernity: A Critique* (Cambridge, MA: MIT Press, 1999), 23.
57. Andreas Huyssen, *After the Great Divide: Modernism, Mass Culture, Postmodernism* (Bloomington: Indiana University Press, 1986), 67.
58. R. L. Rutsky, 'The Mediation of Technology and Gender: Metropolis, Nazism, Modernism', in *Fritz Lang's Metropolis: Cinematic Visions of Technology and Fear*, ed. Michael Minden and Holger Bachmann (Rochester: Camden House, 2000), 218.
59. Rutsky, 220.
60. Rutsky, 233.
61. Leo Marx, *The Machine in the Garden: Technology and the Pastoral Ideal in America* (Oxford: Oxford University Press, 1964), 228.
62. Marx, 127, 130–1, 244.
63. Marx, 129–36.

CHAPTER FOUR

Imitation of Life *and the Depiction of Suburban Space*

In *Theory and Design in the First Machine Age*, architectural historian Reyner Banham points out that the twentieth-century flight from the centre of the city to the periphery didn't result in less dependence upon machines. Commuters were still heavily reliant upon the latest generation of 'light, subtle, clean' devices that were meant to be deployed 'by thinking men in their own homes in the new electric suburbs', a process that would later be accelerated by the introduction of 'miniaturization, transistorization . . . television and the computer'.¹ Topping this list of mechanisms as a potential agent of change was the automobile, an individually owned and operated piece of machinery that people could 'literally' 'take into their own hands'.² According to Edward Dimendberg, the motor-driven flow from the metropolitan core to the suburbs that resulted from increasing car ownership would have a massive impact upon the shape of the 'post-1945 American city'. Since the latter's 'spatial dispersion, increased automobile traffic, and large-scale federally supported construction projects differed fundamentally from earlier urban forms', he would eventually conclude that the more densely concentrated 'metropolis portrayed in the film noir cycle' usually 'emerges as a highly rationalized and alienating system of exploitative drudgery permitting few possibilities of escape'.³

Yet during this period the city still had many prominent defenders, including the well-known American critic Lewis Mumford, who in an article published in the *Architectural Record* observed that urban agglomeration is much more likely to provide employment, cultural diversity, face-to-face social interaction and mutual co-operation than the much more thinly populated countryside.⁴ Towards the end of a landmark text that was first drafted during the 1930s, Mumford described the potential benefits of the large-scale 'world city' in the following glowing terms:

> Metropolitan massiveness and congestion have a deeper justification, though it is not fully recognized . . . it has brought together, within a relatively narrow compass, the diversity and variety of special cultures: at least in token quantities all races and cultures can be found here, along with their languages [and] their customs . . . The complexity and cultural inclusiveness of the metropolis embody the complexity and variety of the world as a whole.⁵

Sirk's cinematic depictions of New York, Mumford's only North American example of this kind of 'metropolitanism' in a subsequent work on municipal development, appear to bear these conclusions out.[6] In *Final Chord*, we observe a very disparate group of tenants living in a high-rise apartment building that is located in Manhattan, which includes a poor German widow and a prosperous American oratorio singer. Two decades later, Sirk's New York still encompasses an economically and ethnically diverse collection of residents who commingle with strangers as well as friends in a whole series of shared urban spaces. These range from the common hallway of a brownstone apartment building, to the corridors of a university research hospital, to a downtown public school classroom, to a busy railway terminus, to a wide variety of theatres, restaurants, nightclubs, parks and other relatively unrestricted places of entertainment. In particular, the director's multi-layered evocation of this highly diverse city contains both a replica of the '"21" Club' (where Kyle Hadley first tries to impress 'executive secretary' Lucy Moore in *Written on the Wind*) and the 'poor man's' version of this exclusive establishment, a cheap basement eatery frequented by unemployed actors in *Imitation of Life*.[7]

In those films that unfold at least partially within an urban setting, an important relationship may suddenly arise from the accidental crossing of paths with an unknown person from another social strata in a public place. For instance, at the beginning of *Weekend With Father* (1951) a lonely Manhattan advertising executive meets an amiable widow on the platform of Grand Central Station quite by chance when they are each putting their respective offspring on a train to summer camp. Soon afterwards, they run into one another again walking their dogs in Central Park, both attempting to console a family pet that is missing its usual playmates. The couple's romance gradually blossoms as they explore the metropolitan area together, while their children remain unaware of their parent's burgeoning relationship. A number of equally fortuitous encounters occur during the opening scene of *Imitation of Life*, which has been set in the teeming and even more heterogeneous surroundings of Coney Island. In the first sequence, an attractive blonde widow searching for her missing daughter on the crowded beach enlists the aid of a handsome male bystander (the photographer destined to become her major love interest). She will finally locate Susie eating a hot dog under the pier alongside the mixed-race child of an African-American woman who is graciously watching over them both. A relatively free interaction between classes had already been suggested by the distinct dissimilarities in the way in which people are dressed (some men wear business suits, while others are clad in more proletarian shorts and sport shirts or bathing trunks). When Lora Meredith offers to bring Annie Johnson and her daughter Sarah Jane back to her apartment later that evening, two single-parent families have managed to come together across the nation's deep-seated racial divide. Indeed, without the financial support, organisational skills and childcare contributed by her most constant adult companion, Lora's acting ambitions would never have been realised.

This is not to say that Annie and Sarah Jane don't face any racial discrimination within New York's municipal boundaries, since their African-American ancestry does clearly limit how far they are able to progress. While Annie and Lora start out at the same poverty-stricken level (the former taking over the latter's piecework job of hand-addressing a mail order company's envelopes at home) the actress will eventually become a star on the Broadway stage. By contrast, in Sirk's bitter assessment of the current political climate, Annie can only aspire to fulfilling the subservient roles of indispensable housekeeper and surrogate parent to Lora's only child. This is quite unlike John Stahl's 1934 film adaptation of the original Fanny Hurst story, in which both mothers receive a portion of the profits that were generated by selling the black woman's pancake recipe. Sirk apparently thought that the audience would never understand the extreme vehemence of the light-skinned Sarah Jane's desire to 'pass' unless her mother was 'just the typical Negro, a servant, without much she could call her own but the friendship, love and charity of a white mistress'.[8] He succeeds in provoking a sense of outrage over their 'whole uncertain and . . . oppressive situation' in the viewer by making the saintly Annie and her tormented daughter (who can only obtain the privileges attached to her skin colour by renouncing her darker mother) the most sympathetic characters in the film. Yet however compromised Annie and Sarah Jane's metropolitan prospects might have been, their situation becomes even more untenable after Lora has shifted both families to a single-family home in the secluded confines of an exclusive suburb.

I SOME LIMITATIONS OF THE TYPICAL AMERICAN SUBURB

Lewis Mumford once defined 'suburbia' as a distant dormitory where 'by and large, life is carried on without the discipline of rural occupations and without the cultural resources that the Central District of a large municipality still retains in its art exhibitions, theatres, concerts, and the like'.[9] Since they were conceived in reaction to the perceived evils of the modern city (greater congestion due to industrialisation and mass immigration, increasingly ruthless business competition and political manipulation and escalating levels of poverty and crime), these bedroom communities were generally designed to fulfil only a few restricted functions. Again according to Mumford, the residential drift to the ex-urban hinterland that has plagued the twentieth-century

American city was symptomatic of 'the temptation to retreat from unpleasant realities, to shirk public duties, to find the whole meaning of life in the most elemental social group, the family'.[10] In these over-specialised peripheral districts, where municipal buildings and services, institutes of higher learning, workplaces and even shops were often deliberately eschewed, the possibilities for human activity were largely confined to child rearing, gardening, interior decorating and personal recreation. Therefore, after Lora buys an expensive house in a semi-rural subdivision in *Imitation of Life*, she must still commute to New York in order to sustain her career (just like the husbands who own homes in Stoningham in *All That Heaven Allows*). To a much greater degree than the much more densely populated metropolitan centre, Sirk's suburban neighbourhoods are often places of extreme regimentation and monotony.

For instance, Cary Scott's problems in *All That Heaven Allows* largely stem from the cultural barrenness of her cloistered Connecticut enclave: what is a woman to do in such an intensely domestic environment after her husband has died and her children have gone away to university? Once her designated social duties are no longer required, even the 'serious business' of 'play' that provides Stoningham's primary reason for being becomes a threat to the widow's fragile self-identity. Her continuing presence at 'the country club' and 'the cocktail parties' that represent the 'frivolous counterparts of a more varied and significant [civic] life' (according to Mumford) either draws attention to her anomalous aloneness or exposes her to the sexual advances of her neighbours' husbands.[11] In this respect, Sirk's fictitious character's predicament mirrors the situation of many of her real-life counterparts who were stranded in similar housing developments located on the outskirts of New York. According to an article that was published in *Harper's Magazine* during this period, in many prosperous outlying suburbs, such as Bronxville, Scarsdale and Bedford, women outnumbered men by at least three to two. The sons of the families who lived in these sequestered communities usually left home to further their education and establish corporate careers, while their fathers often preferred to move closer to their offices in the city after losing their wives, or so the author of this investigation claimed. Since 'polygamy' was not in 'good repute' in such fastidious neighbourhoods, which tended to contain people who disapproved of marriages that transgressed class or ethnic boundaries, there seemed to be no easy solution to this frustrating gender imbalance.[12]

Within the context of *All that Heaven Allows*, Cary breaks off her engagement to her former gardener primarily because her children are afraid of being ostracised by their rather snobbish circle of friends.[13] Since she had already rejected a proposal from a more socially acceptable older businessman who had promised her companionship instead of passion, the lonely widow's chances for emotional fulfilment appear slim. Even Cary's diminished post-engagement expectations are soon dashed, however, when her children confess on Christmas Day that they will no longer be returning to their family home on the weekends. Kay announces her own impending marriage (finally demonstrating some awareness of what her mother had given up) and Ned tells his family that he intends to study in Paris for a year before taking up a position with a company based in Iran.

This scene ends with one of the most poignant visual evocations of emotional isolation that I have ever seen, which comes into view just after Cary's son has presented her with a television set as a substitute for genuine human contact. The camera tracks in until Ned and the accompanying salesman have vanished and the solitary widow's ghost-like reflection trapped in the rectangle of its darkened screen fills the frame. Earlier in the film, Cary had resisted the same agent's efforts to sell her one of these electronic devices directly, since at that point her relationship with Ron had removed her from the category of bored suburban 'ladies' who needed 'something to do with their time'. Now, overwhelmed by the void left by the loss of her fiancé and the sudden departure of her children, the despondent widow can only contemplate her phantasmagoric alter ego in silence. Without Ron, the best that Cary could hope for was a pallid simulacrum of the sympathy, tenderness and affection that she might have possessed, filtered through the one-way receiver of an impersonal electronic contrivance. The substance of the salesman's soothing off-screen monologue ('Turn that dial and you can have all the company you want . . . , life's parade at your fingertips') is clearly belied by the picture that we simultaneously observe, an attenuated likeness that mirrors nothing but Cary's desolation. By cutting out almost every vestige of the external world, the director seems to be implying that this home-based technology will only exacerbate the solipsistic turning inward that was already endemic in the suburban housewife's experience. Unlike the melodrama that contains it (which urges us to apply the moral lessons that we have learned), this image suggests that television's ceaseless stream of illusions may well short-circuit the viewer's ability to act.

If one ignores the fact that the latest broadcast medium was itself an instrument of social control, it could be argued that the withdrawal from the larger public arena that this very private form of entertainment represents constituted a logical form of self-defence in Cary's censorious community. Unlike Fritz Lang's *Metropolis* or Mabuse films, in Sirk's cinematic corpus it is the suburb that functions like a gigantic surveillance machine, enabling its residents to assess, discipline and correct their neighbours' 'inappropriate' conduct. As I will discuss at greater length in the final chapter of this book, the 'picture' window that reveals the interior of the Scott family's Colonial

Revival home is just as penetrable to the outside gaze as the glass cells of the contemporary Modernist apartment blocks that were parodied in Jacques Tati's 1967 comedy *Playtime*.[14] Moreover, like most North American suburbs, where detached houses are surrounded by open lawns rather than fences or walls, Stoningham's relatively unobstructed streets make it possible for the local inhabitants to keep a close watch on anyone who is passing through them. While Cary (and every other resident) is also subject to this surveillance and will be punished for violating the local codes of propriety to some degree, there is no question of the affluent widow fitting in if she simply chooses to comport herself with more decorum. Yet since most suburban subdivisions were sorted by economic status and race, this increased visibility also made it immediately apparent when someone did not belong in that particular district. Cary might be hurt by the vicious gossip engendered by her relationship with Ron and upset by being shunned by her neighbours, but no one would ever try to drive her out by bombing her home or burning crosses on her lawn. Throughout the 1950s, these and many other violent kinds of deterrent were unleashed against African-Americans attempting to infiltrate white housing developments all across the country, sometimes with fatal consequences.[15]

II Stahl versus Sirk and the Emergence of the Colour Line

After 1920, even northern black professionals (who before 1900 had mingled freely with their white counterparts) had become increasingly confined to buying properties located within a few carefully circumscribed inner-city neighbourhoods. According to Douglas Massey and Nancy Denton, the sheer volume of African-Americans moving to the rapidly industrialising cities of Chicago, Detroit, Cleveland, Philadelphia and New York had provoked the intense social antagonism that was responsible for imposing this state of virtual apartheid. Moreover, a disproportionate percentage of this massive influx consisted of the most utterly deprived southerners, who had been drawn to these manufacturing centres by the relatively high wages paid for unskilled labour.[16] Hence, as Massey and Denton have observed, during this initial period of transition northern 'middle-class whites were repelled by what they saw as the uncouth manners, unclean habits, slothful appearance, and illicit behaviour of poorly educated, poverty-stricken migrants who had only recently been sharecroppers'.[17] Since many factory owners had also employed rural black labourers as strikebreakers, who even in the best of times were competing with other groups of immigrants for jobs, white working-class enmity was often just as strong.[18]

The growing entrenchment of this kind of bigoted attitude culminated in sporadic outbreaks of violence, which included the beating, shooting and lynching of African-Americans who strayed into the wrong part of the city. Northern whites had become 'increasingly intolerant of black neighbours and fear of racial turnover and black "invasion" spread', to the degree that all 'Negroes' were now expected to live in the clearly designated precincts that had been dubbed '"black belts", "darkytowns", "Bronzevilles" or "Niggertowns" ... no matter what their social or economic standing'.[19] Towards the end of the 1940s, this spatial isolation was greatly intensified by 'white flight' to the dormitory communities that had begun to spring up just beyond the municipal boundaries.[20] The result was the distinctive racial distribution pattern that still dominates the built environment of the United States today, which one group of sociologists has dubbed 'Chocolate City, Vanilla Suburbs'.[21] Finally, by a variety of means, African-Americans were even excluded from the much less costly mass-produced housing tracts that post-dated World War II (such as Levittown on Long Island).[22] For black suburban residents like Annie Johnson and Sarah Jane in *Imitation of Life* (who during this period were generally restricted to the live-in domestic help), the leafy streets beyond the limits of their white employer's property harboured nothing but hostility and potential danger.[23]

This animosity was at least partially due to the policies that had been developed by the body that was established to implement the National Housing Act of 1934, which hardened the resistance of many builders, real estate brokers and home owners to the idea of allowing African-Americans into white communities. In accordance with the detailed system of appraisal that the Home Owners Loan Corporation had worked out during the previous year, the Federal Housing Administration decided that only certain types of dwellings located in particular kinds of neighbourhoods would receive support from a scheme that was designed to 'insure long-term mortgage loans made by private lenders for home construction and sale'.[24] Hence, although this key piece of New Deal legislation (supplemented by the Serviceman's Adjustment Act of 1944) did significantly increase the number of ordinary citizens who could afford to purchase a house, the standard method of assessment also consistently devalued older building stock and multi-family residences, as well as any homes that had been erected in more densely populated or mixed-use municipal zones. This preference for extreme homogeneity even extended to the ethnic make-up of the neighbourhood, since any region that contained pockets of people from many different cultural backgrounds was deemed to be in transition and therefore unstable. Moreover, even a tiny sprinkling of Jewish occupants would prevent that particular vicinity from receiving the highest rating no matter how expensive or well-maintained its constituent properties.[25] The HOLC definition of a First Grade (A or green) region clearly specified that districts 'in demand as residential locations in good times and bad' must be entirely populated by 'American business and professional men'.[26] Jews were obviously not 'American' enough, and blacks were considered to be even more beyond the pale, since the presence of any non-white families whatsoever would automatically consign that whole precinct to the lowest possible category.[27]

The resulting Fourth Grade (D or red) HOLC rating effectively ended the possibility of obtaining an amortised mortgage for a house that was situated in that area (making it very difficult to sell), which caused real estate prices to plummet and speeded up the decay of these often unfairly depreciated structures. Since private banks read this classification as indicating a 'hazardous' environment that had suffered an irreversible decline, they generally refused to lend money to the residents of the African-American, interracial or ethnically diverse urban neighbourhoods that had been placed in this category or to anyone else who wished to buy a property there. Consequently, the owners of dwellings located in recently constructed white suburban enclaves were the major beneficiaries of the national government's FHA mortgage guarantees and VA-sponsored building programs.[28] Moreover, most of the residents who had been attracted to these privileged developments came from middle-class districts in the city rather than 'from the slums or from rural areas', which meant that they knew just how quickly the HOLC rating of any neighbourhood could turn from good to bad.[29] Even after the Supreme Court had declared that the restrictive covenants preventing African-Americans from buying or renting houses in many outlying suburban communities were unenforceable in 1948, the colour line that protected white investors remained essentially in place.[30]

Northern builders, real estate boards and neighbourhood associations had already devised a complex series of strategies to prevent blacks from moving into certain locations by the 1950s. In Levittown, for instance, the construction company's sales representatives refused to give out application forms to African-Americans hoping to acquire one of the homes that were currently being completed.[31] Similarly, real estate agents often engaged in the practice of 'steering' when selling or renting houses to non-whites, which meant that they showed these clients only those possibilities that were available in existing black and mixed race neighbourhoods while pretending that listings in other areas had already been taken.[32] Finally, many suburban residents banded together to form 'homeowners' or 'improvement' associations that were charged with the task of protecting the value of their properties.[33] This mainly involved cleansing the immediate vicinity of any hint of an African-American presence, a goal that was unwaveringly pursued through a variety of means. For example, the association's members might organise a boycott of a realtor who sold a local property to a family of blacks, pool their resources to buy this house back, and then re-sell it to a more acceptable white candidate. They could also fight for zoning laws that excluded multiple family dwellings, public housing and other low-income residential developments that might entice African-Americans into their region.[34] According to Thomas Sugrue's analysis of post-World War II Detroit, if all else failed neighbourhood associations 'resorted to . . . harassment and violence' to drive unwanted residents away. During this period, the city's white inhabitants 'instigated over two hundred incidents against Blacks attempting to move into formerly all-white neighbourhoods, including mass demonstrations, picketing, effigy burning, window breaking, arson, vandalism, and physical attacks'.[35] While these clashes would have been less frequent in regions that were further from the ghetto, suburban residents employed equally extreme measures (including dynamiting the unwanted family's home) in order to discourage African-Americans from settling in their area.[36]

Perhaps because the shooting of John Stahl's earlier version of *Imitation of Life* pre-dated the founding of the Federal Housing Administration, the four main characters appear to be much more sanguine about the prospect of living in an interracial environment. After Bea Pullman's business has begun to flourish, she offers to give her devoted black housekeeper her own home and car, paid for with part of the proceeds earned from selling boxes of the pancake mix that was based upon the latter's recipe. At this time (1933, before the tacit institutionalisation of the ghetto) and place (metropolitan New York), the two families could still have occupied separate dwellings within the same neighbourhood. Of course, the faithful Delilah tells Bea that she has no desire to live apart from her beloved mistress, exclaiming, 'How 'm I gonna take care of you and Miss Jesse if I ain' here?' Both women (and their daughters) would eventually move from the cramped apartment behind their Coney Island storefront into the same elegant Manhattan townhouse.

Through the windows of the parlour of the white widow's new home, the intricate silhouette of the Queensboro Bridge can frequently be observed, especially in the lengthy cocktail party scene during which she meets an intriguing top-hatted ichthyologist. The prominence of this distinctive landmark locates Bea's refined Colonial Revival row house (complete with delicate wrought iron balconies and railings) within a small upper-class enclave that overlooks the East River. According to Paul Goldberger, this urbane New York neighbourhood was the haunt of the very rich during the 1930s, and yet Delilah and Peola Johnson's presence in the glamorous businesswoman's residence is accepted without question.[37] Despite the economic, ethnic and racial complexities that were inherent in their metropolitan address, the wealthy inhabitants of this district still seemed confident of their own ability to dominate their urban context. Perhaps this was because the system of ranking that positioned them at the top of the social hierarchy was also inscribed into the elevation and plan of their dwellings. Just like many of its genuine Manhattan counterparts, Bea Pullman's row house features a raised stoop leading to a formal front entryway that has been placed almost a full storey above the sidewalk. Below this entrance on the main façade, an inconspicuous door located a few steps down from the street opens onto the servants' quarters, which occupies the lowest portion of the building. In keeping with the status implications of this rather transparent spatial hierarchy, Delilah and Peola have been allocated the downstairs region of their impressive new residence, while Bea and Jesse inhabit the upper storeys.

In a sharp contrast with the opulent furnishings of the Pullman's salon on the floor above, the Johnsons make do with the homely Chintz-covered furnishings that the two families had brought with them from Coney Island. Although Delilah and Peola are not expected to behave like servants in Bea's midtown row house (where a white butler and waitresses cater for the needs of her guests), they remain cut off from their ex-mistress's high-society activities. From the modest surroundings of their basement apartment, the two African-American women can only comment on the quality of the jazz music that is wafting down to them from on high ('they don't play too bad for a bunch of white boys'). As soon as the cocktail party is over, Bea will tell Delilah about her romantic encounter with Stephen Archer, but this does not erase the fact that her former cook (and current business partner and friend) was not free to attend this event herself. Regardless of the affection that has grown up between the two families, the vertical stratification that has been built into the structure of their home keeps the non-white characters in their place.

In Sirk's 1958 version of *Imitation of Life*, the same group of protagonists establish their first joint household in a very similar area, only now we glimpse the Manhattan Bridge in the initial establishing shot of their building. The inclusion of this distinctive monument reveals that Lora, Annie, Susie and Sarah Jane have started their life together in Brooklyn, on the third floor of one of the richly ornamented row houses that began to be erected there during the 1850s.[38] This neighbourhood technically constitutes New York's first suburb (made possible by the ferry service to Manhattan that began in 1814 and the completion of John A. Roebling's earlier bridge in 1883), but it was annexed by the city in 1898.[39] Nevertheless, as Robert Fishman has noted, in comparison with their nineteenth-century British equivalents 'the American bourgeoisie' showed 'a surprising loyalty ... to the urban row house and mixed-use neighbourhood' even when they were building beyond the existing municipal limits.[40] Most Brooklyn homes (including Lora's building) were patterned after their attached Manhattan counterparts rather than the freestanding villas that had already begun to appear on the outskirts of London by the 1790s.[41] Despite 'the poverty and commercialism pressing in on them', at this juncture few wealthy New Yorkers had chosen to withdraw from increasing metropolitan tensions by retreating to a detached dwelling located in a more pastoral landscape.[42]

Yet long before the 1940s (when the narrative of Sirk's version of *Imitation of Life* begins), the detrimental effects of mass industrialisation and immigration had convinced government officials and the more affluent classes that there was no cure for metropolitan congestion, disintegration and disorder except avoidance. Under the influence of Taylor's *Principles of Scientific Management*, Herbert Hoover's 1922 Advisory Committee on Zoning had proposed a blueprint for future metropolitan development that called for dividing the city into separate areas that would each be dedicated to what they perceived to be conflicting functions.[43] Later that year (on the basis of the Advisory Committee's findings), the federal government published 'A Standard State Zoning Enabling Act', which laid out the procedures that local municipalities had to follow in order to curtail individual property rights by imposing land use controls. This national examination of the legality of zoning restrictions was at least partly inspired by the attempts that had already been made by several metropolitan centres to preserve 'detached house districts on the outskirts of the city where children can play on the earth without going to public playgrounds, where there can be some vegetation and where there can be an abundance of light and air'.[44] In this brief statement, Edward S. Bassett (speaking on behalf of the 1917 New York Committee on the City Plan) succinctly outlined the domestic paradigm that many Americans now preferred, which would inevitably lead to the decline of the urban row house. A subsequent US Supreme Court judgment even ruled that multiple family dwellings could be excluded from these ideal residential precincts (along with industrial buildings and businesses), on the basis that the increased traffic and noise that they produced 'intensif[ied] nervous disorders' and were detrimental to 'the safety and security of home life'.[45]

For the struggling white and African-American families who still remained in the older boroughs, the passing of New York's first zoning laws in 1916 would only have compounded their relatively high population densities. All of the apartment blocks, semi-detached and attached houses that could no longer be constructed in the outlying areas that were reserved for single family dwellings now had to be crowded into existing urban neighbourhoods. Moreover, as soon as the New York bourgeoisie had begun to shift their families into the freestanding homes that were situated beyond the existing municipal boundaries, each floor of the row houses that they left behind was often subdivided into separate apartments.[46] This would have been the fate of the once-fashionable late nineteenth-century terrace that Lora Meredith and her daughter moved into soon after arriving in the city. Unlike Bea Pullman's East River townhouse, by the late 1950s the aspiring actress's Brooklyn brownstone (with its characteristic elevated stoop and scooped out 'English basement') would have been considered an inappropriate dwelling for someone of an upper- or even a middle-class social standing. In an age of soaring steel-framed skyscrapers equipped with elevators (like the building where Lora's playwright-mentor is a tenant next to the theatre district), living in a walk-up apartment on the third floor of a four-storey brownstone was no longer a sign of privilege. Moreover, New York's ageing metropolitan neighbourhoods (where each structure often sheltered many households and children played on the street) were no longer thought to provide a suitable environment for raising a family.[47] Hence, the fictitious actress's purchase of a detached suburban home as soon as her finances would allow reflects the predominant view of this period.

Nevertheless, it is within the small rooms and compact layout of their single level 'cold water flat' that the two families in Sirk's version of *Imitation of Life* seem to be most at ease. The spatial limitations of their shabby five-room apartment constantly bring the characters together, communicating a very palpable sense of intimacy that the director reinforces through his composition of the image. Over and over again, an American shot reveals the integration of at least three of the four main protagonists into a close-knit group that has gathered around the kitchen table, the telephone in the hallway, the old fashioned padded chair in the lounge or Susie's large brass bed. During the shot/reverse shot exchanges that record Lora and Annie's heartfelt dialogue about their troubled past and their hopes for the future, both characters are usually still visible within the frame, even though this series of over-the-shoulder shots ostensibly represents each individual's point of view. Whether they are shown together or apart, both women often appear in the centre or the foreground of the film's Brooklyn mise-en-scène and they are usually depicted on a similar scale. The levelling effect of this visual equivalence is also supported by the sheer physical containment of the setting, which does not allow for enough spatial layering to cause either mother to recede into the background. If any figure is accorded a sort of transitory dominance in these scenes it is Annie, who soothes the distraught actress like a weeping child after she has rejected the sexual advances of a prospective agent. Until Lora's theatrical career has finally taken off, the two mothers appear to regard each other as commensurate partners in the running of their shared household.

Even more significantly, Annie's acceptance by the external metropolitan community enables the housekeeper to earn small amounts of money in her own right to deposit in the collective 'kitty'. After taking over Lora's initial job of hand-addressing envelopes, the resourceful African-American woman generates some additional income by laundering a 'persnickety' gentleman's shirts. In return for cleaning their building's common halls and stairways, she also receives a reduction from the landlord on their rent. When all else fails, it is Annie who manages to extract milk and eggs on credit from the deliveryman, Mr McKenney. Moreover, from her base in Brooklyn she can even participate in several African-American organisations, becoming a member of a large inner-city Baptist church and several lodges. Here too, both children attend local public schools and try to catch squirrels in the park under the watchful eyes of their mothers. While it is true that Annie and Sarah Jane are obliged to sleep in a storage area off the kitchen, they are never actually shown occupying that confined space. Throughout their stay in this tiny Brooklyn apartment, both the Johnsons and the Merediths appear to be equally at home, especially in the kitchen, lounge and Susie's bedroom (where both girls play). Hence, I would argue that the walls and doorways that segment this space are not meant to represent either psychological estrangement or obstacles that cannot be overcome. Similarly, the relatively open interior of Lora's rustic, vaguely Colonial Revival suburban dwelling (a stylistic fusion that Alan Gowans has described as Georgian/Homestead) does not indicate the end of status distinctions or a new tolerance of racial diversity.[48]

Unlike in the 1934 version of *Imitation of Life*, social inequalities are less evident in the elevation and ground plan of the two-storey house that Lora Meredith acquires in an idyllic rural subdivision during the late 1950s. In the private area of this typical 'servantless' design (without separate quarters for the domestic help), all four residents sleep in adjacent bedrooms on the second floor.[49] On the ground level, the sparing use of partitions (which define only one more room than the public zone of their previous apartment) means that much of this sprawling space remains relatively undefined. In this respect, Lora's house is the perfect incarnation of the twentieth-century middle-class home, which generally contained fewer, larger rooms than its Victorian predecessor, to the degree that the entire downstairs area might only consist of a living room, dining room and kitchen (as in this case, omitting even an enclosed front hallway in which to inspect one's guests). A number of factors were responsible for this widespread simplification: a growing demand for ease of cleaning (another side-effect of the 'servant problem'), the covert influence of architectural modernism (especially of the Prairie School), and an increased desire for a more relaxed, informal way of life that spills over into the surrounding landscape.[50]

Yet as Alan Gowans has noted, historical detail continued to be applied to the twentieth-century period house although it was far less specific or profuse, which had more to do with rising costs and falling standards of workmanship than 'progressive' aesthetics.[51] Lora's main living area has been adorned with classical mouldings and other decorative vestiges of past historical styles, and many of its elaborate wooden braces (complete with drop pendants) appear to perform no structural function whatsoever. Moreover, before we interpret the swift induction of visitors into the relatively unimpeded interior of this house as a sign of social inclusiveness, it should be remembered exactly where this building has been erected. During the 1950s residents of this kind of exclusive white housing development would have already been rigorously pre-screened, which means that they could afford to be more open with their neighbours. Once only 'people like us' (with similar incomes, careers, educational attainments and racial backgrounds) are allowed to buy properties in a neighbourhood, it is no longer necessary to invest in a set of intermediate rooms to filter out unwanted guests. Moreover, from the vantage point of Lora's brightly illuminated front lounge, the residents can easily see, classify and identify anyone who walks across the lawn or passes by the cut-away wall that has been placed beside the main entrance. In other words, what this lack of solid internal and external barriers connotes in this instance is an opening up to visual penetration and surveillance. As we have seen, African-Americans were the most vulnerable targets of this kind of scrutiny, since their households had to be eliminated as soon as possible in order to prevent a decline in the local real estate values. Hence, a black woman had to have a good reason for venturing into this kind of ethnically expurgated residential district, which was usually employment by a white homeowner as a domestic servant.

Consequently, in order to justify her continuing presence in the white actress's home, Annie takes on the role of the hired help whenever Lora entertains guests. On the majority of these occasions, the housekeeper stays out of sight in the kitchen, preparing food in the one room that was still largely closed off from the rest of the ground floor. Several members of her extended family (including Steven Archer) stop in to see her there, before returning to the main living area to join the rest of the party. All except Sarah Jane, of course, whose indeterminate position leaves her hovering on the threshold of the kitchen, equally shut out of these formal receptions unless she is acting as her mother's go-between.[52] We observe Annie in the front room with Lora and an outside visitor only once, when David Edwards drives up from Manhattan in order to discuss the casting of his latest theatrical project. Although the self-effacing African-American housekeeper helps the actress to dress backstage and has known the playwright for more than a decade, she stands behind the bar near the far wall mixing drinks for the full duration of the meeting instead of joining the others on the sofa. In other words, *Imitation of Life*'s black and white characters inhabit the amorphous space of the twentieth-century 'living room' quite differently, and for the Johnson family it does not represent a site of relaxation and ease. The enlarged floor area of their new home simply increases the number of steps that Annie must take when travelling from task to task. It also allows plenty of scope for her to be sidelined, marginalised and placed in the background of the composition, as the two families begin to drift further apart.

For her own protection, Annie never hesitates to put on this mask of public deference as long as she remains marooned in such a hostile environment. This is despite the fact that over the past ten years she had become Lora's most treasured confidant and friend. Of course, the actress has to pay for her housekeeper's loyal support after choosing to relocate both families to a white suburban neighbourhood where neither of the Johnsons could ever find outside work (at least while Sarah Jane is still living with her mother). Although Lora has been generous to her longstanding companion, giving her a pearl necklace, a mink collar and enough money to send her daughter to college (as well as to pay for a lavish funeral), she has also denied her any involvement in the running of their joint affairs once they have moved into this semi-rural home. During the scene in which the two women are arranging their newly purchased furniture soon after their arrival, Annie wonders aloud if they can afford to pay for all of this as well as to send Susie to a boarding school. Lora then locks the bills for her daughter's education in a desk drawer and refuses to discuss the matter any further, electing to ignore Annie's advice about what the teenager really wants (to be back with her mother). The actress now being the only breadwinner, she alone would decide how her money would be spent, thus eliminating any possibility that the two mothers could continue to manage their household together. While this lack of financial autonomy might have disempowered the African-American housekeeper no more than the average housewife, unlike the widowed Cary Scott in *All That Heaven Allows*, she could not have stayed on in this area if anything had happened to her white benefactor. Indeed, even under Lora's protection Annie never really felt completely safe, opting to make the long trip to the city to see her non-white friends rather than inviting them back to this forbidding outpost.

Sarah Jane unequivocally voices this bitter truth when she tries to explain to Susie why her boyfriend must never know the real identity of her mother. Under the Jim Crow laws, being optically white was not enough to obtain the privileges of that race, since even a drop of African-American blood was sufficient to justify classifying a mulatto child as black. Sarah Jane had to pretend to be as light-skinned as she appeared (something that her mother's complexion would immediately contradict) in order to be fully accepted in her restricted neighbourhood, and to gain access to a broader range of careers. After a preamble in which she confides, 'I don't want to have to come through back doors or feel lower than other people or apologise for my mother's colour', the troubled young woman then points out that racial discrimination was a fundamental tenet of their artificial 'village'. She asks rhetorically, 'What do you think people would say where we live if they knew my mother?' and answers her own question with the blunt statement 'They'd spit at me and my children'. Unfortunately, Sarah Jane's boyfriend does find out that her mother is a 'nigger' (to use Frankie's terminology), which he forces her to concede in a strikingly Expressionist scene that rips through the peaceful serenity of the preceding brightly-lit Arcadian idyll. The raven-haired beauty will soon discover that she can't pass for white while remaining with her family, and that the punishment for the threat of miscegenation is even crueller than she could ever have imagined.

In an interview published in 1978, James Harvey told Sirk that he was puzzled by the strange vehemence of the scene where Sarah Jane is beaten by her white boyfriend in *Imitation of Life*, which has been infused with such a heightened emotional, psychological and stylistic intensity that it stands out from the rest of the film. The critic would eventually conclude that Frankie's dialogue ('Is your mother a nigger?') and behaviour (raining down repeated blows on the defenceless teenager's body and face) seemed 'blaringly exaggerated'.[53] Yet we know from the historical record that Sarah Jane's white boyfriend's actions were not so ludicrously excessive. The penalty that an African-American might have to pay for moving into a white neighbourhood could be as high as his or her own life, whether it was taken inadvertently through the destruction of property or as the direct result of a physical attack.[54] Frankie's despicable treatment of the young woman that he had now recategorised as black (and therefore somehow subhuman) was not an inexplicably disproportionate response to the situation at all, given the social and geographical context. If white suburbanites weren't usually obliged to thrash African-Americans in the street, this had more to do with the atomisation of 1950s civic society than anything else. Frankie's family had decided to settle in an upper-middle-class suburb that was located far from the ghetto, which meant that they would never have expected to meet any blacks in their neighbourhood except for domestic servants. From their perspective, the light-skinned Sarah Jane had invaded this white residential bastion by stealth, threatening to contaminate the purity of its carefully guarded homes.[55]

In addition to this pronounced fear of racial mixing, since most African-Americans were immured within the crumbling inner city core (which no one could borrow the money to repair), they had also become inextricably associated with the urban problems that many commuters were attempting to flee. These were both moral ('integration . . . [of] a previously all-white neighbourhood . . . [will cause] an immediate rise in crime and violence . . . of vice, of prostitution, of gambling and dope') and physical (which will lead to 'blight and decay, and the . . . loss of [the existing residents'] home and savings').[56] Thus, Frankie would have convinced himself that he was guarding his sequestered community against the introduction of a potentially lethal contagion, and that the violence of his rejection of Sarah Jane was entirely warranted. In fact, as soon as the vengeful young man's assault on his terrified ex-girlfriend begins, the director's depictions of Frankie's body become so utterly depersonalised that he ends up standing in for the entire white race. The handsome youth who interrogates Sarah Jane in the initial two shot is immediately transformed into a succession of disconnected parts: a writhing, headless torso glimpsed from behind, a pair of severed hands that seize the unfortunate woman by the collar and whack her on the side of the head, and an unseen presence holding her limp body erect in order to sustain this buffeting (Figure 4.1). Even after he has dropped the shocked teenager to the ground where she falls forward into a pool of dirty water, the director still refuses to show us her attacker's face.

By choosing to represent Frankie through the use of synecdoche for much of this sequence, Sirk blocks any real possibility of the spectator ever identifying with his character. He is the disembodied arm beating Sarah Jane down and, as the camera swivels to the left of her whimpering figure, the pair of grey-flannel-clad legs that we see walking nonchalantly away. The director does not reframe the image in order to reveal Frankie's full silhouette until just before he turns to briefly survey his handiwork. By that time, the heart-

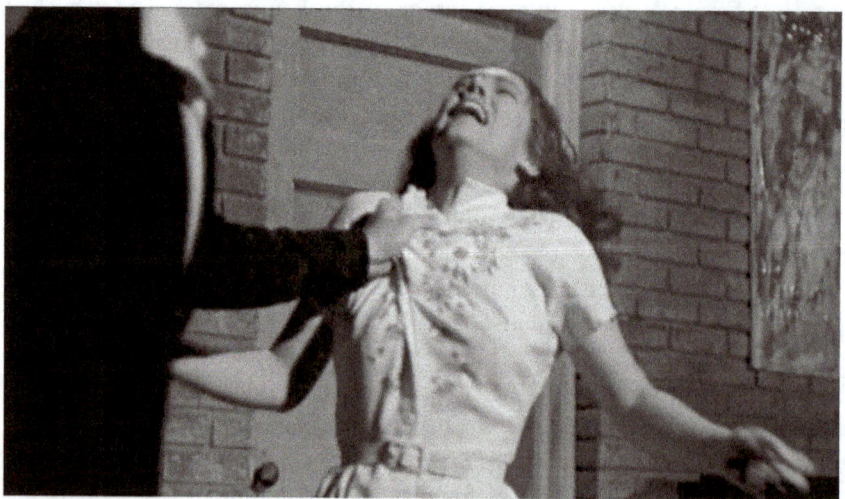

Figure 4.1 Frankie's brutal beating of Sarah Jane in *Imitation of Life*.

less adolescent has travelled some distance and has his back to the viewer, which again makes his features impossible to distinguish. When Frankie does momentarily glance back at Sarah Jane (and us), the lighting casts his face in darkness while picking out an aureole of disturbingly Aryan-looking blonde hair.

Twenty years after *Imitation of Life* was first released, the director couldn't remember if he had been able to make the mixed race girl's 'degradation' extreme enough, but this brief scene remains shockingly brutal. In his faceless anonymity and the cold implacability of his fury, Frankie does become the all-encompassing personification of 'Whitey' that Sirk had asked his scriptwriters to provide.[57] In the director's own words, he wanted 'the audience to get the feeling that this is not just the boy knocking [the mixed race teenager] down but society', and there is no doubt that he has succeeded in his intention.[58] The theme of racial oppression is also underscored by the words that are visible on the glass front of an empty building, just before Sarah Jane's ordeal begins. When Frankie initially leads his former sweetheart to believe that they will both run away to 'Jersey', her joyous smile (shown mirrored on the window behind him as if this huge pane were a screen) is immediately cancelled out by the phrase that surrounds her reflected image. The combination of the words 'liberty' and 'bar' sums up Sarah Jane's whole deplorable racial patrimony, an inheritance so pernicious that it threatens to destroy all of her hopes. Once the light-skinned mulatto's African-American ancestry has been revealed, it will present an almost insurmountable obstacle to her freedom to pursue an entertainment career, to engage in a romantic liaison with a white man, or to remain in what is essentially a segregated neighbourhood.

Whatever reflexivity was evinced in the director's decision to film the prelude to Frankie's barbaric attack as a reflection (in the second such shot, he backs the frightened girl up against a brick wall), I would argue that it does not impair the spectator's ability to empathise with his victim.[59] This was not the opinion of Michael E. Selig, who concluded that these two indirect images (along with what he has described as the 'excessively contrived action' of this sequence) have the effect of qualifying 'the viewer's engagement'. To my mind, this abrupt switch to a completely different visual register, with its sombre tonality, accelerated pace of editing, unusual fragmentation and odd perspectives, serves to denaturalise the situation rather than to alienate the observer. This remarkable degree of stylisation forces the viewer to recognise the problem of racial discrimination, while at the same time enabling us to experience something of the suffering of its victims.

In particular, the many reaction shots of Sarah Jane's imploring face, the helpless curve of her back when Frankie suspends her in the air and the crumpled heap formed by her body after she has been tossed aside all elicit our sympathy. This emotional connection is further enhanced by the keening wail of the 'hot' jazz saxophone and trumpet playing that accompanies these images of the unfortunate teenager's vicious assault. Unlike the anodyne dance tune being broadcast over the radio while Sarah Jane tells Susie about her attempts to 'pass' for white, this non-diegetic music highlights the jazz musician's ability to tap into more visceral feelings, in this instance manifesting a deep-seated rage against social injustice. While there is no doubt that the viewer's response to the allegorical figures of 'a White man beating a Black woman' has been 'overdetermined' (according to Selig), I would argue that we are still genuinely touched by the pathos of Sarah Jane's plight.[60]

In this way, the director provokes the audience into caring deeply about an issue that might otherwise have remained on a more abstract philosophical plane, galvanising us into taking action or at least into re-examining our own ideas on the question of race. Moreover, by mobilising the affective power of melodrama in order to persuade his viewers to 'think with the heart', the director has managed to temporarily create a new public sphere that is capable of overcoming the sheer physical dispersion of the mid-twentieth-century American community, however briefly.[61] By this time, in the United States at least, the major crises of modern life did not arise from the overstimulation, dissociation, disciplining and control of the urban crowd by the state, industry or any other entity, as Simmel or Kracauer had once predicted. Rather, the democratic citizen's main vulnerability was post-World War II American society's undue emphasis on intimacy and privacy and the withering away of any sense of mutual responsibility or conception of a greater public good. This is not to deny the increasing ascendancy of the large corporation, but the triumph of the capitalist-industrialist hegemony was only assured when the atomisation of suburban existence had reduced the possibility of achieving the collective solidarity that was necessary to resist it.

Therefore, Sirk's much-vaunted success in attracting urban and suburban patrons back to the cinema during this period could be considered something much more significant than simply understanding the kind of entertainment that appeals to 'the ladies'.[62] From the director's perspective ('you can't move masses by abstract thinking'), attracting a sizeable number of people to a motion picture that condemns racial discrimination, as well as placing too much emphasis on personal wealth and ambition, constitutes the first step in the reconstruction of the political equivalent of the civic square.[63] If the isolated monads of mid-twentieth-century American society could be brought out of their homes and into this 'alternative public sphere', then perhaps there was still hope.[64] As well as prompting us to reflect on our own experience of modern life, many of this director's most important melodramas also ask the viewer to consider what kind of communities we should be building. This important question is the main focus of the two detailed architectural case studies with which I will conclude this book.

Notes

1. Reyner Banham, *Theory and Design of the First Machine Age* (Cambridge, MA: MIT Press, 1980 repr. of the 1960 edn), 10–11.
2. Banham, 12.
3. Edward Dimendberg, 'From Berlin to Bunker Hill: Urban Space, Late Modernity and Film Noir in Fritz Lang's and Joseph Losey's *M*', *Wide Angle*, 19, No. 4 (October 1997), 65–6.
4. Lewis Mumford, 'Megalopolis as Anti-City', *Architectural Record*, 132, No. 6 (December 1962), 107–8. This article is largely a critique of Frank Lloyd Wright's low-density Broadacre City.
5. Lewis Mumford, *The City in History: Its Origins, Its Transformations, and Its Prospects* (London: Secker & Warburg, 1961), 561.
6. Lewis Mumford, *City Development: Studies in Disintegration and Renewal* (London: Secker & Warburg, 1946), 22–5.
7. In the production notes for *Written on the Wind* [Box 424, File 11977, Universal-International Pictures archives], the anonymous author notes that 'probably the greatest interest to anyone who has ever visited or lived in New York is the detailed reproduction of the famous "21" Club. With the complete co-operation of [the] ... owners, 100 photographs of the internationally known bistro were made exclusively for Art Director Robert Clatworthy and even such details as menus, napkins, glass ware and ... [any other] appointments necessary for authenticity [were] flown to Hollywood.'
8. Halliday, 148.
9. Mumford, *City Development*, 20.
10. Mumford, *The City in History*, 494.
11. Mumford, *The City in History*, 495. In devising a new type of community that had become more and more committed to 'relaxation and play as an end in themselves', Mumford argues that twentieth-century urban planners had created a residential milieu that was suitable for only 'a single phase of life, that of childhood' [495].
12. Frederick Lewis Allen, 'The Big Change in Suburbia, Part I', *Harper's Magazine*, 208, No. 1,249 (June 1954), 22–3.
13. In *The Status Seekers* [Harmondsworth: Penguin, 1959], Vance Packard reproduces a partial list of a 1956 ranking of 'approximately 300 occupations' that was co-authored by several University of Chicago sociologists and published in the *Chicago Tribune*. According to this rating, which was purportedly 'based on the skill and responsibility involved', 'Gardener' belonged in the 'Lowest-status group' (the seventh of seven possible categories) alongside 'Janitor' and 'Scrub woman'. The 'Highest-status' group was reserved for occupations such as 'Medical Specialist', 'Executives, top level, large national concern' and 'Law

partner in prestige firm' (pp. 104–5). Both this poor regard for Ron Kirby's initial occupation and the typical American's excessive respect for successful businessmen (also according to Vance, p. 103) are reflected in the dialogue of *All That Heaven Allows*.

14. The anonymous author of a 1950 magazine article entitled 'Is There a Picture in Your Picture Window?' described this current American predilection as an alarming 'fad'. Unless this broad area of glass actually frames an aesthetically pleasing view, it will rob you of your privacy and reduce your home to 'a gold fish bowl'. This feature, along with a companion piece entitled 'Do Your Neighbours Know Your Business?' details various methods for screening a suburban living space from the street. See *House Beautiful*, 92, No. 1 (January 1950), 33–5.
15. See Douglas S. Massey and Nancy A. Denton's *American Apartheid: Segregation and the Making of the Urban Underclass* (Cambridge, MA: Harvard University Press, 1993), 30, 34–5 and Thomas Sugrue's 'Crabgrass-Roots Politics: Race, Rights, and the Reaction against Liberalism in the Urban North, 1940–1964', *The Journal of American History*, 82, No. 2 (September 1995), 560.
16. Massey and Denton, 26–9.
17. Massey and Denton, 29.
18. Massey and Denton, 28–9.
19. Massey and Denton, 30.
20. In *Crabgrass Frontier: The Suburbanization of the United States* (Oxford: Oxford University Press, 1985), Kenneth T. Jackson points out that most American cities had initially grown by annexing the settlements that had sprung up beyond their original boundaries. He argues that the 'failure' of twentieth-century urban planning stems from the fact that these outlying developments began to refuse to be incorporated into the greater metropolitan area. Suburban commuters obviously wanted to live in a carefully controlled environment that was different from the city in terms of its visual and cultural homogeneity and relative affluence. By the 1950s the population of many large municipalities had begun to fall, as urban residential districts were increasingly abandoned to first-generation immigrants, African-Americans and the poor. See *Crabgrass Frontier*, pp. 148–56.
21. Reynolds Farley, Howard Schuman, Suzanne Bianchi, Diane Colasanto and Shirley Hatchett, '"Chocolate City, Vanilla Suburbs": Will the Trend towards Racially Separate Communities Continue?', *Social Science Research*, 7 (1978), 319.
22. Rosalyn Baxandall and Elizabeth Ewen, *Picture Windows: How the Suburbs Happened* (New York: Basic Books, 2000), 174–9. In 1950, according to Gwendolyn Wright, 'William J. Levitt ... was easily the largest developer in the country', building 17,450 houses in Levittown between 1947 and 1951 [*Building the Dream: A Social History of Housing in America* (Cambridge, MA: MIT Press, 1983), 251–2]. As Baxandall and Ewen observe, Levitt justified Levittown's whites-only policy mainly on economic grounds, arguing, 'most whites preferred not to live in mixed communities' [p. 177]. In an article that was published in *Harper's Magazine* [207, No. 1,243] in December 1953, however, Harry Henderson asserted that many of the residents he interviewed claimed they would not have minded

buying homes in a more racially-mixed suburb. Nevertheless, because their community was originally segregated, most Levittowners were afraid to change this 'abnormal' policy in case it resulted in a lowering of property values. See pages 85 and 86 of Henderson's 'Rugged American Collectivism: The Mass-Produced Suburbs, Part II'.
23. In order to prevent African-Americans from buying or renting their own accommodation in the 'exclusive Chicago suburb of Wilmette', 'a committee of citizens went so far as to ask wealthy homeowners to lodge all maids, servants, and gardeners on the premises, or else to fire all Negroes in their employ'. See page 36 of Massey and Denton's *American Apartheid*.
24. Jackson, 204.
25. For a lengthy discussion of the HOLC rating criteria, and the use that the FHA and private lending institutions made of them, see Jackson, 195–218.
26. Jackson, 197.
27. Jackson, 197–8. On pp. 208 and 209 he notes that a map of Brooklyn dated March 1939 indicated that the presence of just one non-white family on a block was enough to prompt the FHA to label that whole block 'black'. In other words, even the tiniest percentage of African-Americans in any given neighbourhood immediately lowered its HOLC rating.
28. Jackson, 215.
29. Jackson, 210.
30. As George Lipsitz points out on page 26 of *The Possessive Investment in Whiteness: How White People Profit from Identity Politics* (Philadelphia: Temple University Press, 1998), the 'Supreme Court ruled in *Shelley v. Kraemer* that state courts who enforced these deed restrictions against the will of buyers and sellers violated the Constitution'. He went on to note that this rather limited ruling 'did not make it illegal for property owners to adhere to them voluntarily, and it did not ban the registration of restrictive covenants with local authorities'.
31. Baxandall and Ewen, 178.
32. Lipsitz, page 26 and Massey and Denton, page 50.
33. Massey and Denton, 35.
34. Thomas J. Sugrue, 'Our Town: Race, Housing, and the Soul of Suburbia' [review], *The Journal of American History*, 84, No. 1 (June 1997), 316. See also Lees, 60–3.
35. Sugrue, 'Crabgrass Roots Politics', 560.
36. Massey and Denton, 35 and Packard, 81, 83–4.
37. Paul Goldberger, *New York: The City Observed* (Harmondsworth: Penguin, 1979), 151–2.
38. Charles Lockwood, *Bricks and Brownstone: The New York Row House, 1783–1829* (New York: Abbeville Press, 1972), 211–14.
39. Robert Fishman, *Bourgeois Utopias: The Rise and Fall of Suburbia* (New York: Basic Books, 1987), 117 and Ann Douglas, *Terrible Honesty: Mongrel Manhattan in the 1920s* (New York: Noonday Press, 1995), 154.
40. Fishman, 116.

41. Fishman, 53, 117.
42. Fishman, 118.
43. M. Christine Boyer, *Dreaming the Rational City: The Myth of American Planning* (Cambridge, MA: MIT Press, 1983), 197–8. This was long before *La Charte d'Athènes* was conceived at the 1933 meeting of the *Congrès Internationaux d'Architecture Moderne* in Paris, which suggested a similar division of functions.
44. Boyer, 159.
45. Boyer, 160–1.
46. Lockwood, 254–6.
47. Even the most palatial New York apartment could not provide an adequate environment for family life, according to institutions such as the *Ladies' Home Journal* and Better Homes in America. The executive director of the latter group told the 1921 National Conference on Housing that 'a child's sense of individuality, moral character and intellectual efficiency could only develop in a private detached dwelling'. Moreover, women who chose to bring up their children in an apartment (which not only contained a smaller area to clean, but also lacked the time-consuming amenities of a lawn and garden) were also accused of being lazy and shirking their domestic duties. See Gwendolyn Wright, pp. 150–1.
48. According to Alan Gowans, this contradictory fusion of 'the Georgian mansion's formal symmetry with Colonial homestead hominess of proportion, material and ornament' represented a typically American desire to combine upward mobility with comfort. See his *The Comfortable House: North American Suburban Architecture 1890–1930* (Cambridge, MA: MIT Press, 1986), 147–8.
49. In 'Three-Way Mirror: Imitation of Life' [in *Imitation of Life*, ed. Lucy Fischer (New Brunswick, NJ: Rutgers University Press, 1991), 9] Lucy Fischer remarks that the 'percentage of black women engaged in private service steadily decreased from 1890 as opportunities arose in factories, laundries, offices, and stores'. According to Steven Mintz and Susan Kellogg [*Domestic Revolutions: A Social History of American Life* (New York: Free Press, 1988), 124], the ratio of domestic servants (both black and white) to the general population fell by half between 1890 and 1920, 'thereby greatly affecting the life-styles of many middle class families'. This lack of live-in help contributed to the development of the simplified ground plan that is characteristic of the twentieth-century suburban house, a trend that Lora Meredith's new home reflects.
50. Gwendolyn Wright, *Moralism and the Model Home: Domestic Architecture and Cultural Conflict in Chicago 1873–1913* (Chicago: University of Chicago Press, 1980), 244–6, Alan Gowans, *Images of American Living: Four Centuries of Furniture and Architecture as Cultural Expression* (New York: Harper & Row, 1976), 422–4.
51. Gowans, *Images of American Living*, 424.
52. Sarah Jane makes her awareness of the racial discrimination of the surrounding suburb quite plain, when at one point she sashays into the living room carrying a tray of canapés on her head and addresses 'Miss Lora' in the dialect of a plantation slave. The actress is enraged, since this embarrassing incident occurs in front of her agent and a famous Italian film director. Lora follows Sarah Jane back to

the kitchen and forces her to admit that the Meredith family has always treated her with respect. This does not alter the fact that the neighbours think Annie and Sarah Jane have no business being in this district unless they are genuinely live-in servants.
53. Harvey, 'Sirkumstantial Evidence', 57.
54. To cite a Californian example of this kind of violence, Mike Davis records that Los Angeles civil rights activist O'Day Short was killed (along with his wife and children) when the Ku Klux Klan firebombed his recently purchased home in a whites-only section of Fontana, California in 1945. See *City of Quartz* (New York: Vintage Books, 1990), 400.
55. This fear of racial mixing would have evoked Sirk's experiences in Nazi Germany, where Jews as well as Communists, blacks, Gypies, homosexuals and other marginal groups were deliberately dehumanised by being likened to a bacterial contamination or disease or any other form of pestilential invasion. See Volume Two of Klaus Theweleit's *Male Fantasies* (Minneapolis: University of Minnesota Press, 1989), pp. 3–26.
56. These quotations have been taken from the testimony given by Thomas Poindexter (a founder of the Greater Detroit Homeowners' Council) to the United States Senate Committee on Commerce (convened in opposition to the Kennedy administration's civil rights legislation). His statement was not delivered until 1963, but it represents a cogent summation of the anti-integration sentiment that had been in existence for decades. See Sugrue, 'Crabgrass-Roots Politics', 575.
57. Harvey, 57.
58. Harvey, 57.
59. Michael E. Selig, 'Contradiction and Reading: Social Class and Sex Class in Imitation of Life', *Wide Angle*, 10, No. 4 (1988), 21.
60. Selig, 21
61. Lehman, 47.
62. During a decade when theatre owners were finding it harder and harder to wrest people away from their television sets, many of Sirk's films were immensely popular. According to the director, his version of *Magnificent Obsession* made ten times more money than John Stahl's original, and was considered to be 'Universal's most successful enterprise for years'. See Halliday, 106. Barbara Klinger confirms this statement in *Melodrama and Meaning: History, Culture and the Films of Douglas Sirk* (Bloomington: Indiana University Press, 1994), noting that '*Magnificent Obsession* grossed eight million dollars, and [Rock] Hudson reportedly started receiving three thousand fan letters a week' [p. 99]. In a studio press release for *Imitation of Life* dated 9/12/58 and credited to 'banker', Sirk was described as 'a ladies' man because he has directed every highly successful "woman's angle" picture at U-I in the past decade'. See Box 696, File 23704 of the Universal-International Pictures archive.
63. Lehman, 47.
64. In 'The Mass Production of the Senses: Classical Cinema as Vernacular

Modernism', *Modernism/Modernity*, 6, No. 2 (1999), Miriam Hansen defines the 'specifically modern type of public sphere' represented by the cinema (after Siegfried Kracauer) as an 'alternative to both bourgeois institutions of art, education and culture, and the traditional arenas of politics – an imaginative horizon in which, however compromised by capitalist foundations, something like an actual democratization of culture seems to be taking place' (p. 70).

Part Three

Two Architectural Case Studies

CHAPTER FIVE

Final Chord *and* 'Die Neue Welt': *The Mise-en-scène of* Aufbruch[1]

Final Chord or *Schlussakkord* was the only film from Douglas Sirk's German period to depict twentieth-century urban life. In the prologue that the director added to the existing script, two antithetical aesthetics appear to underscore the philosophical and political disparities that distinguish a democratic New York from a Fascist Berlin.[2] Since it consists of nothing but luminous skyscrapers and all-white 'non-bourgeois' interiors, *Final Chord*'s Manhattan seems to represent the egalitarian '*Neue Welt*' or 'New World' that had been predicted by Machine Age architects during the previous decade. By contrast, Berlin's grandiose Imperial monuments and luxurious Art Deco residences suggest a highly inequitable society that has chosen to preserve received hierarchical distinctions. Of course, given the repressive nature of the current political regime, the director could only criticise its authoritarian tendencies indirectly. Consequently, in *Final Chord* the architectural symbolism of each of these cities may be read both positively and negatively (from a Modernist and a National Socialist point of view). After outlining some of the most significant arguments on either side, I will then attempt to address the vexed question of which metropolis exemplifies the most desirable 'New World' of the future, on the basis of the formal and narrative evidence that is provided by the film itself.

In this lengthy preliminary section (which takes up more than a third of the total running time), Sirk introduces the key characters and sets out the major dramatic conflicts by cross-cutting between New York and Berlin. After a montage sequence highlighting the giddiness of Manhattan's New Year's Eve revelry, a drunken passer-by stumbles across a dead man seated on a bench in Central Park. The audience soon discovers that the well-dressed suicide was a fugitive living under an assumed name who had fled Germany after being convicted of embezzling funds from his employer. Although his wife had accompanied him into exile, they were forced to leave their young son behind. We subsequently see this engaging child being taken to an orphanage in Berlin after the police department confiscated the money that had been left with a foster mother for his care. Convinced that Peter's parents would never be found, the head of the children's home (Professor Obereit) agrees to allow him to be adopted by his friend and musical companion, Erich Garvenberg. As well as acknowledging his genuine fondness for the boy, the orchestra conductor was also speculating that the arrival of their new son would save his marriage to a beautiful, but childless socialite. By providing his wife with a more seemly way to pass the time while he was off communing with 'Bach and Beethoven', he had hoped both to assuage her loneliness and to reduce the allure of her rather raffish circle of friends. Under more propitious circumstances this strategy might have worked (Charlotte does try to reform, and later confides to an unsavoury baron that she enjoys being a mother), but a discarded lover tries to extort money from her and finally hounds the poor woman to her death.

By the end of Sirk's extended preamble we are already asking ourselves which woman is more deserving of this cherubic boy, the person who gave birth to him (Hanna Müller) or the glamorous creature who has taken him into her home (Charlotte Garvenberg)? Which of these protagonists truly belongs with the noble Erich Garvenberg, Frau Müller (who shares his love for classical music and for Peter) or his wife (who can't really begin to fathom either)? Moreover, since one of the first things Sirk discovered at UFA was that 'a set is an expression of the people in it, as well as the people being an expression of the set', why does he initially choose to locate each of these women within a very different kind of architectural space?[3] Given the limited number of times that these characters are glimpsed outside (never, in the case of Charlotte; during one fleeting exchange at the beach with Professor Obereit, a short scene in which she sees the conductor off at the airport, where the noise of his plane's engine drowns out her attempt to tell him the truth about her relationship to Peter; and a single brief shot at the gate of the Garvenberg residence after she has returned to kidnap her son in the case of Hanna), the director's astute use of the built environment takes on an unusual symbolic resonance in this film. Throughout *Final Chord*'s American prelude and long after her return to Berlin, Hanna continues to be linked to the tall, curtain-walled buildings and austere 'non-bourgeois' interiors that had once held out the promise of a more equitable world to come. In particular, the militant plainness of Hanna's New York apartment provides a sharp contrast with Charlotte's chosen haunts, which betray the lingering fascination with luxury that is the defining feature of the Art Deco style.[4] While both Modernist and Art Deco architecture reflected the tenor of twentieth-century urban life to some degree, only the former had attempted to move beyond stylistic innovation in order to transform the city's underlying socio-economic systems. Charlotte's favourite Berlin haunts might appear to be equally up to date, but their reliance upon pre-industrial handiwork clearly negates the superficial look of contemporaneity.

Since much of the meaning of a Modernist interpretation of *Final Chord* turns upon this architectural distinction, the importance of Hanna's association with the most dissident strand of twentieth-century design cannot be overstated. Among other things, it brings to mind Ernst Bloch's analysis of the crucial role performed by *Spuren*, or traces, as outlined in *The Utopian Function of Art and Literature*.[5] When filtered through an 'anticipatory' consciousness, allegorical objects that are embedded in the present offer intimations of a more exemplary society than might otherwise have been imagined. In the case of *Final Chord*, Hanna's architectural *Spuren* constantly admonish us to look ahead towards a yet to be realised 'New World' of the future, an orientation that obviously refutes the nostalgic invocation of the past that is evident in National Socialism's most prominent monuments.[6]

Of course, even in Bloch's more forward-looking conception of allegory, these fragments of an ideal future needed to be examined by a receptive viewer in a relatively sympathetic environment in order to perform this liberatory function. If, as the exiled German philosopher would later write, openness was the essential feature of twentieth-century Machine Age design, then 'this will towards an adjustment with the outside world was undoubtedly premature'.[7] Why replace dark stone façades with 'light glass walls' when all that will be disclosed by this expanded field of vision is acts of Gestapo violence? Bloch's rather blunt reappraisal of the '*Neues Bauen*' or 'New Architecture' contradicts a number of other revolutionary theories by arguing that the context of these innovative structures remained equally paramount: 'The broad window full of nothing but outside world needs an outdoors filled with attractive strangers, not . . . Nazis.'[8] If Berlin's Machine Age buildings seemed 'detached and keen to depart' after the founding of the Third Reich, was there any place left where Modernist architecture might still appear to be at home?[9] In other words, under what circumstances would the 'lifeless functional forms' of the abstract 'New Objectivity' gain content and metamorphose into the 'socially animated' city of Le Corbusier? According to Bloch, only when they are the embodiment of a truly 'collective' society would these 'chalk-white tenements' no longer seem hollow, gaining colour and substance from the accompanying political reforms.[10] For this reason, the dedicated Marxist went on to nominate the Soviet Union as the most appropriate site for the ongoing Modernist project. If a similar logic is applied to Douglas Sirk's 1936 film *Final Chord*, however, then another portion of the globe seems to offer a place where 'the beginnings of a different society will make true architecture possible again'.[11] To any viewer who could still admire the transparency of Sirk's creative reinvention of New York's scintillating skyline, the classless community that fulfils the promise of this Modernist cityscape appears to be firmly located in the United States.[12]

I VISIONS OF MODERNITY: INTERPRETING THE NEW YORK SKYLINE

Final Chord's first real establishing shot consists of a distant bird's-eye view of New York that stretches out towards infinity. This slowly moving aerial perspective reveals a city that has been doubly defined by geometry, in which a series of rectangular buildings rise up from an equally rigorous gridiron street plan. Although much of this scene unfolds after midnight, artificial light spills out of the windows of many of these translucent structures and irradiates the surrounding darkness. It is an image that seems to recall Fritz Lang's rhapsodic paean to New York by night, which was published in *Filmkurier* (the 'leading German film journal') shortly after the director had returned from his first trip to America in 1924. In Lang's opinion, this nocturnal view constituted 'a beacon of beauty strong enough to be the centrepiece of any film . . . [with] streets full of moving, turning, spiralling lights, and high above the cars and elevated trains skyscrapers . . . in blue and gold, white, and purple and still higher above . . . advertisements surpassing the stars with their light'.[13]

Three years later, Joachim Teichmüller would coin the term 'light architecture' to describe this kind of synthetic fusion of space, structure and artificial illumination, which he admitted was already a well-established artistic practice.[14] By the mid-1920s, German books, journals and magazines had begun to routinely include both day and night exposures of the same architectural perspective.[15] In other words, a brightly-lit edifice shining through the darkness had become emblematic of the transfiguring energy of modernity, which meant that many contemporary urban buildings were now being designed with this perception in mind. Consequently, I would argue that *Final Chord*'s New York (which in the case of the exterior views is only glimpsed at night) represents the apotheosis of this process. Given the increased regularity of its fenestration and the widespread diffusion of its electrical glow, Sirk's image of Manhattan captured the 'fantastic beauty' of the 'the flaming script' that architect Erich Mendelsohn had ascribed to Fritz Lang's photographs of the actual place even more perfectly.[16]

Final Chord's first external shot of New York focuses only upon the upper portion of the nocturnal vista that Lang had so eloquently described, however, as the camera glides across a succession of rooftops and gleaming towers that are often illuminated from within. Later in this scene, Sirk's mobile framing even exposes the equivalent of Lang's advertising signs picked out in light. After the camera has passed through Hanna's apartment window and panned along the row of skyscrapers that is located across the street, the spectator can't help observing that one of these buildings has been emblazoned with two carefully selected English words. Together, they form the phrase 'Yes Times', a verbal conjunction that appears to be urging the viewer to accept 'the new spirit' of 'this new epoch' (in the words of Le Corbusier), along with the unadorned steel-framed architecture that embodies it.[17] Only then are we shown the culmination of this relatively constricted sequence of shots, an aerial view of a completely Modernist metropolis that appears to go on forever. To my mind, this light-filled Manhattan panorama offers a transnational crystallisation of the 1920s avant-garde's dream of the ideal city, since it conflates the set-back skyscrapers of Hugh Ferris with the layout of Le Corbusier's *Plan Voisin*.

Rosemarie Haag Bletter has convincingly argued that the dematerialised tall building held a privileged place in the utopian parlance of the early twentieth-century German architectural avant-garde.[18] Whether one was a 'romantic' Expressionist or a 'rational' proponent of the New Objectivity, soaring curtain-walled façades continued to stand for spiritual aspirations and for 'the social transformation of a new society'.[19] Although the shape of *Final Chord*'s Manhattan towers appears to have been derived from a specifically American source, Hugh Ferris's architectural renderings were often just as visionary and just as oriented towards the future as those of his European Modernist counterparts. In response to a request to draw a series of high-rise building profiles that would conform to New York's 1916 zoning laws, the well-known delineator produced a collection of stepped-back or pyramidal configurations that had an immediate impact upon the characteristic silhouette of the skyscrapers that were later erected in the downtown core.[20] While the ziggurat-like shape of these influential architectural schemata could be loosely described as Art Deco, in other respects they were just as stripped down and forward-looking as their International Style equivalents.

For instance, Ferris' studies of height and massing were completely devoid of ornament, a quality that he predicted would be carried over into the 'coming generation' of young architects' designs in his widely circulated 1929 book *The Metropolis of Tomorrow*. Echoing the moralistic rhetoric of his European peers, the prominent American draughtsman had urged his colleagues to abandon their current practice of 'evasion and deception' by refusing to add columns and other decorative 'forms that no longer serve functions' to this kind of steel-framed building.[21] In other words, the 'new beauty' that issued from the discovery of this 'new truth' will no longer be applied to the architectural façade as a supplementary afterthought. Instead, it would emanate from the harmony of the fundamental proportions or the way in which the various structural elements (now 'honestly' exposed) intersect. Moreover, in the 'Imaginary Metropolis' that is outlined in the final section of Ferris's influential publication, architecture no longer reflected the chaos of unbridled competition and the individual property owner's 'urge – for money'.[22] Instead, the lofty civic towers that formed the focal point for each of its distinct zones (Art, Business and Science) would be 'consciously employed for no less an object than the elevation and the evolution of man'.[23] Just like many of his European contemporaries, this American visionary believed that the 'forthright structural simplicity', 'scale' and 'power' of many recent American skyscrapers 'announces' nothing less than 'the coming of a new order'.[24]

With regard to *Final Chord*, it seems to me that the widespread artificial effulgence, set-back or rectilinear shapes and unadorned quality of its New York architecture reflect this more progressive conception of modernity. Although Eric Kettlehut was responsible for designing the breathtaking American panoramas that were filmed in UFA's studios, they bear little relation to his previous dystopian imaginings.[25] When compared with the cityscapes he had created for *Metropolis* at the end of the previous decade, *Final Chord*'s bird's-eye view of New York exhibits a number of marked dissimilarities.[26] The earlier film's oppressive jumble of Expressionist, Neo-Gothic or Neo-classical towers looming over the streets below has disappeared, along with the nucleated *Stadtkrone* city plan; individual corporate or Imperial aggrandisement appears to have given way to a more egalitarian social order regulated by a co-operatively organised state. Although some of *Final Chord*'s curtain-walled structures are taller than others (and only these have a set-back silhouette), no single piece of architecture seems to stand out as the dominant focal point. Nor do any of this film's skyscrapers appear to overshadow their surroundings in such a threatening way, due to their relative weightlessness and the orderliness of their spacing (which even allows for a gap between the foundations of adjacent buildings). Finally, the non-hierarchical tenor of these unornamented American buildings has been further magnified by the gridiron street plan, which to some Modernist architects represented the visible manifestation of a fundamentally re-engineered society. Conveying at once democratic equality, an infinitely extensible decentred collectivity and the 'grip of man ['s reason] upon nature', according to Le Corbusier, the gridiron's perfect geometry also evokes the more equitable world to come.[27]

By avoiding the *Stadtkrone*'s emphasis on a select group of official monuments in *Final Chord*'s New York cityscapes, Kettlehut also eliminated its feudalistic overtones, which included a tacit acceptance of the onlooker's subordination to an overwhelming authority. Instead, in the standardisation of its architectural forms and the infinite extension of its limits, his idealised bird's-eye view of New York suggests a much more democratic tolerance for mobile, liminal states that are flexible enough to allow for adaptation and progressive social change.[28] Philip Fisher has argued that in a specifically American context, where successive waves of immigrants often didn't share the same racial origin, language or history, it was this gridiron land survey and city plan that instilled in its citizens a sense of 'common identity'. He would go on to claim that because this kind of subdivision was non-hierarchical, unbounded and identical from place to place, it actually made physically manifest the formation of a democratic national space.[29]

Of course, during this period more conservative-minded viewers would have disputed such a reading of *Final Chord*'s New York, arguing not only that the 'New Architecture' was incapable of achieving such rarefied social goals but also that this type of structure had had a detrimental effect upon many traditional European civilisations. As early as 1925, Stefan Zweig had claimed in the *Berliner Börsen-Courier* that an endemic spiritual bankruptcy was the result of the 'monotonization of the world' that had occurred with the progressive Americanisation of every other contemporary industrial society. In his view, 'millions of people, from Capetown to Stockholm, from Buenos Aires to Calcutta', now 'dance the same dance to the same short-winded, impersonal [jazz] melodies'.[30] In architectural design and city planning as well as everything else, this international mass culture's taste for 'uniformity' was supposed to have erased any trace of 'individuality' along with any geographically specific artistic traits. Some German observers had already asserted that the symptoms of this precipitous global decline were even more apparent in the United States, where immigrants from a 'mish-mash of nations without race and culture' had adopted an 'unfeeling form of business behaviour' that was 'devoid of common decency and of common trust'.[31] According to Adolf Hitler, this lack of a discrete national identity and of any shared sense of a higher cultural purpose would have been compounded by the problems that are intrinsic to any democratic system. In his view, parliamentary assemblies were essentially too transient and weak to forge a more enduring 'People's State', which is only made possible by the ratification of a supreme leader whose edicts must be obeyed.[32]

II The Weight of History: Germany's Imperial Monuments

According to Émile Durkheim, in the absence of any more constructive socio-political ideals the possibility of upward mobility introduced by industrial capitalism excites 'appetites ... [that] no longer recognize the limits proper to them'. The pioneering French sociologist would go on to observe that 'with increased prosperity, desires increase [and] overweening ambition always exceeds the results obtained, great as they may be'.[33] Ironically, in *Final Chord*, the cultural malaise that incites these unbridled appetites is most in evidence in the city where vestiges of older architectural traditions are still readily apparent. With the exception of Hanna, Professor Obereit and Erich Garvenberg, few residents of 1936 Berlin demonstrate any loyalty, even to their most intimate family or friends, never mind to any members of the larger community.³⁴ In the opinion of those who had been schooled in 'the authoritarian ... state of Imperial Germany' and tempered by the firestorm of the World War I, this kind of social disintegration could only be countered by imposing a militaristic discipline upon the lax civilian population.³⁵ Therefore, in addition to their shared racial and cultural inheritance, the German people needed to be 'brought to political unity' by the binding dictates of the omnipotent leader who most perfectly embodied their common spirit or *Volkgeist*. This totalitarian conception would finally be realised when Adolf Hitler became both *Führer* and *Reichkanzler* in 1934. From this moment onward, although his subjects were expected to bask in the reflected glory of their leader's achievements, they could no longer question his policies because both he and his Party now stood above the State.³⁶

For all those who were convinced (like Albert Speer) that 'tight public order was in our blood', the absolute power of the new dictatorship would have stimulated a vicarious pride, since it was meant to exemplify the more forceful confluence of the People's aggregated will.³⁷ Perhaps as an extension of this fundamental precept, Hitler had also declared that the 'self-respect' of 'each individual German' would only be 'restored' by building a few outstanding ceremonial structures that belonged to the entire nation (or at least to all right-thinking Aryans).³⁸ Only these 'magnificent edifices' could unite the 'individual inhabitant with his city' because they 'seemed made ... for all eternity' and were 'intended to reflect, not the wealth of an individual owner, but the greatness and wealth of the [whole] community'. Quite unlike his European Modernist counterparts (who during this period were obsessed with the problem of designing an adequate living space for everyone), Hitler believed that when it was 'compared to ... [these official monuments] the [private] dwelling house ... sank to the level of an insignificant object of secondary importance'.³⁹ By the late 1930s Hitler and Albert Speer had begun to collaborate on an elaborate plan to remodel the nation's capital (to be subsequently renamed Germania). At the time of *Final Chord*'s initial release, however, the drawings of the enormous *Volkshalle* or People's Hall that was meant to anchor the architect's projected north–south grand avenue had yet to be finalised.⁴⁰ What Sirk's film highlights in its place is the remnant of a previous effort to transform Berlin into a more imposing European capital: the *Domkirche* or Protestant Cathedral that was designed by Julius Raschdorff and erected by Kaiser Wilhelm II between 1894 and 1905.

This enormous building dominates the aerial perspective of the German city that was shot on location and immediately succeeds *Final Chord*'s bird's-eye-view of New York (separated only by a brief travelling shot of the Atlantic Ocean). Against the radical indeterminacy of the film's imaginary Manhattan skyline (where no distinction has been made between office towers, apartment blocks and publicly owned buildings), Sirk has chosen to juxtapose an image of one of Berlin's most well known emblems of authoritarian control (and civic *Kultur*, according to Hitler's stylistic lexicon). Commissioned in 1893 to replace a much smaller church on the same site, the inflated grandeur of this Neo-Baroque religious edifice was intended to glorify 'the monarchy, the new state run by aristocrats, the military and the church'.[41] As planning historian Wolfgang Sonne has noted, the *Domkirche* (or *Berliner Dom*) was part of a whole series of post-unification monuments that were supposed to symbolise the city's increased status as the capital of a pan-German Empire. In particular, the cathedral's massive silhouette evoked 'the traditional connection between throne and altar . . . on a new urban scale' by echoing 'the cupola of the castle' in its 'dome'.[42]

The colossal dimensions of this grandiloquent Imperial structure would explode the continuous fabric of modestly-scaled buildings, pedestrian promenades and axial perspectives that Karl Schinkel had envisaged earlier in the century.[43] Even before its construction was finally completed in 1905, at least one critic had begun to mock the pomposity of Raschdorff's design by describing it as a 'cathedral in World-Exposition style'.[44] In a newspaper article that was ironically entitled 'The Most Beautiful City in the World', Walter Rathenau wrote that the *Domkirche*'s mixture of decorative eclecticism and immense size offered the perfect summation of the parvenu exaggeration that had come to typify Wilhelmine Berlin.[45]

Unlike the *Berliner Dom* (and despite the *Führer*'s own taste for the Neo-Baroque), the official architecture of the Third Reich was generally Neo-classical in style.[46] Yet it is precisely this overblown quality that made Raschdorff's turn-of-the-century landmark the ideal substitute for the many National Socialist monuments that had not yet been built. According to Wolfgang Schäche, this disproportionate (and very untraditional) giganticism was of even greater significance than the fact that the so-called 'Nordic' embellishment of many civic monuments proclaimed the kinship of Nazi Germany with 'the . . . perfection of Ancient Greece'.[47] Moreover, after analysing the plans that were drawn up between 1937 and 1943 for a new museum district in Berlin, Schäche even denies that these National Socialist designs should be interpreted as classical at all. For instance, while conceding that 'structurally antique elements' such as Doric columns and a triglyphic frieze are apparent in the preparatory drawings of a proposed Museum of Ethnology, he argues that these are so 'distorted by scale and proportion' as to have 'become unrecognisable'.[48] After adducing the analogous findings of several previous scholars, Schäche would eventually conclude that 'Whatever classical elements actually *were* used [in the design of this didactic cultural district], the grotesque exaggeration of their proportions forced them into a monumentality whose "effect was more akin to Egyptian tyranny than Hellenic humanism'".[49]

In the end, the latter contends (by quoting a previous article by J. Petsch) that the 'National Socialist Style' can only be defined as a 'monumentalism' that has evolved (both 'formally and thematically') from 'the "architecture of *Wilhelminisch* Germany"'.[50] Just like Hitler's most megalomaniacal structures (in which 'the suppression of the lone architectural feature' signals 'the social suppression of the individual'), the Kaiser's massive Imperial buildings had sought to absorb every onlooker into a regimented order that would 'prepare them for war and death' on behalf of their new nation.[51] Moreover, by demanding such ponderous 'community' edifices as the concrete embodiment of the 'eternal values' of their respective regimes, these autocratic leaders were sending out a message to the world as well as to their own people. When it was deployed in Germany during the Third Reich, this extraordinary architectural magnitude was intended to express the *Führer*'s belief that 'We are . . . the complete equals of every other nation'.[52] Foreigners (and dissenting residents) were meant to be overwhelmed and somewhat daunted by the formidable power that these enormous monuments implied. Loyal supporters who already identified with the racist and militarist ideology that they encoded would be filled with a sense of collective pride.

Since *Final Chord*'s bird's-eye view of Berlin was shot before many of the city's more 'heroic' National Socialist edifices had been erected, I would argue that Kaiser Wilhelm's Protestant Cathedral appears to be standing in for this kind of totalitarian design. From the director's chosen vantage point, the spectator can't help noticing that the *Berliner Dom* towers over the neighbouring buildings, which was something that Hitler required of any civic monument (citing several classical and medieval examples that he admired as precedents in *Mein Kampf*).[53] Only a structure that eclipses its surroundings could function as the theatrical backdrop for the semi-liturgical spectacles that the Nazis were constantly staging in order to reignite their believers' faith. Although Raschdorff's Imperial cathedral could not encompass a crowd of 150,000 (the projected standing capacity of Hitler and Speer's proposed Berlin *Volkshalle*), these material constraints would eventually be overcome by appropriating the adjacent public space.[54]

By 1936, the plaza in front of the *Domkirche* had been converted from an extensively landscaped park into a barren Nazi parade ground.[55] While *Final Chord* was still in the process of being made, Hitler delivered a highly millenarian May Day speech from a raised podium that had been placed at one end of this same recently paved civic square. Within plain sight of one of Kaiser Wilhelm's most important landmarks, he declared in 1933 that a 'Revolution [had] passed over Germany' that had been 'legalized by the people's confidence' in voting for National Socialism and further legitimated by their ongoing readiness to submit to their *Führer*'s will.[56] Together with the figure of Adolf Hitler himself, the *Domkirche* would have provided the necessary 'visible focus' for this re-creation of the 'visible force' that Speer claimed had been generated by the huge crowd that attended the National Socialist government's very first May Day celebration (which was also held in Berlin).[57] As Benjamin Warner has noted, on 'these occasions all sense of individual responsibility was removed; the apocalyptic visions of the regime were to substitute individually meaningful thoughts or actions with total self-sacrifice and participation in the communal *volk* entity'.[58]

Hence, for many viewers, *Final Chord*'s Berlin would have appeared to be steeped in just this kind of reactionary political ideology, whether it originated with the Prussian monarchs, the German Emperors or the existing totalitarian regime. Each of the sumptuous Neo-Baroque or Neo-Classical monuments that the film reveals implicitly asks us to accept a highly inequitable society and to submit to an imperious autocrat's demands. Within these symbolically-loaded 'community' spaces, even Erich Garvenberg's masterful conducting of Beethoven's 'Ode to Joy' may be read as invoking 'the leadership principle' that the *Führer* was meant to encapsulate.[59] Moreover, Hitler's emphasis upon revivifying selected remnants of an '*unrefurbished past*' in order to reshape the nation's destiny meant that he (and many other disaffected members of German society) risked the prospect of 'losing time in the Now' completely, to quote Ernst Bloch.[60] As the eminent philosopher would go on to remark, how can we discover the '*prevented future contained in the Now, the prevented technological blessing, the prevented new society with which the old one is pregnant in its forces of production*' when the 'temporal alienation' of the ruling class at once 'facilitates . . . 'revolution' and reaction'?[61] When even the processes of industrialisation have been diverted into satisfying the archaic 'needs . . . of olden times' then every possible alternative political configuration has been effectively closed down.[62]

Previous appeals for an architecture of 'home, soil and nation' would have shaded imperceptibly into the atavistic 'untimeliness' that was so central to the communal rituals of the National Socialist state. Again according to Bloch, Germany's surviving 'pre-capitalist' 'impulses and reserves' had unleashed 'non-contemporaneous elements [that emanated] from [an] even "deeper" backwardness, namely [that of] *barbarism*'. Thus, the totalitarian government's revival of ancient 'campfires and sacrificial smoke burn[ing] in the folkish hall' represented not mere play-acting but a genuine 'conspiracy against civilisation'. When the national consciousness was divided between the irrational myths of the past and the dream of an expurgated future, then the sacrifices that one had to make in the present would remain perpetually unexamined. In resurrecting aspects of the 'darkest primitivization', the Nazis had suspended not only current standards of justice and decency, but also reason itself. Bloch went on to observe that when he and his peers recall 'the tune "When Jewish blood spurts from the knife", which drifts over the SA troops as a swastika in music, we feel the dream of preserved insanity ... in this kind of National Socialism'.[63] Hence, to any viewer who was averse to the institutionalised savagery of the Third Reich, the sense of anomie that might arise from being assimilated into the standardised surroundings of an American democracy would have seemed tame by comparison.

III Determining *Final Chord*'s 'New World': The Textual Evidence

If *Final Chord*'s representations of a Modernist New York and a historical Berlin can be interpreted both positively and negatively, which of these conflicting viewpoints is best supported by the narrative events? Perhaps one way of beginning this process of evaluation would be to compare Hanna's encounters with the police in each of these cities, since the differences between them highlight the progressive erosion of her political rights. In New York, Hanna is treated by these figures of authority with the utmost kindness and solicitude, to the degree that the uniformed officer who begins to tell her about her husband's suicide soon becomes too overcome with emotion to go on. After the detective in charge finishes informing the widow that her husband has been found dead in Central Park, out of consideration for her grief he allows the heartbroken woman to turn, walk across the room and sink into a chair by the window. This means that he will then be obliged to step forward towards Hanna, which establishes the pattern of their interaction for the rest of the sequence. Instead of attempting to dominate the poverty-stricken immigrant, this surprisingly egalitarian municipal official now allows his movements to be governed by hers. During the initial two shot in which Hanna identifies her husband's gun, the detective continues his investigation only after he has placed himself on the same level by sitting down on the bed just behind her. As the widow recounts the story of her husband's piteous downfall while looking away from her interlocutor, the side-on alignments of their profiles and bodies parallel one another almost exactly. The director then cuts to a more frontal view that begins with a close-up of Hanna's agitated hands before tilting up to a similar perspective of her tear stained face, which is again mirrored by a corresponding close-up of the kindly detective who appears to be located right beside her in this tightly compressed space.

In addition to revealing the depth of the widow's complex feelings and strengthening the audience's identification with her character, this double close-up also emphasises the plainclothes officer's evident sympathy as he inclines his head inward towards hers. The detective then glances off-screen and the director cuts away in order to show us what he sees: Hanna's neighbour and the tipsy stranger who had accidently stumbled into her apartment both regarding this soft-spoken woman with an equally intense empathetic gaze. Hence, even during what is essentially a police interrogation, by drawing together a group of concerned observers and oscillating between their respective points of view, a circle of compassionate listeners is born that foreshadows the community of co-equals that will later be formed by the radio broadcast of Beethoven's Ninth Symphony. In particular, the composition within the frame establishes a visual equivalence between the widow and the detective that appears to signify both freedom from subservience and a cohesion that is founded upon mutual respect, regardless of her husband's transgressions.

Once her American neighbours have arranged Hanna's passage back to Berlin, she soon discovers that Erich and Charlotte Garvenberg have already adopted her son. The heartbroken widow will be hired to work as his nanny only after agreeing to fulfil the orphanage director's rather cruel conditions, that she cannot divulge the fact that she is Peter's mother to his new family. In other words, Hanna's inability to fight the arbitrary rulings of the local authorities is being underscored from the very moment that she disembarks in Germany. Unlike in her New York interview, when a Berlin policeman arrives at the Garvenberg villa in order to inquire about her husband's death, Hanna must descend the stairs to meet him and stand stiffly at attention for the full duration of this inquiry. Far from being sympathetic to her plight, all of the incidental bystanders (with the exception of Erich Garvenberg) decide that the nanny must be guilty by propinquity as soon as they learn of Christian Müller's embezzling.

In a sharp contrast with the relative equality implied by the formal construction of her American investigation, the framing and editing of this scene expose the power imbalance that dominates Hanna's life after her return to Germany. Even before the police had appeared on her doorstep, the frustrated mother had complained to Professor Obereit about the insecurity of her position as an employee, observing that she could be dismissed at any time without the need for any further justification. At one point during the nanny's subsequent grilling by the lone Berlin inspector, Sirk cuts from a medium shot of Charlotte and an aristocratic friend looking down on them from the second storey landing to a long shot that depicts their point of view; diminished both by distance and by the elevated camera angle, Hanna stands awkwardly in the foyer of the Garvenberg residence, where she is required to undergo a very public cross-examination.

Unlike her previous encounter with the New York authorities, after the initial two shot in which the widow and the German policeman first confront one another, the spectator never actually sees this peremptory public official's face. Although a slightly later shot reveals a more frontal view of Hanna looking intently at her interrogator (who now has his back to the camera), there is no subsequent point-of-view shot that shows us what she sees. Particularly in relation to the previous scene, where a shot/reverse shot structure that focuses increasingly tightly on each of their faces signalled Erich Garvenberg's growing awareness of Hanna as a person, this distanced presentation of the Berlin inspector turns him into a shadowy, anonymous and somewhat implacable figure. Just like Charlotte and the Baroness (who rushes into the nursery to tell the conductor that Herr Müller had been a 'convict'), the German policeman had already labelled the defenceless widow the wife of a criminal, which meant that he automatically assumed that her character had been tarnished by association. Consequently, in this sequence there is not a single close-up of Hanna's face as well, which seems to suggest that in returning to Berlin she has suffered both a loss of individuality and a reduction of her rights as a citizen.

Perhaps not unexpectedly, given her own susceptibility to her perfidious lover's threats, Charlotte is more concerned with the potential damage to her own reputation than with justice by this stage. As soon as Christian Müller's illegal activities have been exposed, she resolves to dismiss Hanna without cause the next time her husband leaves town. The prospect of losing her son forces the nanny to admit that she is Peter's real mother, although this startling disclosure is not enough to change her mistress's mind. Moreover, even Erich Garvenberg will betray his doubts about his former employee's character, after an unfortunate chain of events results in Hanna being accused of Charlotte's murder. Although the conductor's growing love for the widow prompts him to tell the judges that she could not have been responsible for his wife's death, what Garvenberg really believes has already been telegraphed by his previous actions. Upon arriving home from a performance in Sweden and finding Charlotte's lifeless body in her room, he had destroyed the glass vial that contained the morphine that her doctor had prescribed as a sedative. Unlike the conductor, the spectator knows that this tiny bottle was covered with Hanna's fingerprints, but only because she had administered the correct dose after returning to kidnap her son. By disposing of this crucial piece of evidence, Garvenberg indirectly reveals that he thinks his ex-nanny might have actually killed his wife. Only when the conductor is himself at risk of imprisonment as an accessory to the crime will his housekeeper finally concede that Charlotte confessed on her deathbed that she had committed suicide by taking this drug overdose herself. If Erich Garvenberg's future hadn't also been at stake, then

Freese would probably have kept the vow of secrecy that she had made to her late mistress forever. Although Hanna is cleared by this sensational revelation as well, the machinations of the German justice system are made to seem very capricious indeed. There seems little doubt that without the housekeeper's last-minute intervention, an innocent person would have been sentenced to an extended period of incarceration, or worse.

Of course Charlotte had already been destroyed by this oppressive atmosphere, which appeared to offer such a morally compromised woman no hope of redemption no matter how hard she tried to change. At a crucial moment in the prologue, two of Erich Garvenberg's point-of-view shots highlight the empty chair that discloses his wife's absence from the performance of Beethoven's Ninth Symphony that will prove to be a turning point in Hanna's life (albeit via a radio broadcast in New York). Charlotte had lingered too long listening to her lover's strangely mesmerising lecture on astrology, arriving at the Berlin *Staatsoper* or State Opera House only after the concert had begun. Consequently, one of the theatre's younger ushers, who didn't realise that this glamorous socialite was the conductor's wife, would prevent her from entering the auditorium.

After an illuminating digression, in which Charlotte justifies her behaviour to Freese by explaining that her inaccessible husband will always be a stranger since he would rather be 'with Bach and Beethoven' than with his wife (a plight that does eventually garner her some sympathy), Sirk returns to the concert that is unfolding inside the State Opera House.[64] As a tuxedo-ed baritone sings the first verse of Beethoven's musical version of Schiller's 'Ode to Joy', the camera tracks sideways along the front row of the chorus in order to explicitly link this figure with the conductor who is controlling his performance. In the following crane shot, the camera glides past a much more distant view of the orchestra and audience before curving upward to halt on a caryatid that has been placed near the ceiling, continuing to skim across the first layer of the picture plane. Whatever the spectator's opinion of the hierarchy that is implied by Erich Garvenberg's elevated position or by the richly carved Neo-Classical sculpture that gazes down upon the concertgoers far below, we never really manage to infiltrate the closed ranks of this expurgated assembly. Even when the camera's forward momentum has not been blocked by the planar arrangement of the composition, it still seems to divert our visual perception along the surface of the image rather than taking us deeper into the depicted space. While this mobile perspective may tie those who are already inside the theatre closer together (as the orchestra merges with the audience, a larger choir sings 'All mankind shall be as brothers/'Neath thy tender wings and wide'), it makes no attempt to integrate the viewer into this leader-fixated congregation.[65]

At this crucial juncture, Sirk dissolves from a close-up of the Berlin State Opera House's monumental goddess to a shot of the Atlantic Ocean to a close-up of a tiny model of the Statue of Liberty that is located in New York. This mass-produced miniature is surrounded by a cluster of equally diminutive American flags, which reinforce its widely-held association with the Enlightenment principles of 'freedom' and 'brotherhood' (the major themes of the Schiller poem that provided the libretto for the 'Ode to Joy').[66] Against Berlin's autocratic distinctions and rigorous exclusions, New York's most widely recognised allegorical figure holds out the promise of political emancipation to everyone, regardless of class, ethnicity, religious creed or country of origin (whether or not this was actually the case). Unlike *Final Chord*'s portrayal of German society, this standardised American effigy suggests a 'New World' that is a very merciful place.[67] Within these shores fragile individuals would not be eliminated in order to preserve the superiority of an autochthonous race.[68] Instead, foreign émigrés weakened by poverty and oppression would not only be taken in and cared for, but their rekindled hopes for the future should also revive their strength.

In the case of *Final Chord*, this is exactly what happens to Hanna during her crucial hiatus in the United States. After Christian Müller's unexpected death, her neighbour (Washington Smith) and his equally compassionate friend (Dr Smedley) scrupulously tend to the traumatised widow's needs for a full six weeks, despite the fact that she hasn't any money. Although her husband's suicide has liberated Hanna to some degree since it will allow her to change course and return to Berlin, she is initially unable to make any such decision and simply languishes in bed. The poor woman's flagging will to live is finally restored on 16 February, when she hears the strains of the 'Ode to Joy' through the party wall of her apartment. While the music that triggers her ultimate recovery was being broadcast from Berlin, it wouldn't have been nearly so effective if she hadn't already spent such an extended period recuperating in the much more sympathetic environment of New York.

I should also point out that the director shows us the widow's ecstatic response to this celebrated German symphony only after the viewer has already seen that Washington Smith and Dr Smedley (who are both Americans) seem to feel just as profound a sense of connection to Schiller's (and Beethoven's) chosen themes. Consequently, the spectator is obliged to recognise that this rhapsodic tribute to 'friendship', 'freedom' and 'brotherhood' still has the ability to erase international boundaries, so that 'its magic bring[s] together/ All whom earth-born laws divide' (the sentiment expressed in the words that we hear just before the wave-borne transition to New York). Finally, in Sirk's fictitious depiction of the United States at least, the composer's most fundamental philosophical tenets (at least as they are expressed in this work) appear to have been fully integrated into the ordinary citizen's everyday experience. When the two Americans take on the responsibility of caring for a poor German immigrant that they barely know, they are building a microcosm of the worldwide society that Beethoven had envisioned in the 'Ode to Joy'. The spectator is drawn into New York's more cosmopolitan and inclusive community just like Hanna, due to the way in which this sequence has been shot and edited together.

If we return to the close-up of the tiny Statue of Liberty, the camera tilts down to reveal a medium close-up of Washington Smith's head in profile. After registering the intensity of his concentration, the director then pulls back in order to reframe this image as a medium shot. Although the well-dressed American is listening to a radio transmission of the same concert that we have just seen in progress in Germany, Smith evidently feels free to conduct this symphony for himself (thus supplanting Erich Garvenberg, who is no longer visible).[69] Along with waving his hands in the air in time to the music, the classically trained singer also reads a copy of the written notations upon which all performances are based. Therefore, I would argue, when it has been filtered through a radio in New York and examined alongside the 'universal language' of the composer's pre-existing score, the *Staatsoper* orchestra's version of Beethoven's *magnum opus* loses its visceral immediacy and begins to transcend the specificity of its German origins.[70] As the well-known Modernist architect Hannes Meyer once proclaimed, the 'Radio ... [has liberated] us from our national seclusion and [made] us part of a world community'.[71] In other words, what might have been a highly emotive induction into Germany's cultural patrimony at home, becomes in America a broader appeal for a more global form of comradeship that is no longer grounded in racial affiliation or a strong sense of territoriality.

This conclusion will be further reinforced in a later sequence, when the director cuts from a close-up on the orchestral score, to a medium shot of Smith looking away from its pages to listen to the music, to a matching shot of Hanna on the other side of the wall mirroring his upturned gaze and listening to the music just as intently, to a more distant perspective in which the camera explicitly brings the seated figures of the oratorio singer and Dr Smedley together by tracking from one to the other.[72] A harmonious international collective has already been formed through the editing, but the widow is even implicitly present in the mise-en-scène of the two shot, when the doctor rises from his chair and stands next to the exit that leads to her adjacent apartment. Although he is at first immersed in the composer's joyous anticipation of a 'brotherhood' that spans the globe, Dr Smedley will turn, glance at this door and remember Hanna, then immediately walk out of the room in order to check on her condition. Unlike Beethoven's Berlin acolytes, his New York disciples try to put the composer's theoretical fellow-feeling into practice here and now, by acknowledging that citizens have a duty to care for one another as well as individual rights.

Just before Dr Smedley enters her space, the camera tracks in from a medium shot of Hanna sitting bolt upright on her bed to a close-up of her face, which again emphasises this character's passionate reaction to Beethoven's music. Although she has already become a part of this perspicacious New York audience (even before they have all assembled in the same place), Hanna will translate the sentiment that lies behind the 'Ode to Joy' somewhat differently. In particular, the widow concentrates on a single line taken from the libretto that she repeats to the doctor soon after he has arrived for the second time, '*Und der Cherub steht vor Gott*' ('And the Cherub stands before God'). Hanna obviously associates Schiller's angelic being with her son and it is at this point that her health begins to take a turn for the better.

When Dr Smedley discovers the restorative effect that listening to this music has had upon the grieving widow, he returns to Smith's apartment, dismantles the radio and brings it into her room followed by his friend. For the rest of the broadcast, the kind-hearted doctor, the classical singer and the German émigré will share a state of contemplative beatitude that has been inspired by the uplifting exultation of the 'Ode to Joy'. It should also be noted that not once during the entire sequence in which Hanna's remarkable improvement is being played out did Sirk choose to cut in any footage of the State Opera House performance that is the source of this music. Even after the widow has settled back on her pillows after deciding to rejoin her son, the director edits in two relatively static shot/reverse shot exchanges that further delay the crossing to Germany for the climax of the symphony. Hence, this whole process of revitalisation takes place within the confines of Hanna's white-walled apartment, which would seem to suggest that her pellucid American surroundings might have also had something to do with her recovery. In particular, the widow's clean light-filled Modernist dwelling prefigures a community that has been liberated from both poverty and excess consumption, especially in comparison with *Final Chord*'s Berlin. Whether she is being cared for by her neighbours or left in peace to plan ahead and dream, it seems clear that Hanna can only subsist without any income or savings as she remains in New York. By contrast, in her lavish Art Deco bedroom in her husband's elegant upper-class *Landhaus* in Berlin, Charlotte will ultimately die by her own hand. In other words, these two distinct architectural idioms encode equally divergent conceptions of the society of the future, which I will now discuss in the concluding section of this chapter.

IV Fashion or Revolution: Towards a Non-bourgeois Interior

Le Corbusier was the first to point out the ideological divide that separates the 'New Architecture' from Art Deco in *The Decorative Art of Today*, but this antagonism was subsequently amplified and endorsed by many other critics.[73] In what was essentially an apocalyptic rejoinder to the *Expositions des Arts Décoratifs et Industriels Modernes*, the architect established an antithetical relationship between an unadorned Modernist aesthetic and Art Deco ornateness that has obvious political implications. Since it was synonymous with hand-crafted luxury goods during the 1920s, he insisted that the Art Deco style utilised rich gilding, expensive veneers and simplified historical motifs to disguise more than design flaws. Extending the logic of a maxim that had already been coined by Adolph Loos ('ornament and crime'[74]), Le Corbusier condemned the Art Deco aesthetic not only for its wasteful flourishes, but also because it represented nothing more than an 'accidental surface modality' that tacitly confirmed received hierarchical distinctions. Linking a taste for decoration to both aristocratic surfeit and the deprivations of the slums, he argued that the democratic citizen 'abhors display'. Only the pure contours of the Modernist 'type-object' have been imbued with 'the life of the great machine age [that] has profoundly stirred up society ... cut through all the locks [and] thrown open all of the doors'.[75] Echoing a key phrase from his previous manifesto ('Architecture or Revolution?'), the architect implies that the widespread introduction of a Machine Age aesthetic would effect such sweeping social changes that actual rebellion would be rendered unnecessary.[76]

Architectural critic Sigfried Giedion described the interior of one of these Modernist 'machines for living' in an article entitled 'The New House' that was published in *Das Kunstblatt* in 1926. After deploring the 'abundance of furniture and sequence of fragmented rooms' that typified the homes of the prosperous upper-middle classes, he declared that 'the standardization and simplification wanted by the architecture of the future' would give rise to a 'house that is as lean and spare as possible, as empty as possible ... [with] absolutely no ostentation ... [that would primarily consist of] one big room'. Nevertheless, what the early twentieth-century 'non-bourgeois' interior (containing 'few partitions, few doors, few rugs, few pictures, few curtains; little furniture') ultimately represented was a much broader socio-economic transformation, nothing less than the advent of a more co-operatively based, cosmopolitan and classless community.[77]

To my mind, the sparse furnishings of Hanna Müller and Washington Smith's white-walled New York apartments should not be interpreted as a sign of poverty or cultural lack, but rather as a reflection of the progressive ideals of 'The New House'.⁷⁸ Moreover, as Theodor Adorno has noted, these unadorned Modernist spaces harboured a 'dream of the totally technological world, free of the shame of work . . . that points beyond the commercial [marketplace]'.⁷⁹ In a society that has been emancipated from the false yearnings induced by bourgeois capitalism and 'cleansed of human domination and exploitation', domestic objects would simply reify their functions and be accumulated for their use-value alone.⁸⁰ Citizens of this reconfigured state will content themselves with the few possessions necessary to satisfy their basic needs, thereby reducing the number of hours that must be devoted to exhausting or unpleasant labour. While the tasks performed by industrial workers are often de-skilled and repetitive, the free time gained through more extensive mechanisation could be devoted to their own spiritual, intellectual or physical improvement. Finally, if energy and materials were no longer squandered on superfluous decoration, the proper utilisation of these resources should ensure that mass-produced 'type-objects' are available to everyone. The result would be a 'vision of useful things which have lost their coldness' because they have been created to serve a beneficial purpose in a world that has been purged of the profit motive.⁸¹ Consequently, if 'the issue of the New Dwelling is primarily spiritual and the struggle for the New Dwelling [is] but one part of the larger struggle for new ways of living',⁸² then *Final Chord*'s standardised Manhattan tenements provide an apt symbol of how we should be living now.

From a Modernist perspective at least, how we should not be living is perfectly summed up in the strikingly eloquent poster that Willi Baumeister designed for the 1927 Stuttgart *Werkbund* exhibition, which was meant to provide a showcase for this groundbreaking form of domestic architecture (Figure 5.1).⁸³ The sheer number of possessions that have been crowded into the more conventional salon that the artist has chosen to depict (and negate, by splashing a large red X across the entire space) recalls Walter Benjamin's caustic description of the 'MANORIALLY FURNISHED TEN-ROOM APARTMENT' as the 'site plan of deadly traps'. Moreover, in this upper-middle-class interior the viewer may easily discern the kind of lavish accoutrements that had made the influential German critic's flesh crawl: the inlaid cabinet and other wooden furnishings that are 'distended with carvings', the hanging lamp, Persian carpet and heavy tapestries that transformed the 'master of the house' into an 'indolent pasha in the caravanserai of otiose enchantment'.⁸⁴ Hence, in *Final Chord's* Berlin, Charlotte's will to resist Carl-Otto's predatory sexual advances is clearly sapped by the 'otiose enchantment' effected by the opulent Oriental inflected décor of his home. After attributing the 'only . . . adequate analysis' of the hidden menace of the Orientalist interior to 'the kind of detective novel that began with Edgar

Figure 5.1 Willi Baumeister, *The Dwelling* (1927).
Staatliche Museen zu Berlin, Kunstbibliothek; photograph: Dietmar Katz
[CC BY-NC-SA] Willi Baumeister Stiftung

Allen Poe', Benjamin would go on to observe that its 'soulless luxuriance . . . becomes true comfort only in the presence of a dead body'.[85] Again, just as the critic had predicted, in *Final Chord* Charlotte dies alone in 'the soulless luxuriance' of her overstuffed *haute-bourgeois* room where the sinuous curves of her bedstead form the outline of a tomb.

Finally, unlike the more radical 'New Architecture' of the 1920s, Art Deco could quite happily coexist with industrial capitalism since it had always represented the 'confluence of commerce and desire'.[86] Hence, the denizens of *Final Chord*'s Berlin are almost all obsessed with wealth, status and pleasure, qualities that are reflected in the sumptuousness of their Art Deco surroundings.[87] For example, Carl-Otto's elegant salon has been adorned with richly grained wooden panels and Japanese masks, which provide the backdrop for a gleaming effigy of Shiva and an elongated statue of a cat. Similarly, Charlotte's lavish bedroom contains hand-painted arabesques on the walls, a glistening padded door and matching satin quilt, lush floral patterns on the deeply upholstered armchairs, a sylph-like glass figurine and glittering perfume bottles strewn across a shiny lacquered vanity.[88] At first these interiors seem to exude a sybaritic sensuality and affluence, but this glowing impression turns out to be a false one, since the woman who is most closely associated with both of these locations will soon be ruined by a lack of affection and money. Her astrologer lover's ever-escalating demands for payment could not be met from Charlotte's restricted means, which forces the desperate socialite to commit suicide before her sexual infidelities could be revealed to her husband. In *Final Chord*'s Berlin, the splendour of the surroundings can't disguise the fact that Germany is a deeply divided society, whose fissures can't be papered over by an application of ornament.

By contrast, long after her return to Berlin, Hanna continued to be identified with the few traces of architectural Modernism that were still in evidence. These include the white-walled communal living spaces of Dr Obereit's orphanage, and the Garvenberg nursery, where the widow cared for a child who did not know that she was his mother.[89] Dressed in a series of pared-down ensembles that reflect this International Style aesthetic, Hanna will eventually retrieve her son against all the odds. But she has also fallen in love with his adopted father, whose wife's suicide will enable them to marry. The last sequence in this film obviously ritualises Hanna's reabsorption into a male-dominated nuclear family by staging her final reunion with her son in a Neo-Baroque cathedral. As a choir sings excerpts from Handel's *Judas Maccabeus*, this unassuming woman appears in a vaguely medieval costume for the very first time. Yet I would argue that Hanna's apotheosis as a traditional Madonna with child (complete with sculpted angels blowing trumpets) is countered by the very different promise of renewal that was offered by

Final Chord's American prologue. When it has been interpreted in the light of the architectural codings that have already been established, this image simply confirms that Hanna has returned to a place that is still held in thrall by outmoded conventions. Despite the hyperbole of the ending, the widow's last-minute assimilation into 'official Nazi cultural discourse' as an 'idealized mother figure' must also be read as banishment from a better world to come.⁹⁰

Notes

1. *'Die Neue Welt'* means 'The New World' and this phrase was also the title of an influential essay published by the Modernist architect Hannes Meyer in *Das Werk* in 1926. In this vision for the future (which could be applied anywhere) he states: 'Large blocks of flats, sleeping cars, house yachts and transatlantic lines undermine the local concept of the "homeland"'. See p. 107 of 'The New World', in *Form and Function: A Sourcebook for the History of Architecture and Design, 1890–1939*, ed. Charlotte and Tim Benton (London: Open University Press, 1975. A rough translation of *Aufbruch* would be something like 'new beginnings'.
2. Sirk told Jon Halliday that he wrote *Final Chord*'s New York prologue himself, which was the most important change made to the original script that had been submitted by a 'well-known screen-writer called Oberländer'. See Halliday, 41–2.
3. According to Sirk, at UFA the director had a great deal of influence on the look of the final sets. Moreover, since the director 'had experience as a set designer . . . [he] felt quite strongly about the sets'. See Halliday, 37.
4. Charlotte is closely associated with a very prominent Art Deco motif, a sylph-like glass figurine. Sabine Hake points out this connection on page 140 of 'The Melodramatic Imagination of Detlef Sierck: *Final Chord* and its Resonances', *Screen*, 8, No. 2 (1997) but she doesn't link this symbolic attribute to an Art Deco aesthetic. Alistair Duncan's summary of the standard Art Deco iconography is as follows: 'stylised bouquets of flowers, young maidens, geometric patterns including zigzags, chevrons and lightning bolts and the ubiquitous *biche* [doe]'. See his *Art Deco* (London: Thames & Hudson, 1988), 8.
5. Ernst Bloch, *The Utopian Function of Art and Literature* (Cambridge, MA: MIT Press, 1988) 101–11, 120–7.
6. According to Bloch, a truly modern perspective required this admixture of the future with the present. 'In other words: contemporaneity is not such if it is not also super-contemporaneous; it is not the capitalist of the uncontrolled changeable Today who stands at par with the real present but only the knower and controller of the Tomorrow in the Today together, in short, the active Marxist.' See 'Transition: Berlin, Functions in Hollow Space', in his *Heritage of Our Times* (Cambridge: Polity Press, 1991), 195–6.
7. 'Transition: Berlin Functions in Hollow Space' and 'II. Buildings on Hollow Space' [in *The Principle of Hope*, vol. 2 (Cambridge, MA: MIT Press, 1986), 735]. Bloch labels this mode of building New Objective or Objective in deference to

the rationalism of *Neue Sachlichkeit* paintings. His description is synonymous with European Modernist architecture of the 1920s, in which a lack of ornamental detail was combined with highly abstract geometric shapes; additional characteristics included a relatively unobstructed ground plan, flat roofs, smooth, white rendered or glass curtain walls and large areas of gridded or strip windows.

8. Bloch, 'II. Buildings on Hollow Space', 734.
9. Bloch, 'II. Buildings on Hollow Space', 734.
10. Bloch, 'Transition: Berlin Functions in Hollow Space', 200–2.
11. Bloch, *The Utopian Function of Art and Literature*, 190.
12. It should also be noted that the rhetorical force of *Final Chord*'s New York skyline would have been magnified by its lack of resemblance to the actual site. Throughout the 1920s and beyond, European Modernist architects such as Erich Mendelsohn, Ludwig Hilberseimer and Le Corbusier had published damning critiques of many twentieth-century American cities, where an absence of regulation had led to a disorderly fragmentation of their original plans. For example, Le Corbusier published a 1923 photograph of the Manhattan skyline on page 45 of *The City of Tomorrow and Its Planning* (New York: Dover Publications, a 1987 repr. of the 1929 American translation of Le Corbusier's 1924 French text) because he thought that it represented the epitome of 'confusion, chaos and upheaval'. The American scenes in Luis Trenker's 1934 *Heimat* film *The Prodigal Son*, which were actually shot on location, would have conveyed a similar impression.
13. Quoted by Dietrich Neumann, 'The Urbanistic Vision in Fritz Lang's *Metropolis*', in *Dancing on the Volcano: Essays on the Culture of the Weimar Republic*, ed. Thomas Kniesche and Stephen Brockmann (Columbia, SC: Camden House, 1994), 147.
14. Werner Oechslin, 'Light Architecture: A New Term's Genesis', in *Architecture of the Night: The Illuminated Building*, ed. Dietrich Neumann (Munich: Prestel, 2002), 28.
15. Oechslin, 32–3.
16. In his large-format 1926 book *Amerika: Bilderbuch eines Architekten*, Mendelsohn reproduced one of the double-exposed photographs with which Lang tried to approximate the experience of looking at New York's brightly-lit downtown streets with the following caption: '[It] is the backdrop for the flaming script, the rocket fire of mobile illuminated advertising, emerging and vanishing, disappearing and erupting above the thousands of cars ... Still disorganised, since exaggerated, yet still full of fantastic beauty, which will one day be perfected.' See page 33 of Oechslin's essay.
17. Le Corbusier, *Towards a New Architecture* (London: The Architectural Press, a 1974 repr. of the 1927 English translation of Le Corbusier's 1923 French text), 12. In the introduction to the slightly later *The City of Tomorrow and Its Planning*, he describes an exchange with a 'terribly disillusioned Viennese architect who maintained that the death of old Europe was imminent [and] only young America could feed our hopes'. Le Corbusier apparently replied, 'The architectural problem of old Europe ... lies in the great city of to-day. There lies the Yea or the Nay, life or slow extinction. One or the other, but it will be Yes if we wish it'

[pp. xxv–xxvi]. In my opinion, *Final Chord* is saying (quite literally) 'Yes' to the modern city in this sequence, though of course a Nazi sympathiser would not necessarily read New York's stripped-down architecture in this way.
18. Her most significant publications on this subject include 'The Interpretation of the Glass Dream – Expressionist Architecture and the History of the Crystal Metaphor', *Journal of the Society of Architectural Historians*, 40 (1981), 20–43 and 'Expressionism and the New Objectivity', *Art Journal* 43 (1983), 108–20. See also Reyner Banham's 'The Glass Paradise' in *Design by Choice* (New York: Rizzoli, 1981), 29–33 and Clark V. Poling's *Kandinsky: Russian and Bauhaus Years, 1915–1933* (New York: The Solomon R. Guggenheim Museum, 1983), p.74.
19 Bletter, 'Expressionism and the New Objectivity', 113.
20. 'In order to preserve a measure of light and air in the city's canyons, the [New York Zoning] code dictated that after a fixed vertical height, a building had to be stepped back in accordance with a designated angle drawn from the centre of the street; a tower covering no more than a quarter of the site could then rise to an unlimited height' [see Carol Willis's 'Drawing Towards Metropolis', an essay that appears at the end of the facsimile of Hugh Ferris's 1929 publication *The Metropolis of Tomorrow* (Princeton: Princeton University Press, 1986), 157]. Ferris was asked to collaborate on these 'zoning envelope studies' in 1922 by the New York architect Harvey Wiley Corbett. The resulting drawings were first exhibited at the New York Architectural League in 1922 and then published in the American architectural journal *Pencil Points* the following year, along with an essay by Corbett. According to Corbett's 1926 observations in the *Saturday Evening Post*, 'The drawings have had the curious effect of opening [the architect's eyes] to the hitherto unsuspected possibilities of beauty of mass and proportion' [quoted by Willis, p. 159].

Willis also observes, 'these drawings were shown in a number of German cities, including Berlin at the Academy of Fine Arts, in an exhibition on progressive American architecture and illustrated in the catalogue *Ausstellung Neuer Amerikanischer Baukunst*, January 1926; they also appeared in a feature article on Ferris in the German magazine *Baukunst* in January 1926' [p. 181, fn. 40]. Finally, they formed the centrepiece of Ferris's famous 1929 book *The Metropolis of Tomorrow*, dividing the preceding illustrations of existing skyscrapers from the later delineations of 'An Imaginary Metropolis' of the future. Hence, both Eric Kettlehut and Sirk may well have been familiar with these iconic images.
21. Ferris, 60.
22. Ferris, 16.
23. Ferris, 61,124.
24. Ferris, 36.
25. Halliday, 44.
26. See Dietrich Neumann's 'The Urbanistic Vision in Fritz Lang's *Metropolis*' for an insightful analysis of the series of sketches that Kettlehut made of the same urban intersection while he was creating the exterior settings of Fritz Lang's well-known 1927 film. During this process, the Emperor's Headquarters replaces

a cathedral on a key site, which led Neumann to conclude, 'Kettlehut's final version not only stood for the most conservative approach to skyscraper design and city planning, but it also clearly harked back to the German Empire with its connotations of nationalism, imperialism and a centralised system' [p. 152].

27. Le Corbusier, *The City of Tomorrow and its Planning*, xxi.
28. In a fascinating essay on the German population's perception of their own post-World War I topography, Peter Fritzsche imported the term '*Machbarkeitswahn*' from Detlev Peukert's writings because he thought that it encapsulated the Weimar Modernist's heady sense of future possibilities [p. 42]. A preoccupation with *Machbarkeitswahn* was not strictly the prerogative of the political left during the 1920s and early 1930s, however. The National Socialists also thought that the contemporary city was infinitely malleable and open to revision, although their models required a great deal of subordination to a centralised authority. See Peter Fritzsche's 'Landscape of Danger, Landscape of Design: Crisis and Modernism in Weimar Germany', in *Dancing on the Volcano: Essays in the Culture of the Weimar Republic*, 29–46.
29. Philip Fisher, 'Democratic Social Space: Whitman, Melville and the Promise of American Transparency', in *The New American Studies: Essays from Representations*, ed. Philip Fisher (Berkeley: University of California Press, 1991), 70, 72, 76, 81, 85, 94.
30. Stefan Zweig, 'The Monotonization of the World', in *The Weimar Republic Source Book*, ed. Anton Kaes, Martin Jay and Edward Dimendberg (Berkeley: University of California Press, 1994), 397. In the 'New World' Hannes Meyer viewed the results of this standardisation in a much more positive light. He rather optimistically predicts, 'The standardisation of our requirements is shown by: the bowler hat, bobbed hair, the tango, jazz . . . and illustrated by the crowds going to see Harold Lloyd . . . Grock and the three Fratellini weld the masses – irrespective of class or racial differences – into a community with a common fate' [p. 107].
31. See the excerpt from Heinrich Class's 1912 book *If I Were Emperor* (published under the pseudonym Daniel Fryman) entitled 'Americanism' on page 11 of *The Nazi Years: A Documentary History*, ed. Joachim Remak (Englewood Cliffs, NJ: Prentice-Hall, 1969).
32. See the excerpts from a speech that Hitler delivered in Hamburg on 17 August 1934 and to the Association of Newspaper Proprietors in Berlin in June 1933 in *The Speeches of Adolf Hitler, April 1922–August 1939* (Oxford: Oxford University Press, 1942), 452–4, 455.
33. Émile Durkheim, *Suicide: A Study in Sociology* (New York: Free Press, 1951), 253.
34. Some New Yorkers do exhibit signs of drunkenness, since *Final Chord* opens on New Year's Eve, but they almost always do what is right in the end. The tipsy reveller who found Christian Müller dead in Central Park immediately goes for help. The raucous partygoers who burst into Hanna's apartment take off their masks and bow their heads in sympathy as soon as the police detective tells Hanna that her husband is dead. By contrast, in Berlin Hanna's husband embezzled money from his employer and then abandoned his son in order to

avoid going to prison. The city's opulently dressed demi-monde seem to do nothing but throw lavish parties and take a keen interest in astrology. The Berlin-based astrologer Grigor Carl-Otto includes many upper-class wives (including Charlotte) among his sexual conquests, and so on.

35. Albert Speer, *Inside the Third Reich* (London: Weidenfeld & Nicolson, 1970), 33.
36. Norman Baynes described the political implications of the Constitution of the National Socialist State on pages 413–19 of *The Speeches of Adolf Hitler, April 1922–August 1939*.
37. Speer, 33 and Hitler's 'Speech to the Reichstag on 23 March 1933', as well as his 'Proclamation read at the Nuremberg *Parteitag* of September 1934' in *The Speeches of Adolf Hitler, April 1922–August 1939*, 424, 457.
38. Berlin was chosen as the capital of the newly united Germany in 1871, around the same time that it became a major industrial centre. In 1880 the city had over one million inhabitants, but by 1910 the population was over 2 million. A major housing crisis was one of the side-effects of this exponential growth, which 'was unprecedented in Europe in both its extent and speed' (according to Iain Boyd Whyte). During the 1920s, many German Modernist architects such as Bruno Taut and Walter Gropius thought that the development of standardised government-subsidised housing estates would provide the answer to this problem, but Hitler was only interested in building elaborate official monuments. See Boyd Whyte's 'Berlin 1870–1945: An Introduction Framed by Architecture', in *The Divided Heritage: Themes and Problems in German Modernism*, ed. Irit Rogoff (Cambridge: Cambridge University Press, 1990), 223–39. Hitler's words may be found on page 69 of Speer's *Inside the Third Reich*.
39. *Mein Kampf* (Boston: Houghton Mifflin, 1943), 264. Doug Clelland has estimated that between 100,000 and 130,000 dwellings would have had to be erected in Berlin in the years immediately after World War I to ease the congestion caused by the growing population ['Berlin: An Architectural History', *Architectural Design Profile*, No. 50 (1983), 13]. The poorest occupants of the city were still subject to severe overcrowding when Hitler was writing *Mein Kampf* in the mid-1920s.
40. Hitler's obsession with creating a ceremonial north–south axis for Berlin that would be lined with formal government buildings pre-dated his association with Speer. The architect recalls that the *Führer* first showed him sketches of this broad street and of the Triumphal Arch and People's Hall that were to be its most significant architectural features in 1936. Speer would not be formally commissioned to further develop these inchoate ideas until 1937. See his *Inside the Third Reich*, 73–80.
41. Iain Boyd Whyte, 225.
42. Wolfgang Sonne, *Representing the State: Capital City Planning in the Early Twentieth Century* (Munich: Prestel, 2003), 102–3.
43. Hermann G. Pundt, *Schinkel's Berlin: A Study in Environmental Planning* (Cambridge, MA: Harvard University Press, 1972), 191–2.
44. See Sonne, 103 and Lothar Müller, 'The Beauty of the Metropolis: Toward an Aesthetic Urbanism in Turn-of-the-Century Berlin', in *Berlin: Culture and*

Metropolis, ed. Charles Haxthausen and Heidrun Suhr (Minneapolis: University of Minnesota Press, 1990), 39.
45. Müller, 39.
46. Benjamin Warner, 'Berlin – the 'Nordic Homeland' and the Corruption of the Urban Spectacle', *Architectural Design Profile*, No. 50 (1983), 75.
47. Warner, 75.
48. Wolfgang Schäche, 'Nazi Architecture and Its Approach to Antiquity: A Criticism of the "Neoclassical" Argument, with reference to the Berlin Museum Plans', *Architectural Design Profile*, No. 50 (1983), 84.
49. Schäche, 86.
50. Schäche, 87.
51. Schäche, 84, 87.
52. Speer, 69.
53. *Mein Kampf*, 265.
54. For a description of Speer and Hitler's domed Berlin *Volkshalle*, which would have been sixteen times larger than St Peter's Cathedral in Rome had it been built, see Speer, 152–4.
55. Pundt, 191–2.
56. *The Speeches of Adolf Hitler, April 1922–August 1939*, 213–14, 224–5.
57. Warner, 76.
58. Warner, 78.
59. Hake, 'The Melodramatic Imagination of Detlef Sierck', 136. Nevertheless, when Garvenberg is not actually conducting, his behaviour often seems to contradict the domineering manliness that National Socialism prescribed. The conductor obviously desires a much more companionate marriage, recognises his own complicity in Charlotte's inappropriate conduct, demonstrates an almost feminine affinity with children and offers to sacrifice his freedom for the woman that he loves rather than for the good of his country.
60. Ernst Bloch, 'C. Non-Contemporaneity and Contemporaneity, Philosophically', in *Heritage of Our Times* (Cambridge: Polity Press, 1991), 104, 108.
61. Ernst Bloch, 'C. Non-Contemporaneity and Contemporaneity, Philosophically', 113, 108.
62. Ernst Bloch, 'C. Non-Contemporaneity and Contemporaneity, Philosophically', 107. In this essay, Bloch states that 'Germany in general, which had managed no bourgeois revolution up to 1918, is – unlike England, and especially France – the classical land of non-contemporaneity, i.e. of unsurmounted remnants of older economic being and consciousness. Ground rent, large landed property and its power, were almost universally integrated into the capitalist economy and its political power in England, and differently in France; whereas in long backward and even longer diverse Germany the victory of the bourgeoisie did not even develop to the same extent economically, let alone politically and economically' [p. 106].
63. Ernst Bloch, 'C. Non-Contemporaneity and Contemporaneity, Philosophically', 106–7.

Final Chord *and* 'Die Neue Welt'

64. Neither of Peter's potential mothers is presented as being wholly good or bad in *Final Chord*. Following her fugitive husband to New York meant that Hanna had to leave her son in Berlin with a caregiver, who winds up placing him in an orphanage. After she has kidnapped Peter from his adoptive mother (while the conductor is away in Sweden), Hanna dreams that she has killed the woman that she wishes to replace in the Garvenberg household with morphine. Although we later learn that Charlotte has taken this fatal drug overdose herself, the fact remains that the seemingly proper nanny wanted her mistress dead, at least on a subconscious level.

    As for Frau Garvenberg, she is presented as being weak-willed rather than evil. Left alone and unprotected by her music-obsessed husband (who even spends his leisure time playing classical duets with Professor Obereit), Charlotte is seduced by an unscrupulous astrologer who later blackmails her. It is Carl-Otto's repeated attempts to extort money from his unfortunate victim that repeatedly diverts his ex-lover's attention away from her duties as a wife and mother.

65. This translation of the German lyrics has been taken from *The Beethoven Companion*, ed. Thomas K. Scherman and Louis Biancoli (New York: Doubleday, 1972), 927.

66. In 1905, Georges Pioch described Beethoven's Ninth Symphony as 'the "Marseillaise" of the regenerated ... societies which are to come' because it had been alleged for more than sixty years 'that the real subject of Schiller's "*An die Freude*" is not Joy (*Freude*) at all but Freedom (*Freiheit*)'. Nicholas Cook has traced this 'Ode to Freedom' reference back to a novel entitles *Das Musikfest* by Wolfgang Griepenkerl, which was published in 1838. He states that 'In this novel one of the characters refers to the true meaning of Schiller's "Ode to Joy", and an author's footnote reads: "It was freedom"'. See page 94 of his *Beethoven: Symphony Number Nine* (Cambridge: Cambridge University Press, 1993).

67. In Schmidt's 1980 interview Sirk spoke of the enormous impact that reading some of the 'giants' of American literature had had on him while he was still living in Germany. '[These writers] wrote from larger spaces [and their] books breathed an exotic freedom that filled all of us with a longing for this country. In our imagination [the United States] was first of all a great continent of huge size, limitlessness ... [that filled us with] wishful longings ... especially in Germany' where 'this transformative moment in history' was 'futile and heavy' and from which the 'element of freedom was disappearing by the day'. See the first section of Schmidt's documentary, which has been entitled 'Entering a New World'.

68. In the words of the verse from a poem by Emma Lazarus that were attached to the statue's base in 1903, 'Give me your tired, your poor,/Your huddled masses yearning to breathe free,/The wretched refuse of your teeming shore,/Send these tempest-tos't to me./I lift my lamp beside the golden door!' See Marina Warner's *Monuments and Maidens: The Allegory of the Female Form* (London: Picador, 1985), 10–11.

69. In *Towards a New Architecture*, Le Corbusier declares that the inhabitants of his Machine Age dwellings should be listening to a more standardised type of music

that is in keeping with their modern way of life. He points out on page 115 of this text that 'the gramophone or the pianola or the wireless [radio] will give you exact interpretations of first-rate music, and you avoid catching cold in the concert hall, and the frenzy of the virtuoso'.

In other words, the calculated emotional response that is generated in the audience by the conductor or the musicians' 'frenzy ' may be superseded by a more reasoned (and possibly even critical) judgement when the listener encounters only the sound of this music, filtered through some sort of technological device. I would argue that this is exactly what seems to be happening in *Final Chord*, when Sirk cross-cuts between the Berlin concert hall and the New York apartment dwellers listening to the same performance of the 'Ode to Joy' being broadcast over the radio.

70. Theodor Adorno's 1934 appraisal of 'The Form of the Phonograph Record' was generally negative (since the technical limitations of the period resulted in an inferior quality of sound), but he thought that its ability to fix a particular rendition of a composition that could then be endlessly reproduced would 'some day become readable as the "last remaining universal language since the construction of the tower"' [Thomas Levin's translation, as published in *October*, No. 55 (Winter 1990), 59]. I would argue that the point-of view-shots of the orchestral score that Sirk has edited into this sequence offer the spectator another version of this musical 'universal language', which subtly transmutes our aural experience.
71. Meyer, 106.
72. The German words '*Ja – wer auch nur eine Seele/Sein nennt auf dem Erdenrundt!*', which Linda Schulte-Sasse translates as 'Oh, whosoever can speak of having a soul on this earth', are clearly visible on this page. See her 'Douglas Sirk's *Schlussakkord* and the Question of Aesthetic Resistance', *The Germanic Review*, 73, No. 1 (Winter 1998), 10.
73. The *Exposition des Arts Décoratifs et Industriels Modernes* held in Paris in 1925 provided the catalyst for the codification of this crucial conflict. Le Corbusier's own *Pavillion de l'Esprit Nouveau* offered a rare example of Modernist architecture amid the sea of Art Deco construction that dominated this fair. For a summary of the contemporary assessments of the *Exposition* itself, see Nancy Troy's *Modernism and the Decorative Arts in France: Art Nouveau to Le Corbusier* (New Haven: Yale University Press, 1991), 191–2. Richard Striner's 'Art Deco: Polemics and Synthesis', *Winterthur Portfolio*, 25 (1990), 24–33 surveys the arguments for and against Art Deco that followed upon Le Corbusier's scathing indictment.
74. Adoph Loos, 'Ornament and Crime', in *The Architecture of Adolf Loos*, ed. Yehude Safran and Wilfred Wang (London: Arts Council of Great Britain, 1985), 100–3. Loos's essay was originally published in German in 1908, but Le Corbusier published a French translation in a 1924 issue of *L'Esprit Nouveau*. Loos's ideas were directly quoted on page 85 of the French architect's anti-Art Deco diatribe *The Decorative Arts of Today* (London: Architectural Press, 1987 translation of the 1925 French edition).
75. *The Decorative Arts of Today*, 41–2, 118.

76. Le Corbusier, *Towards a New Architecture*, p. 13.
77. Giedion, 'The New House', in *Le Corbusier in Perspective*, ed. Peter Serenyi (Englewood Cliffs, NJ: Prentice-Hall, 1975), 32–3, Laslo Moholy-Nagy, 'Constructivism and the Proletariat', in *Moholy-Nagy*, ed. Richard Kostelanetz (London: Allen Lane/Penguin, 1970), 185 and the 1928 document 'CIAM: La Sarraz Declaration', in *Programmes and Manifestoes on Twentieth-Century Architecture*, ed. Ulrich Conrads (London: Lund Humphreys, 1970), 109–13. The twenty-four celebrated Modernist architects who signed the La Sarraz Declaration in 1928 (including Le Corbusier, Hugo Haring, Hannes Meyer, Mart Stam and Gerit Rietveld) also called for a radical rethinking of individual priorities. As well as calling for a system of economic rationalisation and standardisation that was intended to deliver shorter working hours (rather than the maximum amount of commercial profit) they included an additional caveat that was directed at the consumer. The responsible client must accept 'a revision of his demands . . . [by] readjust[ing] to the new conditions of social life. Such a revision will be manifested in the reduction of certain individual needs henceforth devoid of real justification; the benefits of this reduction will foster the maximum satisfaction of the greatest needs for the greatest number, which are at present restricted' [p. 110]. In other words, the inhabitants of the 'New World' that they envisaged were obliged to recognise that one person's surplus could only be obtained at another person's cost.
78. Before he began to design his own furniture with the assistance of Charlotte Perriand in 1927 [Mary Mcleod, 'Undressing Architecture: Fashion, Gender and Modernity', in *Architecture in Fashion*, ed. Deborah Fausch et. al. (Princeton: Princeton University Press, 1991), 82], Le Corbusier advised his readers to furnish their Machine Age interiors with simple, mass-produced wicker or Thonet bentwood chairs. Against the 'false taste' of richly adorned historicist or Art Deco objects, he pitted the European Modernist corrective of a 'bright clear [room with] white walls [and a] good chair – wickerwork or Thonet'. See his *The Decorative Arts of Today*, page 90. Of course Hanna's New York apartment does contain such a wicker chair, as well as an unadorned metal bed that is consistent with this advice. Smith's décor is a bit more elaborate, but his apartment is still relatively uncluttered and his wooden furnishings are all rather plain, which is again in keeping with the Modernist aesthetic of the setting.
79. Theodor Adorno, 'Functionalism Today', *Oppositions*, No. 17 (Summer 1979), 35.
80. Adorno, 'Functionalism Today', 39.
81. Adorno, 'Functionalism Today', 39.
82. A statement published by Mies van der Rohe in 1927, quoted in Richard Pommer and Christian F. Otto's *Weissenhof 1927 and the Modern Movement in Architecture* (Chicago: University of Chicago Press, 1991), 136.
83. In 1927, the German *Werkbund* organised its second exhibition in the city of Stuttgart. It included the construction of an actual residential district (called the *Weissenhofsiedlung*) that was erected on a hill on the outskirts of town. This model suburb contained an extraordinary array of Modernist dwellings that were

designed by some of the most famous architects of the day, such as Le Corbusier, Walter Gropius, Mart Stam, J. J. P. Oud, Peter Behrens and Mies van der Rohe. It is from the concordance that was evident in this crucible of Modernist housing design that the main tenets of the 'International Style' were later defined. See *Weissenhof 1927 and the Modern Movement in Architecture* for a detailed history of the genesis and subsequent influence of this important German *Siedlung*.

84. Benjamin, 'One-way Street', in *Reflections: Essays, Aphorisms, Autobiographical Writings*, ed. Peter Demetz (New York: Schocken Books, 1986), 65.
85. Walter Benjamin, 'One-way Street', 64–5.
86. Charlotte and Tim Benton, 'The Style and the Age', in *Art Deco: 1910–1939* (London: V & A Publications, 2003), p. 13. In Berlin, even Charlotte's sexual indiscretions have been commoditised, and she is unable to pay the high price that Carl-Otto has placed on his silence.
87. On page 254 of an article entitled 'Le Problème du luxe dans l'architecture moderne' that was published in *Cahiers des Arts*, no. 5–6 (1928), Sigfried Gidieon observed that the more privileged classes had traditionally used hand-crafted objects made of precious materials (such as those typical of Art Deco) to separate themselves from the masses. Sirk would use the Art Deco style as a marker of upper-class pretension again in *Has Anybody Seen My Gal?*, which is set in the fictitious small American town of Hilverton during the 1920s. As soon as the Blaisdell family has received $100,000 from an unknown donor, Harriet pressures her husband into buying an expensive Beaux-Arts mansion 'on the hill' that she proceeds to decorate with fashionable Art Moderne (an American variation on Art Deco) furnishings as a sign of their newly elevated social status.
88. Charlotte Garvenberg's clothing is in keeping with the sensual elegance of her Art Deco surroundings. Her evening gowns are invariably glamorous, since they feature the rich textures and light-catching surfaces of glittering sequins or drifting clouds of tulle. Even her day dresses have been fabricated from such voluptuously tactile materials as satin, brocade, lace and fur. To many Modernist architects, Charlotte's aversion to the simple, tailored, menswear- or sportswear-inspired clothing that the 'New Woman' was supposed to wear would have signalled her tacit acceptance of sexual inequality. See p. 107 of Meyer's 'The New World' and pp. 233–4 of Le Corbusier's 'The Furniture Adventure', in Charlotte and Tim Benton's *Form and Function*.
89. Professor Obereit's harmonious orphanage clearly demonstrates that a child's mental and physical development may be fostered by anyone with suitable training or an innate vocation, regardless of gender. The good doctor actually jokes at one point that Erich Garvenberg would make an excellent '*kinderfräulein*' or childcare worker. Although they are not related by blood, Garvenberg will later claim that Peter's talent for putting on elaborate puppet shows came from him. In other words, Sirk's film appears to demonstrate that consanguinity was less important than empathy and love in forming a strong bond with one's child. This notion obviously disputes one of the key theories of National Socialism.
90. Hake, 137.

CHAPTER SIX

Back to the Future: Modernist Architecture and All That Heaven Allows

In a prominent two-page pictorial spread that was published in a March 1948 issue of *Life* magazine, an anonymous writer credits a New York architect with transforming an 'old-fashioned dwelling' into a 'striking modern home'. According to the brief text that accompanied this rather dramatic set of photographs (which included a full-page view of the most transparent elevation lit up at night), a 'moldering' Connecticut farmhouse has been made 'new' by the installation of an enormous glass window in one façade and by leaving the partially demolished interior relatively open-plan.[1] The reconstruction of the Old Mill in Douglas Sirk's 1955 melodrama *All That Heaven Allows* produces a similar effect, since Ron Kirby will eventually build both of these elements of the ideal contemporary home into his renovated dwelling. In what constitutes the film's most important domestic setting, since it makes visually manifest the tree farmer's love for Carey Scott, he will combine aspects of two competing Modernist idioms (according to Elizabeth Gordon, the current editor of *House Beautiful* magazine).[2] At first, the Old Mill's rough timber and masonry walls evoke the 'home-grown variety' that Gordon associates with Frank Lloyd Wright, who was the major source of the mid-century American preoccupation with 'natural' finishes and irregular shapes.[3] By the end of the narrative, however, these raw 'organic' surfaces will have disappeared behind a whitewashed patina that was more typical of the Machine Age dwellings of the 1920s (what Gordon dubs the International Style after Philip Johnson and Henry-Russell Hitchcock's well-known catalogue).[4]

In other words, this pivotal building's hybrid architectural language reveals an underlying connection that *House Beautiful*'s anti-International Style campaign had deliberately obscured: American and European Modernism each contained both 'organic' and 'mechanistic' tendencies, despite their very disparate appearances. For example, in an early public lecture Frank Lloyd Wright praised the machine's capacity to liberate the worker from repetitive drudgery, and many of his most inventive designs could not have been executed without the use of industrial materials such as high tensile steel.[5] Similarly, even in his most speculative urban schemas Le Corbusier had tempered the strict geometry of his buildings with luxuriant gardens and grass-covered playing fields. For instance, in the *City of Tomorrow and Its Planning* he asks: 'Why should not the new spirit in architecture . . . satisfy the deepest human desires by once more covering with verdure the urban landscape and setting Nature in the mist of our Labour?'[6] Hence, the opposition that *House Beautiful* sets out between European Modernism's 'bleak, box-like and mechanistic' structures and an indigenous tradition of '*organic* design' was to a large extent illusory.[7]

Gordon and many of the other writers associated with this magazine had failed to notice that the orientation of International Style architecture had shifted to such a degree that it had almost converged with its 'organic' equivalent. After taking refuge in the United States during the political upheavals of the 1930s and '40s, many European Modernist architects had begun to experiment with more rustic regional building techniques (especially in their smaller suburban residences). As Elizabeth Mock had noted in *Built in U.S.A., 1932–1944*, 'in their first rebound towards natural materials, [these expatriate designers] tended to accept wood in its traditional American form – the light frame surfaced with clapboards or flush siding'.[8] In Mock's opinion, the narrow tongue and groove fir weatherboards that were utilised in Walter Gropius and Marcel Breuer's 1940 House for Henry G. Chamberlain echoed the local Massachusetts vernacular, despite the machine-like precision of its rectilinear shapes.[9] Moreover, not only did cladding an International Style home in a familiar material make the 'New Architecture' seem much less forbidding, but it also prompted the American observer to re-evaluate his or her own indigenous building traditions. Again according to Mock, native-born residents had begun to 'look . . . again at the stone and wood barns of Pennsylvania, the white clapboard walls of New England, the low, rambling ranch houses of the West, and found them good'.

By 1952 (when MOMA would release the next instalment of *Built in U.S.A.*, featuring a selection of the most significant post-war structures), Philip Johnson could safely proclaim, 'The battle of modern architecture has long been won.'[10] After perusing every issue of *Better Homes and Gardens*, *House Beautiful*, *House and Home*, *American Home*, *Interiors* and *Arts and Architecture* that appeared between 1953 and 1956, I would have to agree with this conclusion. Whatever their target audience, the articles that were published in all of these magazines throughout this period focused almost exclusively upon contemporary architecture, whether it had been influenced by an American 'organic' or a European International Style model. Yet how can this overwhelming popularity be explained, given the fact that most people were buying more conventional residences, such as the pseudo-Cape Cod cottages that were being erected by the thousands in suburbs such as Levittown?[11]

Perhaps it was because the 'humanising' process that Elizabeth Mock talked about in her 1944 survey also included relinquishing the radical social agenda that had impelled European Modernist architecture during the 1920s. In the then-current Cold War climate of the United States, probing examinations of the individual's relation to the broader social collective had just about disappeared, which meant that much more emphasis was now being placed on discussing the family in isolation from the rest of the community. For instance, Joseph A. Barry's depiction of the ideal American way of life (which interrupts his meandering report on *House Beautiful's* 'Pace Setter of 1954') is confined to the solitary domestic household. In this very telling digression he writes, 'To come home nightly to a house that refreshes you, to read, to listen to music, to play with your children, to talk quietly to your wife, in a friendly, personal house on your own private land . . . Surely the earth has nothing more fair to show.'[12]

In Barry's oddly rhapsodic evocation of a comfortable suburban existence, there is no longer any anticipation of a cataclysmic break with the dominant political hegemony. Softening the sharp outlines and adding texture, colour and even ornament to the stark planar walls of the 'New Architecture' in order to make it more 'friendly' had also vitiated the movement's original utopian impulses. Earlier attempts to envision a more egalitarian society for all had dwindled into the epicurean pursuit of one's own self-development and pleasure. In other words, mid-century Modernism had re-assimilated many of the social premises that the previous generation had hoped to eradicate: corporate capitalism's uneven distribution of wealth, the divisive displays of luxury that were encouraged by this inequality and the withdrawal of the nuclear family from the problems of the larger community. *House Beautiful* editor Elizabeth Gordon went so far as to claim that it was the duty of 'good' Modernist design to embrace the rampant consumerism (described here as 'freedom of choice') that was a sign of the nation's post-war prosperity.[13] A house that was intended to display one's personal bounty obviously could not be designed in the International Style, since it was an aesthetic grounded in a 'less is more' philosophy (which she translates as 'poverty') that had tried to limit the owner's accumulation of extraneous belongings.[14]

Despite the growing ascendancy of this kind of mid-century Modernist critique, Ron Kirby's gradual reconstruction of the Old Mill in *All That Heaven Allows* seems to imply a much less acquisitive notion of the ideal home. The plainness of this building recalls the stripped-down appearance of New England's early Puritan settlements, Henry David Thoreau's basic wooden shelters in *Walden* (a book that is quoted directly in the film), as well as the 'minimum dwellings' that were being promulgated by European Modernist architects during the 1920s.[15] Unlike the current popular American ideal, the main aim of these more frugal and co-operatively organised communities was the provision of an adequate standard of living for everyone. Hence, the large-scale repetition of 'formulaic' building types that they generally favoured was supposed to produce the opposite of Frank Lloyd Wright's so-called 'mass-man', the type of person who is unsuited for a democratic political system because he can no longer think for himself.[16] Instead of leading to 'vacuity' (as Wright would have it) these standardised forms should give rise to an even greater degree of intellectual and emotional complexity, because their inhabitants' minds would no longer be so fixated on their material possessions.

Robert Woods Kennedy's analysis of a collection of interviews that was published in the *American Sociological Review* in 1948 would seem to support this conclusion. Kennedy observed that those respondents who chose to construct the most innovative residences were motivated by a desire for self-improvement and self-expression as well as for functional living. The Modernist was said to be 'not greatly concerned with what the neighbours think, because he knows what he himself thinks'.[17] With regard to *All That Heaven Allows*, this is exactly what Carey must learn to do when her relationship with her ex-gardener has been exposed after a chance meeting with the town gossip. Ron subsequently urges the widow to become 'more like a man' by taking on the responsibility of making her own decisions (something that he and Mick and Alida Anderson had already discovered for themselves). Even when he is in danger of losing his fiancée for good (who accuses him of forcing her to choose between marriage to him and her children), the tree farmer refuses to help Carey decide what she should do next. In contrast with the residence selected as Joseph A. Barry's 'Pace Setter of 1954', Ron's refurbished home is not a 'comfortable' one, since in order to live there the widow will need to turn 'her back on everything that she has ever known'.

Hence, even when we can still observe the 'organic' substrate of the Old Mill, the spectator will probably not be thinking that the rich tactility of its surfaces would complement furniture from any period (as *House Beautiful* would have us believe).[18] As well as communicating a very Functionalist dedication to a life of 'voluntary simplicity', this rough wood and stone enclosure also conveys a reverence for nature that was not always immediately evident in its European Modernist equivalents.[19] Yet as the narrative of *All That Heaven Allows* unfolds, Ron's living space will be rendered more and more artificial, until in the final scene the viewer discovers that it has been painted completely white. Again, this more urbane conception of plainness (which recalls the Machine Age villas of Le Corbusier) suggests a respect for human agency and intelligence that is not always apparent in American 'organic' Modernism. In fact, the last image of the film (in which we observe a deer lingering in a snow-covered landscape through the window of the Old Mill) seems to propose a dialectical relationship between nature and civilisation that can only be partially resolved though art. To sum up my argument so far, the house that Ron Kirby constructs for the woman he loves blends 'organic' and Machine Age Modernist elements into an aesthetic of modest sufficiency that resists the dominant 1950s American preoccupation with affluence and status. If Carey does elect to marry her ex-gardener and move out of her existing Colonial Revival home, then she will also be cutting herself off from most of her former friends, since they only appear to value men with 'decent money-making vocations'.[20]

I should also point out that the enormous importance of Ron's progressive transformation of the Old Mill is confirmed by the sequence breakdown that may be found in the Universal-International Pictures archives.[21] All of the other locations, such as Carey's living room or the Andersons' nursery, are simply listed in these notes without any further elaboration. By contrast, every time a scene is set in the Old Mill, the condition of the building is clearly specified (i.e. 1st Barn Sequence – Barn in poor shape, 2nd Barn Sequence – Barn in state of repair, 3rd Barn Sequence – Barn still in state of repair, and 4th Barn Sequence – Barn completely remodelled). Moreover, in terms of the structure of the narrative, every major change in Ron and Carey's relationship is marked by an encounter that takes place inside this crucial dwelling. During the first one the couple admit their mutual attraction, during the second the tree farmer asks the widow to marry him, during the third she breaks off their engagement due to external pressures, and during the fourth Carey returns to the man she loves after hearing about his accident. Consequently, the studio's analysis of the reaction cards filled in at the preview screening held in Encino, California showed that the audience thought that the scenes that were shot inside the Old Mill were the most crucial in terms of their own emotional response to the characters too.[22] Finally, although the light-coloured walls and multi-paned windows of Carey's suburban home may superficially resemble the Machine Age traits of Ron's domestic space, they have been derived from a very different set of ordering principles. In this chapter, I intend to examine the disparate architectural systems and associations that have been embedded in *All That Heaven Allows*, a film in which style operates as an important social signifier.

I Modernism Here and There, Now and Then: Deciphering the Old Mill

The Old Mill appears to reflect the 'organic' emphasis of 1950s American Modernism when it is initially glimpsed in *All that Heaven Allows*. During this scene, a lonely widow invited to her ex-gardener's rural property to view his silver-tipped spruces notices the abandoned building and asks to go inside. Light sifts in through tall casement windows and partially illuminates the shadowy interior, which is enclosed by exposed timber beams, unpainted wooden planks and hammer-dressed masonry. At this point, these elements seem to invoke the mid-century domestic architecture of Frank Lloyd Wright: the sense of refuge provided by the thick stone walls, the 'honest' use of undisguised natural materials and the horizontality of the proportions, as long as the overhanging beam suspended across the foreground remains intact.[23]

Yet the rectangular containment of this space was not typical of Wright's later residential ground plans. These homes were better known for their dynamic torsion, since divergent axes often spin out in opposite directions around the ceremonial fulcrum of the hearth. For instance, Wright's conception of Falling Water (1937–9) was deliberately calculated to explode the geometric constraints of 'box architecture' (his pejorative term for the International Style of the 1920s).[24] Rising up from a rocky outcropping over a cascading waterfall, the cantilevered terraces of this dramatic residence expand outward in all directions, aiming for a total reintegration with nature (Figure 6.1). During this period, even the architect's smaller houses tended to pivot around the central core of an imposing fireplace, which now resembled a geological extension of the earth.

Returning to *All That Heaven Allows*, at first the Old Mill seems to evince something of Wright's fascination with primeval petrifaction and this sense of enduring traditions is reinforced by Ron's allusions to his family history. He draws Carey's attention to the millstone where his grandfather used to grind his flour as soothingly lyrical non-diegetic music plays in the background. Yet by the time the widow has made her second visit to this location the tree farmer's seemingly cherished ancestral relic will have gone. In other words, when Ron decides to rebuild this inherited structure he is thinking about his future and not the past, considering where he and Carey will live after they have been married. To adopt Lewis Mumford's terminology, the Old Mill appears to represent a 'utopia of reconstruction' rather than a 'utopia of escape', which may be recognised by the fact that it is 'geometric and planned' instead of 'autarkic and natural'.[25]

There is another aspect of the mise-en-scène that also warns the spectator against reading this building as a simple 'organic' outcropping of an untouched natural world. Although Ron may coexist with the landscape, he is never really absorbed into it. We initially notice the tall, dark-haired gardener standing on the widow's front lawn pruning one of her trees. During the lunch that the couple shares on Carey's terrace, the rigid geometry formed by the espaliered branches of an ornamental vine is often visible just

Figure 6.1 Illustration of Frank Lloyd Wright's Falling Water in *House Beautiful*.
Source: *House Beautiful*, November 1955, p. 246

behind them. Indeed, in many of the shots that make up this sequence, the gardener's profile has been deliberately positioned so as to overlap with this striated pattern, which is presumably the result of his handiwork. While the landscape that surrounds the Old Mill seems much less synthetic, the trees that Ron grows are just as artificial as Carey's carefully trained vine. Inside the laboratory-like space of his glasshouse, the seedlings that the widow stops to admire have been classified and grouped in accordance with their correct genus and species. Moreover, the silver-tipped spruces that provided the reason for her journey to the country were not found flourishing in a forest. Instead, they have been dug out of the earth and arranged in tightly-packed rows against an external wall with their roots wrapped in burlap sacking. When Ron picks up one of these trees to show his guest, its perfectly balanced form and unnatural situation seem to highlight the amount of scientific engineering that was necessary to produce such a fine specimen.

By the time the widow's initial tour of Ron's secluded property has ended, the couple will have acknowledged their mutual attraction. After entering the cavernous interior of the Old Mill, Carey is startled by the flight of a bird and falls from the stairs to the second storey loft into her companion's arms. The decorous 'Mrs Scott' shrinks away from the suddenness of this unexpected intimacy, but after some discussion of whether Ron should move his living quarters here (and of whom he might ask to accompany him) they kiss. To my mind, Carey's nascent ability to cross class boundaries should be directly related to the openness of this interior, a quality that will be retained in the final ground plan. The fluid freedom of movement that it encourages, which is enhanced by the relatively long takes and distant framing of much of this sequence, enables the widow to physically enact her temporary liberation from bourgeois constraints. For the rest of the film, the tree farmer will continue to remodel this space until he has fashioned a suitable home for himself and his prospective wife.

When next we see it, Ron has removed any remaining obstructions from the Old Mill's interior, which militates against the inhabitant's ability to make any social distinctions to an even greater degree. The viewer observes Carey stepping through the door from the outside into a completely undifferentiated space, with no formal front hallway or walls to separate strangers from friends or family or public from private activities. Both of these characters (and their initial free-ranging movements) are shown in a long shot that reveals the full amplitude of this undivided living area. Instead of editing in a series of closer perspectives at this point, the director pans to the right in tandem with the tree farmer's gait, then tracks forward towards the two protagonists in order to convey a true sense of the spatial coherence of this room. By stripping away the extraneous overhead beams and clutter, Ron has uncovered an essentially cubic form that seems to invoke Le Corbusier's Machine Age dwellings of the 1920s.[26]

In an illuminating text that was published in 1930, the pioneering Swiss architect had tried to explain the meaning of the simplified ground plans that were so essential to his conception of the modern home. He concluded:

> *Thus, simplicity is not poverty*, but simplicity is a choice, discrimination, a crystallization having purity itself for an object. Simplicity is a concentrate . . . a fully conscious act, a phenomenon of spirituality.[27]

Hence, in Le Corbusier's compact 'machines for living' not only does the resident 'move . . . and act rapidly', but in his or her 'hour of rest' he or she will '*think of something*, of the harmony of proportions, or of some poem on machinery . . . or a photo of a simple or sublime phenomenon, usual or exceptional [my emphasis]'.[28] With regard to *All That Heaven Allows*, the basic geometry of the Old Mill's main living area appears to elicit a very similar response from its inhabitants. After Ron has completed his renovations and Carey sees the final effect, she will observe to Alida that he has managed to fill this humble shelter with beauty and love. Moreover, the enormous gridiron window that Ron has added to the original structure, which again echoes this early twentieth-century European Modernist aesthetic, seems from the very beginning to operate as a sort of mind-screen that is particularly conducive to thought. The first time that the spectator becomes aware of its presence (during the couple's second meeting in the Old Mill), we don't really see this glass wall directly but simply notice the striking pattern of blue light that it throws across the white rendered surface of the fireplace. As I have already noted, Wassily Kandinsky associated these two colours with a profound sense of spirituality, and in this context they will introduce a period of intense introspection. By asking Carey to marry him slightly later in this scene, Ron forces his more tentative companion to consider the future of their relationship.

At the end of this shot, the camera tracks in closer and halts in a position that still reveals the full length of their bodies as the couple gaze out of the window (Figure 6.2). Standing beside this huge expanse of glass, which is far taller than they are and extends almost down to the floor, Ron and Carey both narrate what they see for one another. The audience observes a snow-covered rural landscape framed by trees, in which a barn and a silo appear in a meadow in the middle distance set against a backdrop of rolling hills. The snow is still falling and it is twilight, so this pristine white vista has been tinctured with the deep blue of the sky. What Carey sees in this icy tableau is a 'view of the pond', which is an aspect of the scenery that the spectator can't quite grasp, since it is currently blanketed with snow. This comment

Figure 6.2 Looking through the window of the Old Mill in *All That Heaven Allows*.

also underscores the link that has already been established between Ron and Henry David Thoreau, since the New England essayist wrote about the two years that he had spent living in a one-room cabin located in a similar landscape in *Walden*.[29] In an earlier scene that took place inside the Andersons' apartment, Carey had read aloud a passage from this book, which was said to constitute 'Mick's Bible' and to represent the model for Ron's liberating material restraint (although the tree farmer 'hasn't read it, he just lives it', according to Alida). What her companion perceives when he gazes out of this window is also a mental geography, since he tells Carey that this opening has been positioned so as to capture the light from the rising sun (something that we will observe to great effect in the final scene).

A short time later, after Ron has proposed to the widow beside the fireplace, they will both walk back to stand in the colder light that is emanating from this glass wall in order to talk about the difficulties that might arise from their marriage. In an exchange that is largely played out in two protracted medium close-ups, the director emphasises the inner journey that is being expressed in his characters' words by showing their upper bodies as black shapes silhouetted against the eerie blue and white glow of the landscape. Just as Le Corbusier had anticipated, these flat panes of glass (through which we glimpse whirling eddies of snow) seem to concentrate and therefore strengthen each inhabitant's capacity for abstract thought. Once Carey has finally agreed to become Ron's wife (after a great deal of hesitation) they will return to this wall, pull the floor-length wooden shutters back and stand looking out at the immaculate winter panorama that fills the screen. In other words, if at times this view through the window seems to mirror the inhabitant's own meditative, internal psychic processes, at other times it appears to be showing them an inspirational vision of an alternative world. From this point onward, whenever the couple are glimpsed inside the Old Mill this strikingly Modernist glass wall is almost always in plain sight.[30]

Although both Ron and Carey are often observed looking out of this window, the director never edits in an unimpeded reverse shot of what they see. Instead, their (and our) perception of the surrounding countryside is conveyed through a series of over-the-shoulder shots, which invariably means that it has been filtered through the mathematical overlay of the gridiron fenestration. Just like Le Corbusier's description of the framed landscapes that may be seen from the windows of the Villa Savoye, looking out at this carefully selected rural prospect from inside the Old Mill seems to tell us that our 'home life will be set in a Virgilian dream'.[31] According to the architect, these intimations of a bucolic utopia could only be achieved through the intervention of reason, imagination and passion, which together 'manifest the poetic powers that animate us and give us joy'.[32] Hence, many important exchanges take place within the immediate range of the Old Mill's architecturally amended view, which Ron especially seems to draw conviction from. During their third meeting in this space, in which Carey tries to persuade him to postpone their marriage, he remains steadfastly by the window even after she has decided to end their engagement. Again, after Ron's accident prompts the widow to return to the Old Mill with Alida, the two women will share their most intimate dialogue right beside this glass wall. During this revelatory conversation, the widow berates herself for failing to recognise the superiority of Ron's way of life (in particular, his refusal 'to give importance to unimportant things') and expresses her regret that she had let others come between them. Alida reminds her that the Andersons had been equally slow to adopt the gardener's anti-materialistic stance, absolving Carey of any residual guilt by telling her not to worry about the past, since it's 'unimportant too'.

When the nurse opens the shutters the following morning, exposing the blinding whiteness of the snow-covered landscape that is visible through the window, it is as if the world has been reborn in the brilliant illumination of the new day. Standing between this transparent aperture and the figure of her beloved, who is lying on the couch that has been placed just below it, Carey swears to the doctor that she has come back to stay. During the closing sequence (which revolves around the couple's final reconciliation), this large expanse of glass and the idyllic prospect that it contains hovers over them until the end. In fact, a planar view of this 'picture' window through which a tame deer looks in from the outside will fill the screen at many key moments: the shot that precedes Ron's return to consciousness, the shot in which Carey decides to take her place by his side and the last shot of the film. The artificial quality of this pastoral 'image' is no doubt ironic, but the spectator has already been warned that redemption cannot be attained through a flight into nature, no matter how much the sight of it refreshes our souls. Only inside the rationalised geometry of this idealised 'house-machine' (and Mick and Alida's apartment, which resembles an equally undivided seventeenth-century Colonial Great Hall) will Ron, his closest friends and later Carey feel secure enough to reinvent both themselves and their community.

The tree farmer will eventually paint every internal surface of the Old Mill white, as may be readily observed in the final scene, thus rendering this building's resemblance to the Machine Age dwellings of the 1920s even more complete. For instance, in *The Decorative Art of Today* Le Corbusier exhorted every citizen to 'replace his hangings, his damasks, his wall-papers, his stencils, with a plain coat of white ripolin'.[33] A universal application of 'whitewash' was supposed have a levelling effect upon the observer, because it 'is the wealth of the poor and of the rich – everybody, just as bread, milk and water are the wealth of the slave and of the king'.[34] Moreover, not only is this stringent aesthetic accessible to everyone, but the white walls that it specifies hide nothing and therefore never lie ('*Everything is shown as it is*'), which induces a process of moral and spiritual purification in the viewer ('Then comes *inner cleanness*').[35] In other words, this luminous plainness does not simply reflect human virtue; it actually creates it by reforming the spectator's values in accordance with the ideological convictions that it encodes.

Within the context of *All That Heaven Allows*, we soon discover that Ron shares Le Corbusier's belief in the power of architecture to stimulate social change. During their third rendezvous at the Old Mill, the tree farmer refuses to move into Carey's existing Colonial Revival residence in order to placate her children. He is so certain that living in his fiancée's upper-class surroundings would affect his character for the worse that he elects to remain in his own home, even though this decision might result in the loss of the woman he loves. In other words, only within the radiant lucidity of the Old Mill's refurbished interior can this spirit of anti-materialism be sustained.

II THE MILL AS ARCHITECTURAL ART AND THE SELLING OF *ALL THAT HEAVEN ALLOWS*

A press release prepared for the marketing campaign of *All That Heaven Allows* by an unaccredited staff member of Universal-International Pictures dubbed the Old Mill 'one of the most interesting sets to grace a major motion picture production in years'. After declaring that it had been designed by 'Art Director Eric Orbom' 'for Rock Hudson to re-build and decorate in the story', the writer went on to say that 'this dilapidated structure which eventually becomes a farm style work of architectural art was designed ... [to be shown] in three different stages of development, all of which are important to the story'. Since it involved the completion, partial destruction and restoration of this crucial location, the building process was actually quite complex, as is revealed in the following excerpt from this document:

> [In order to fabricate the set of the Old Mill] it was necessary, in a manner of speaking, to work backwards. The great high ceilings with gigantic beams, the walls of old timbers and the fireplace of adobe were done to perfection before they were wrecked and aged to simulate a deserted barn which had been standing empty and cobwebby for years. Then, in several stages, it was re-built with paint, furniture and decorative detail until it became worthy of a layout in *House Beautiful*.[36]

Indeed, the main objective of this unknown contributor's publicity strategy is indirectly disclosed in the final sentence: to obtain a high-profile 'layout' in *House Beautiful*, 'American Home, Better Homes and Gardens, or the Sunday

Times Home Section' by providing a studio-authored article on the Old Mill's conversion into a residence that a popular magazine might choose to print. This intention was explicitly stated in another memo that listed a series of architecture- and design-related campaign ideas for the film, which included suggesting that *Better Homes and Gardens* might be interested in reproducing an economical gardening plan that 'Rock Hudson perfected while playing a tree farmer in "All That Heaven Allows"'.[37] In order to increase the likelihood that such a feature would be published, the studio's art department also produced a set of very painterly drawings that depicted the different stages of the Old Mill's transformation.[38]

As early as 1942, *House Beautiful* had published a brief photo-essay that attempted to explain 'Why the Movies are influencing American taste'. A lengthy caption found on the second page of this lavishly illustrated description of the rustic interiors created for a recently released 'romantic comedy' sums up the main argument quite concisely. 'When you go to the movies', the anonymous writer points out, 'you have the opportunity of viewing the work of distinguished decorators, [which has been] conceived with imagination [and] executed with exquisite taste.' Moreover, unlike in the past when 'movie characters inhabited surroundings as unsubstantial as the ray of light that cast their images on the screen', contemporary film sets 'often contain valuable [decorating] ideas that you can adapt to your own purposes'.[39] The aims that the author had in mind appear to be emotional rather than aesthetic, for in the case of the living room, 'the fine proportions . . . the friendly grouping of pieces in a semi-circle around the fireplace, the clear, cheerful colors, and the gracious lines of the furniture' have all been subordinated to the communication 'of an atmosphere of comfort and hospitality, which is the test of the home'.[40]

According to the writer who was charged with the task of reviewing the décor of *When Ladies Meet*, the film's Art Director (Cedric Gibbons) and Decorator (Edwin Willis) had 'created a home, not a mere background for [the] action and dialogue' in their cinematic approximation of 'the American ideal of good living'.[41] Similarly, the architect of the next residence that is surveyed in this issue of *House Beautiful* has managed to construct a dwelling that is as 'friendly as a handshake' from an actress's recollections of her favourite Hollywood sets.[42] A picture of the bedroom found in Michele Morgan's current film ('Joan of Paris') blends almost imperceptibly with the photographs that have been taken of her own house, which is said to combine 'Early American and French Provincial' stylistic influences. Again, the architect and his client were primarily seeking to elicit a certain psychological response from all those who made the journey to this residence that was located on 'a shelf of land high above Beverly Hills'. The informality signalled by the exterior's 'rough stones, earthy brown siding and shingles'

Figure 6.3 Drawing of the Old Mill before renovation.
Source: Universal-International Pictures Archives, Box 434, File 12900, courtesy of NBC Universal

was meant to put visitors at ease, while the deeply padded upholstery of the gingham- or chintz-covered seating inside ministers to their comfort. Despite the spare elegance of the occasional Colonial Windsor chair, J. F. Wadkins' and Michele Morgan's overstuffed evocation of an 'Early American' interior was far removed from the simplicity and restraint of its Puritan sources.

If we return to the three Universal-International Pictures drawings that were meant to reflect the changes that Ron makes to the Old Mill's interior, I would argue that the differences between the various stages seem much less pronounced than might have been expected (Figures 6.3, 6.4, 6.5). Despite the appearance of the large glass wall in the unknown artist's second ink-washed rendering, Ron's open-plan living area still seems very shadowy and cluttered with extraneous details, like the overhead beams and angled braces that are glimpsed only fleetingly in the film. When these elements have been combined with a feature that isn't visible in the motion picture at all (the inward sloping roof supports discernible in the final drawing), they significantly alter the spectator's impression of the overall shape of this space. The rigorous geometry of Ron's ideal home has been considerably softened by the artist's decision to add these oblique wooden struts to the ceiling. Moreover, while the illustration of the finished interior is lighter than the previous two sketches, it doesn't really manage to capture the dazzling radiance that suffuses this room during the film's final scene. Hence, the European Modernist traits that are readily evident in the on-screen depiction of this space, which includes the double height cubic shape of the living area, the large glass wall and the whiteness that has been applied to every surface, are not nearly so apparent in these atmospheric delineations.

Of course, the unknown artist's dappled brushstrokes and chiaroscuro have also magnified the 'organic' aspects of this rural dwelling. Accentuating the distinctive weight, colour and grain of the constituent materials, as well as reducing the viewer's sense of the transparency of the walls, was clearly meant

Figure 6.4 Drawing of the Old Mill during renovation.
Source: Universal-International Pictures Archives, Box 434, File 12900, courtesy of NBC Universal

Figure 6.5 Drawing of the Old Mill after renovation.
Source: Universal-International Pictures Archives, Box 434, File 12900, courtesy of NBC Universal

to make this series of drawings more appealing to the editors of mainstream home decorating magazines.[43] Given the current Cold War-sanctioned clamour for residences that suggested a more 'American' approach to contemporary design (which to *House Beautiful* meant reflecting the 'timeless' rusticity of Frank Lloyd Wright) these shifts in emphasis are easy to understand. Nevertheless, I would argue that they also undermine the meaning that has been inscribed within the film itself.

Most viewers of *All That Heaven Allows* would probably agree that the Old Mill signifies much more than just a pleasant abode that has been 'designed for particular people with [an] understanding [of] ... their special needs, the nature of the site and the materials to be used'.[44] If this structure was merely the solution to a specific set of technical and programmatic requirements (including the desire for comfort and abundance that was so central to *House Beautiful*'s 1950s conception of 'the good life'), then why was Carey so hesitant to take up residence there? By choosing to draw upon an earlier European Modernist aesthetic, Ron appears to be implying that his new home has not been tailored to fit the couple's existing personae, in the manner of the popular mid-century understanding of 'organic' architecture. Nor has nature itself been domesticated and tamed by simply being viewed as the benign source of 'snug' rusticated sandstone walls or 'waxed flagstone floors'.[45] As an alien presence hovering on the other side of the Old Mill's gridiron window, the natural world seems to prick our consciences by pointing to some sort of transcendental ideal that we must measure ourselves against.[46] In other words, the widow, her children and everyone else around them know that in order to move into the tree farmer's house, Carey will need to renounce her bourgeois way of life and adopt an alternative social ethos that is grounded in voluntary simplicity and material restraint.

III STONINGHAM AS MAUSOLEUM: A REPOSITORY OF DEAD CONVENTIONS

Largely set in a railway suburb that was at once wealthier and more established than its automobile equivalent, *All That Heaven Allows* exposes the powerful social forces that almost pressure a middle-aged widow into renouncing her love for her gardener.[47] According to John Stilgoe, the nineteenth-century railway suburb was initially designed to provide the office worker and his family with an opportunity for renewal through a more sustained contact with the land. Beyond the borders of the city, both men and women would have a chance to develop some of the latent abilities that their normal activities tended to suppress. As bourgeois husbands exercised their bodies by working in their gardens, their wives were expected to engage their intellects on botanising expeditions in the nearby forests and fields.[48] Yet Sirk's film portrays the twentieth-century exhaustion of this original impulse, since none of Stoningham's corrupt country club set performs any physical labour, nor are they in touch with their natural environment. Indeed, in the opening scene Carey makes her alienation from her leafy surroundings quite plain by revealing to Ron that she does not know what the 'goldenrain tree' beside her patio is called.

The lonely widow's estrangement from the landscape is clearly demonstrated in the tightly-framed composition of many of the shots that are contained in this sequence. Visual barricades formed by clapboard walls or fences placed parallel to the picture plane seem to crowd in on Carey, especially since she is often presented in the constricted space of a medium close-up or a close-up. This sense of confinement is only relieved once, when Ron takes the box of dishes that her friend Sarah has returned and walks with his upper-class employer towards her house. For the first time, they are both shot from below against an open expanse of sky, while the camera momentarily examines the delicate branches of a tree overhead. The gardener's way of life, which is free of petrified conventions, seems to represent Carey's last chance to escape the snobbery and hypocrisy of her repressive Connecticut community. For the rest of the narrative, Stoningham will remain the most obvious embodiment of the outmoded social mores that threaten to tear the central protagonists apart.

These restrictive traditions have been clearly inscribed into the bird's-eye view of Carey's suburb that has been used to introduce several key scenes. It consists of an aerial perspective of the town square, which is juxtaposed against the soaring white spire of a Colonial Revival church. Lutz Koepnick has inferred from the reiteration of this tableau that the church is the mechanism through which 'small-town America regulates desire and molds conformity'.[49] Yet it is impossible to determine if this tower belongs to a church rather than a secular town hall until its final appearance, when the viewer is finally allowed to see the cross that has been placed on top of the steeple. Therefore, I would argue, on the basis of William Butler's analysis of the changing perception of Litchfield, Connecticut, that Sirk's depiction of Stoningham is more indicative of an idealised conception of 'New Englandness' than of religiosity per se. After the Centennial celebrations of 1876, the image of a Colonial American settlement that became most firmly lodged in the national consciousness was that of the northeastern 'nucleated village of white clapboard houses lining elm-shaded streets, with a simple Congregational church, a general store, and a small schoolhouse surrounding a park-like green'.[50] Hence, it is surely no coincidence that a roughly similar architectural vista may be observed at a number of key moments in *All That Heaven Allows*.

For example, the church and town square feature prominently in the opening shot of the film, in which a moving camera draws a visual link between these emblems of ancestral authority and Carey's Colonial Revival home located on a nearby cul-de-sac. By highlighting the instruments of social control that enforce allegiance to established conventions from the very start, the director heightens the spectator's awareness of the subversive implications of Carey's spontaneous decision to invite her gardener to lunch later in this scene. Similarly, the second shot in which we see these important landmarks (though time has moved on and the village is now covered with snow) precedes a sequence that revolves around Carey turning a television salesman away from her door. She chooses to rush off to join Ron at the Old Mill rather than to settle for television's hollow 'imitation of life', a judgement that foreshadows her eventual rejection of the simulation of friendship that is all that most of her fellow townsfolk can provide. During the cocktail party that was at least partly arranged to introduce Carey's new fiancée to the Stoningham elite, she finally realises the true extent of their narrow-mindedness and bigotry. The spiteful innuendo of Mona (the town gossip) was to be expected, but a condescending disapproval of Ron is openly expressed by almost everyone.[51] In the end, just after our last sighting of this steeple, the widow resolves to leave her privileged community behind. In other words, every sighting of this archetypal New England streetscape is soon followed by a crucial encounter between Carey and Ron, in which the widow must decide whether to resign herself to a life of stultifying conformity or to pursue the more fulfilling possibilities offered by a liaison with her former gardener.

The widely accepted stereotypes that are encapsulated in this view do not present an accurate picture of an early Connecticut settlement, however, as Butler's investigations have shown. For instance, the whiteness that is generally attributed to these seventeenth- and early eighteenth-century wooden structures was not typical of the Colonial era. In Litchfield, which has often been adduced as an exemplary New England village, the first houses were 'painted shades of red, green, and blue – if they were painted at all . . . [and utilitarian] interior rather than [decorative] exterior shutters prevailed'.[52] Moreover, the verdant surroundings that have also been ascribed to this period are an equally romantic misconception. As Butler points out, the 'towering shade trees and inviting parks' of the popular imagination were the product of the nineteenth-century Village Improvement Societies that were founded by the 'wealthy city folk' who had begun to purchase houses in the country.[53]

In these small towns, an elitist Colonial Revival parlance began to crystallise around the more refined Georgian and Federal styles that had superseded the original Puritan vernacular. Moreover, during the tide of 'colonialisation' that swept New England and was in 'full force [in Litchfield] by the mid 1880s', many villages were 'restored' in accordance with the current fantasy of what constituted a genuine early American settlement.[54] White painted clapboard houses adorned with black or dark green shutters and a profusion of classical ornament summed up the most common post-centenary evocation of Colonial design. Finally, by the 1900s it had become just as acceptable to erect a whole new dwelling in a 'modern Colonial' style, which might combine a gambrel-roofed Georgian silhouette with decorative details that had been copied from 'genuine . . . structures or from period design books'.[55] Returning to *All That Heaven Allows*, every house on Carey's street appears to fall into the latter category, since each one is a contemporary restatement of this so-called 'national' architectural idiom. Given the *haute bourgeois* American's predilection for Colonial Revival homes as 'symbols of [superior] ancestry and [elevated] social status', this stylistic homogeneity tells us a great deal about Carey's exclusive neighbourhood.[56]

As Butler has observed, by the early twentieth century the well-to-do inhabitants of many small New England towns were seeking to reconstitute a 'comprehensive colonial environment'.[57] Anything less would undermine their belief that a 'truer' version of America (solely populated by the white Anglo-Saxon Protestant descendants of the Pilgrim fathers) still existed, at least within the borders of their own privileged enclaves. Moreover, by this time contemporary allusions to the first two centuries of American Colonial architecture (at least in the more patrician suburbs) had become equally selective. Only designs that enshrined Neo-classical precedents signifying order, stability and prosperity tended to be erected by the upper-class patrons of this widely disseminated revival style.[58] Consequently, the most radical aspect of the Puritans' worldview, the millenarian yearning for apocalyptic social change, had been completely banished from these sanitised simulacra of historic New England towns. Since many affluent homeowners were attempting to create an image of the past that would justify their own values, they often opted for a formally planned house that reflected the more urbane sophistication of the Georgian or Federal styles. These mid- to late eighteenth-century architectural influences had sanctioned the increasing stratification of American society, registering subtle differences in wealth, rank and status that their twentieth-century emulators had no desire to overturn.

All That Heaven Allows obviously portrays a Colonial Revival suburb that has retained these invidious class distinctions and the hollowness of its traditions is echoed in the rather conventional design of the Scott family home. While 'freer renderings of the Colonial Style' had become commonplace by the 1930s (combining architectural motifs from various periods with a looser, more rambling ground plan), Carey's Neo-Federal dwelling has retained the symmetrical façade and classical details of its original sources.[59] According to a contemporary article by Robert Woods Kennedy that appeared in the *Magazine of Art*, there is a clear correlation between choosing to build a house in a conservative style and a desire to attain a more elevated social standing.[60] Although a Colonial Revival home does not have the venerable patrimony of its eighteenth-century equivalent, it pretends that it does, since 'a house with a distinguished lineage is concrete evidence of upper class status'.[61] Reproducing 'the . . . arrangements of the rooms and their specialization of function help[s] to impress an elaborate ritual on the occupants', even if the actual 'spiritual presence of the ancestors' is absent from a more recent facsimile.[62] Consequently, the orthodox circulation patterns that have been built into the Scott family's suburban dwelling inhibit freedom of thought as well as movement.

For instance, was it proper for a middle-aged widow to invite her gardener into the formal living room that is separated from the rest of the house by the centre hall entryway? In fact, the first time Ron enters Carey's residence (dressed in his work clothes) he lingers on the threshold of the parlour, uncertain as to whether he should enter into this ceremonial reception area or not. Slightly earlier in the same scene, her friend Sarah had exhibited no such qualms about wandering into this space in order to discuss the dinner arrangements for later in the evening. When their conversation is interrupted by the gardener's appearance at the front door, he remains standing in the hallway with Carey, who doesn't invite him to go any further. She will finally introduce Ron to Sarah near the end of this sequence (after some hesitation), but this exchange does not take place until the latter has walked back through the entrance hall on her way out of the house. Unlike the Old Mill, entry into the Scott family home is provisional, and only those visitors who have sufficient status are encouraged to move beyond the foyer into the adjacent rooms.

Yet as Robert Woods Kennedy observed in 1953, 'the traditionalist of today certainly does not come by his style traditionally' through a lengthy apprenticeship with a master of a time-honoured Massachusetts, Pennsylvania or Connecticut architectural style. 'Since the social, economic and technical conditions that created these modes [of building] no longer exist', the contemporary designer could only learn about them with 'the aid of graduate schools, measured drawings, photographs or engineering handbooks'.[63] Consequently, inhabiting the past becomes a kind of virtual mimicry, in which the gestures of one's ancestors are repeated without necessarily being understood, sometimes taking on an entirely different meaning in the process. Whatever democratic associations a Colonial Revival interior might once have had, in a twentieth-century context it was usually linked with ideological conservatism, genealogical prestige and the burnished gleam of old money.[64]

Given the schematic quality of this academic understanding of received forms and motifs, it should be no surprise that Colonial Revival designers often deployed the language of classical architecture for strictly decorative ends. Moreover, when they revisited the already mannered embellishments of the late eighteenth century (as would have been the case with Carey's home), the result was a building that was doubly derivative in its expression. According to Alan Gowans, the suave refinement of the Adams-Federal style's delicate mouldings and white painted details was an indication of 'classical decadence'.[65] Instead of a finely balanced proportional system symbolising order and stability, the Adams' style's lighter variations on classical forms trivialised the gravity of its antique sources. While the architectural details of the Scott family's white painted clapboard house (such as the columned portico, the fan and side lights around the door and the slender colonnettes adorning the fireplace) seem to invoke classical ideals, they will soon prove to be devoid of substance. Even though Carey's son initially urges her to retain their existing residence because it is a repository of past traditions ('This was the place where we were born . . . [How could you] give up a home that's been in the family for I don't know how long . . .'), he later decides to abandon it without a backward glance. After his mother has broken off her engagement to Ron, keeping the building that had anchored his ancestral invocations will turn out to be much less important to Ned than saving money. When Kay's marriage and his own departure for Paris are imminent, he advises Carey to sell off the now overly capacious family home in order to reduce her taxes. As long she remains immured in this Neo-Federal sepulchre, however, the only companion that her children will accept is an exact replica of their deceased father, 'a successful businessman [and] pillar of the community' (in the words of her rueful younger suitor).

With characteristic zeal, Le Corbusier once denounced the typical middle-class home as a museum, temple or sarcophagus dedicated to the '*cult of the souvenir*'. In chaining ourselves to 'these accretions of dead things from our past', our minds are no longer free 'to explore the vast continent before us', because they have been imprisoned by the 'manacles . . . of memory'.[66] Moreover, this is exactly how Carey's memento-filled Colonial Revival residence should be viewed in *All That Heaven Allows*. At one point, her daughter explicitly compares the widow's situation with that of an ancient Egyptian wife who was buried alive in her husband's tomb after his death (although Kay also expresses the hope that her mother will manage to avoid this fate). In order even to contemplate pursuing a new romance, Carey had to first put away some of the more obvious reminders of the late Mr Scott. Her son objects vociferously when a trophy that belonged to his father disappears from the living-room mantelpiece, but Carey will not feel free enough to love someone else until the 'manacles' of 'memory' have been completely left behind.

IV THE EYE OF POWER: WHO IS LOOKING AT WHOM IN THE SUBURBS

When she is alone in Stoningham, Carey often appears imprisoned by the mullions of her 'tasteful' home's multi-paned sash windows. Sometimes the spectator observes the widow from an internal vantage point, watching her gaze into an opaque black void framed by a window that gives back nothing but her own reflection. At other moments, we are shown Carey looking through the cage-like fenestration of this building from the outside, which magnifies the sense of entrapment by making her an object of scrutiny.[67] For instance, as the unhappy widow decorates her Christmas tree alone after renouncing her love for Ron, she hears a group of children singing a carol in the nearby street. In the shot/reverse shot sequence that follows, we do not look out *with* Carey from inside her home at a view that has been filtered through the pattern formed by her mullions (as would have been the case in the Old Mill). Instead, we look in *at* the widow wistfully observing this joyful procession from a position that is located outside the window. Rather than framing a prospect, this intricate latticework now seems to resemble the bars of a cage.[68] Moreover, Carey's feelings of entrapment are further magnified by the surveillance that is implied by the moving camera. At the end of this sequence it tracks in towards the widow's tear-stained face not only to emphasise the depths of her emotion, but also to reinforce the spectator's understanding of the oppressiveness of her situation.

In Carey's patrician suburb her dress, activities and movements are constantly being monitored and commented upon in order to ensure that she performs the social rituals that are expected of a woman of her class. Even before her relationship with Ron has become the target of vicious gossip, the best options open to someone in her position are endlessly discussed on her behalf. Should she relinquish passion and marry an older man of comparable social standing for 'companionship and affection'? Or should she content herself with the electronic solace provided by 'last refuge of the lonely woman', a television set? Her neighbours, friends and family frequently pre-select certain possibilities while voicing their disapproval of others, thereby attempting to restrict the widow's range of available choices. For example, in the opening sequence, Sarah dismisses an unattached man of Carey's own age as a potential date because 'he'll consider any female over the age of eighteen too old'. She then offers to call the elderly Harvey to escort her friend to the country club, a decision that the widow accepts without question. This passivity seems less inexplicable once we realise the degree of Carey's exposure to outside scrutiny; the open, unenclosed lawns and thin, clapboard façades of the typical New England suburb provide no protection from the voyeuristic penetration of its inhabitants' regulating gaze.[69] This is perhaps most apparent at the beginning of the cocktail party that Sarah has organised to celebrate Tom Allenby's engagement to Jo-Ann Frisby, which represented the widow's first official opportunity to 'show off' her new beau. Prior to Carey and Ron's arrival, many of the assembled guests peer intently through the curtained windows, waiting for their inaugural sighting of this much more unconventional pair.

Unlike Michel Foucault, who believed that every area of contemporary society was equally permeable to this 'system of isolating visibility', during the 1950s many writers thought that suburbanites were especially vulnerable to this form of social control.[70] From a purely practical standpoint, *House Beautiful* published a series of articles such as 'Good Living is NOT Public Living', 'Do the Neighbours Know Your Business?' and 'Is There a Picture in Your Picture Window?' that contained valuable tips for warding off the prying eyes of nearby residents or passers-by.[71] More than ten years later, William Dobriner was still arguing that the typically spacious twentieth-century American housing development was governed by a 'Visibility Principle' that enabled 'suburbanites.[to] observe each other's behaviour and general life style far more easily than the central city dweller'. Long before Foucault, Dobriner had noted that 'the omnipresent eye of the community' is neither non-judgmental nor benign but was attempting to instil in the residents a standard of decorum that was so pervasive that they would eventually police themselves. For instance, in suburbs where gardening was '"the thing to do" [then] . . . garden you must [because] a sloppy and inept garden [that does not live up to local expectations] is [exceedingly] visible'.[72]

In the *Death and Life of Great American Cities*, Jane Jacobs also highlights the invasive quality of the inordinate interest that neighbours take in one another's activities in a strictly residential district. Because they lack the more impersonal meeting places that are available in denser metropolitan areas, in many suburbs there is almost no middle ground between a complete absence of social contact and an excessive amount of 'togetherness'.[73] Where few collective amenities exist, the housewife has no choice but to entertain chance acquaintances in the privacy of her own home, for there is nowhere else to get to know one another over coffee. According to Jacobs, this forced intimacy gives rise to the emergence of a much more intolerant society, since 'where people do share much, they become exceedingly choosy as to who their neighbours are, or with whom they associate at all'.[74] By contrast, the wealth of casual public interactions that are available in urban spaces such as sidewalks, shops, restaurants and parks meant that access to a city dweller's residence could be reserved for his or her dearest friends. Under these circumstances, 'it is possible to know all kinds of people without unwelcome entanglements, without boredom, necessity for excuses, explanations, fears of giving offence, embarrassments respecting impositions or commitments, and all such paraphernalia of obligations which can accompany less limited relationships'.[75] Carey's life in Stoningham (especially in the exchanges that unfold within the restricted settings of the country club and Sarah's cocktail party, which is as close as this wealthy community gets to a public arena) seems to display the whole range of uncomfortable emotions that Jacobs has included in this list.[76] While suburban society may deploy 'coercion at the play of a glance', it was the widow's susceptibility to these neighbourhood 'entanglements' that caused her to temporarily renounce her younger lover.

V ET IN ARCADIA EGO: THE DENOUEMENT OF ALL THAT HEAVEN ALLOWS

In 1955, Sirk's former professor Erwin Panofsky published a lengthy treatise on two paintings by Nicolas Poussin that were both entitled *Et in Arcadia Ego*. He began this learned explication by sketching a broad outline of the whole Arcadian tradition, which began with classical literature before turning into a nuanced analysis of seventeenth-century painting. The poet Virgil is credited not only with transforming 'a bleak and chilly district of Greece' into 'an imaginary realm of perfect bliss', but also with the introduction of darker currents of 'frustrated love and death' into this halcyon realm.[77] Panofsky observes that in 'Virgil's ideal Arcady human suffering and superhumanly perfect surroundings create a dissonance' that renders each of these conditions all the more poignant.[78] I would argue that the juxtaposition of Ron Kirby's injured body against the idealised pastoral vista that occurs at the end of *All That Heaven Allows* has a similar effect. This contrast heightens the utopian connotations of the tree farmer's living space, which becomes charged with an even greater philosophical intensity.

In conclusion, both the 'white villas' of European Modernism and the Old Mill's austere interior exhibit the verticality and axial symmetry that Geoffrey Scott interprets as an analogy for the upright form of the human body.[79] In other words, these buildings coexist with an autonomous natural terrain; a separation that is reinforced each time a planar 'view' of the rural scenery is 'pictured' through the exaggerated framing of the window. The denaturalisation of Ron Kirby's dwelling becomes absolute when every internal surface has been painted white by the end of the narrative, which strengthens its resemblance to the International Style architecture of the 1920s. What is the spectator meant to infer from Sirk's retrospective apotheosis of the high artifice of early twentieth-century European Modernism? Perhaps simply the fact that, just like architectural styles, social organisations and cultural mores are man-made constructs that may be disputed and changed. Although Ron and Carey's sylvan idyll is also haunted by mortality, they must resist taking refuge in the landscape and should continue to explore new possibilities as long as they live. Yet the film's final saccharine image, featuring a deer looking through the Old Mill's 'picture' window at the reconciled lovers, seems so freighted with irony that perhaps no such unambiguous message should be proposed. Sirk's fascination with the Machine Age may instead reflect nostalgia for an era that still dreamed of universal reform, before the shadow cast by an atomic war had dimmed the prospect of a progressive future.

Notes

1. 'Old House Made New: A huge glass wall helps to convert an ancient Connecticut farmhouse into a modern dwelling', *Life* (International Edition), 4, No. 5 (1 March 1948), 33. Ron Kirby's Old Mill was also meant to be located in this state. Of course, by 1955 many wholly Modernist buildings had already been erected in Connecticut (including Philip Johnson's infamous all-glass house).
2. Elizabeth Gordon, 'The Threat to the Next America', *House Beautiful*, 95 (April 1953), 126–31, 250–1.
3. Gordon, 250.
4. 'International Style' was a term coined by Henry Russell-Hitchcock and Philip Johnson in a 1932 Museum of Modern Art exhibition catalogue entitled *Modern Architecture: International Exhibition*. It refers to the unornamented European Modernist architecture of the 1920s that often featured flat roofs, smooth white rendered or glass curtain walls and large areas of gridded or strip windows.
5. Frank Lloyd Wright, 'The Art and Craft of the Machine [1901]' in *Frank Lloyd Wright: Collected Writings*, Volume I, ed. Bruce Brooks Pfeiffer (New York: Rizzoli, 1991), 59.
6. Le Corbusier, *The City of Tomorrow and Its Planning*, 78. The preceding paragraph on the same page began with the following exhortation: '*We must plant trees!*' because 'the tree in any case helps our physical and spiritual well-being'.
7. Gordon, 129, 251. According to Gordon's Cold War rhetoric, these minimalist houses weren't just 'unliveable', but the disproportionate amount of praise that they received from an elite group of 'arbiters' of taste had sapped the ordinary American's ability to think for him- or herself (127).
8. Elizabeth Mock, ed., *Built in U.S.A, 1932–1944* (New York: The Museum of Modern Art, 1944), 15.
9. Mock, 36. The vertical orientation of this residence's wooden cladding was more typically used to cover utilitarian buildings such as barns and sheds, which

reflects the Functionalist perspective that its designers had brought with them from Germany.
10. Henry-Russell Hitchcock and Arthur Drexler, ed., *Built in U.S.A.: Post-War Architecture* (New York: The Museum of Modern Art, 1952), 8.
11. See Mock, 12–13. In 'The Six Thousand Houses that Levitt Built' [*Harper's Magazine*, 197, No, 1180, 77–88] Eric Larrabee highlights the irony of Bill Levitt's claim that 'everyone should own a house and lot' by pointing out that the President of Levitt & Sons lived in a Manhattan apartment (p. 84). Larrabee's interviews with Levittown residents revealed that many of them had moved to Long Island mainly because of a shortage of affordable housing in the city. Levitt allowed his tenants to rent their houses for up to two years before deciding to buy, but at the end of that period they were forced to leave if they had not begun to purchase their property. Consequently, some Levittown residents felt that they had been pressured into buying their homes, which means that their acquisition of a 'Cape Coddage' (to use Larrabee's term) did not necessarily represent a free choice. See Larrabee, 78.
12. Joseph A. Barry, 'The Architecture of Humanism', *House Beautiful*, 95 (November 1953), 329.
13. According to Elaine May, 'Between 1947 and 1961, the number of families rose 28 percent, national income increased over 60 percent, and the group with discretionary income (those with money for non-necessities) doubled'. Much of this extra money was channelled into spending on the home, which increased by 240 per cent in the five years after World War II (compared to an increased spending of 33 per cent on food). See May's *Homeward Bound: American Families in the Cold War Era* (New York: Basic Books, 1988), 165.
14. Gordon, 127.
15. As well as asserting that the one-room cabin he built near Walden Pond satisfied the basic need for shelter perfectly adequately, Thoreau also wondered at one point if a six feet long, three feet wide wooden box built by the railway to store tools was large enough for a person to live in. See *Thoreau: Walden and other Writings* (New York: Bantam Books, 1962), 126. This attempt to isolate the smallest amount of space necessary to lead a decent, healthy and fulfilling life was also one of the major preoccupations of European Modernist architects during the late 1920s. In fact, the *existenzminimum* or subsistence dwelling was the main topic of discussion at the 1929 C.I.A.M. (*Congrès Internationaux d'Architecture Moderne*). Of course, the question of how every citizen could be guaranteed the minimum amount of space, fresh air and greenery that was deemed necessary is a highly political one.
16. Frank Lloyd Wright equated the geometric language of International Style architecture with political totalitarianism in a rather heated tirade that was published in *House Beautiful*, even though many of its major practitioners had been forced to flee the National Socialist regime in Germany. See his 'For a Democratic Architecture: A Statement by the Greatest Architect of Today' in *House Beautiful*, 95 (October 1953), 316.

17. Robert Woods Kennedy, 'The Style of Life', *Magazine of Art*, 46, No. 3 (March 1953), 101–4.
18. Joseph A. Barry, 'How Modern Architecture is Returning to the Middle West', *House Beautiful*, 96, No. 11 (November 1954), 236.
19. David Shi, *The Simple Life: Plain Living and High Thinking in American Culture* (New York: Oxford University Press, 1985), 7.
20. In response to a question uttered by a business executive attending the cocktail party where Carey's new fiancé was going to be introduced to her friends ('A gardener, why doesn't he get himself a decent money-making vocation?'), the local doctor (one of the few people on this unorthodox couple's side) responds by asking, 'Do you think that material success is the only end worthy of the pursuit of man?' Both Dr Hennessy and Ron Kirby would obviously answer 'No'.
21. See Box 226, File 07398 in the Universal-International Pictures archives.
22. See Box 508, File 14513 in the Universal-International Pictures archives. In reply to the question 'Which Scenes did you like the most?' a majority of those who answered selected a scene that was located inside this building. The first scene that took place in the Old Mill gained the highest number of votes (17), the second-highest number went to the scene entitled 'Mill remodelling' (8), and the third-highest went to an earlier sequence entitled 'Mill when snowing' (7). All in all, 36 votes were awarded to scenes that were played out inside this crucial setting (including the 4 votes received by the final scene). Only 6 votes were cast in favour of the scene that took place in the next most popular environment, which was described as 'Visiting Kirby's friends, the Andersons, and the dinner party'.
23. The editor of *House Beautiful* strongly supported Frank Lloyd Wright as an individual and the 'organic' Modernist movement in general. Between 1950 and 1955 Wright himself published several essays in this magazine, a travelling exhibition organised by *House Beautiful* ('The Arts of Daily Living') was dedicated to him, a whole issue was devoted to an examination of his houses and their influence on American design and a number of articles praised the 'American' organic mode of building after vilifying some prominent examples of the International Style. See, for example, James Marston Fitch's 'Frank Lloyd Wright's contribution to Your Daily Life' [*House Beautiful*, 98, No. 11 (November 1955), 265–9, 367–71].
24. Wright's animus against European Modernist architecture is well-known. For example, in 1931 he proclaimed: 'Human houses should not be like boxes blazing in the sun, nor should we outrage the Machine by trying to make dwelling places too complementary to machinery. Any building for humane purposes should be an elemental, sympathetic feature of the ground, complementary to its natural environment ... But most "modernistic" houses manage to look as though cut from scissors ... glued together in box-like forms – in a childish attempt to make buildings resemble steamships, flying machines or locomotives ...' Quoted by William Curtis on page 200 of *Modern Architecture Since 1900* (Oxford: Phaidon, 1987).
25. Philip W. Porter and Fred E. Lukermann, 'The Geography of Utopia' in

Geographies of the Mind, ed. David Lowenthal and Martyn J. Bowden (New York: Oxford University Press, 1976), 199–200.

26. In particular, the Old Mill's spatial configuration and circulation patterns appear to echo Le Corbusier's *Maison Citrohan*, which featured a double-height cubic living space entered from the side that is surmounted by a second-storey sleeping loft, with service areas located at the rear. As described in the final chapter of *Towards a New Architecture*, this housing prototype was intended to be as easy to manufacture as a cheap French car (hence the pun on Citroën). During the 1920s, Le Corbusier erected two of his most famous 'machines for living' in the *Weissenhof* model housing district that was sponsored by the *Deutscher Werkbund* in Stuttgart.

27. Le Corbusier, *Precisions: On the Present State of Architecture and City Planning* (Cambridge, MA: MIT Press, 1991 translation of the 1930 French editions), 80.

28. Le Corbusier, *Precisions*, 118.

29. Sirk admired the writings of both Emerson and Thoreau. He told Jon Halliday that 'when I first read *Walden* it was like a sun going up over my youth: this strangely *clean* language'. Moreover, it was the director himself who insisted that this canonical American work be included in a major scene of *All That Heaven Allows*. See Halliday, 113–14.

30. In *The Radiant City*, Le Corbusier called for each residential unit to be enclosed with a 'façade (triumph of modern techniques) [that] is entirely of glass ... [where] the view is right there, from the edge of the floor to the edge of the ceiling and from the left hand wall to the right hand wall; the view is to be seen in front of you, in the foreground (parks and open spaces), and not at the end of a trench-like street' [p. 44]. Moreover, in order to allow the health-giving rays of the sun to stream in through this opening throughout the day, he advised the inhabitants of these apartments to install fully retractable shutters rather than curtains 'for blocking out the light at will' or when privacy is necessary (p. 44). In at least two scenes in *All That Heaven Allows*, we can't help but notice that Ron has equipped the large window that has been inserted into the wall of the Old Mill with wooden shutters that fold back out of sight, just as the architect had suggested.

Finally, during the 1920s and early '30s window mullions would still have been necessary to support the many panes of glass that would have been needed to create this type of transparent wall. It is this kind of gridiron fenestration that Ron installs in the Old Mill, despite the fact that *All That Heaven Allows* was set in the 1950s. By this time, walls covered in larger sheets of unobstructed glass had become commonplace, but the tree-farmer's renovations seem to allude to an earlier period when Modernist architects were committed to more radical social change.

31. Le Corbusier, *Precisions*, 139.
32. Le Corbusier, *Precisions*, 83.
33. Le Corbusier, *The Decorative Art of Today*, 188. Ripolin is the name of a French-manufactured brand of whitewash.

34. Le Corbusier, *The Decorative Arts of Today*, 192.
35. Le Corbusier, *The Decorative Arts of Today*, 188.
36. Box 438, File 13221 of the Universal-International Pictures archives.
37. This typescript may be located in Box 434, File 12901 of the Universal-International Pictures archives.
38. The memo that speculates on the possibility of getting an article on the conversion of the Old Mill placed in a home decorating magazine also includes the following statement: 'Perhaps can get sketches from art department to show how it was done – "before and after"' [Box 434, File 12901, Universal-International Pictures archives].
39. 'Why the Movies are influencing American taste', *House Beautiful*, 84 (July/August 1942), 36, 37.
40. 'Why Movies are Influencing American taste', 37.
41. 'Why Movies are Influencing American taste', 36, 37.
42. 'We call it: "Hollywood Provincial"', *House Beautiful*, 84 (July/August 1942), 38, 39.
43. I didn't find any of these illustrations reproduced in a contemporary American home decorating magazine, even though I looked through every issue that *Better Homes and Gardens*, *House Beautiful*, *American Home*, *Interiors* and *Arts and Architecture* produced between 1953 and 1955. Therefore, to the best of my knowledge, none of these sketches was actually published.
44. This was Joseph A. Barry's definition of 'modern, *organic* architecture'. See page 232 of 'How Modern Architecture is returning to the Midwest'.
45. 'A Center of Living for the Whole Family', *House Beautiful*, 98, No. 11 (November 1955), 204.
46. Thoreau argues that certain bodies of water perform a similar function in *Walden*. After declaring 'A lake is the landscape's most beautiful and expressive feature', he then describes it as 'the earth's eye' since by looking into it 'the beholder measures the depth of his own nature'. See *Walden*, 243.
47. Railway tickets were quite costly, which meant that only relatively wealthy people could afford to travel to their jobs in the city utilising this mode of transport. As Kenneth T. Jackson has noted, 'horsecars ... offered more frequent and less expensive service to outlying towns, but the railroads were twice as fast and their accommodations much more comfortable' [*Crabgrass Frontier*, pp. 101–2].
48. John R. Stilgoe, *Borderland: Origins of the American Suburb* (New Haven: Yale University Press, 1988), 27–37.
49. Lutz Koepnick, *The Dark Mirror: German Cinema Between Hitler and Hollywood* (Berkeley: University of California Press, 2002), 209.
50. William Butler, 'Another City Upon a Hill: Litchfield, Connecticut, and the Colonial Revival', in *The Colonial Revival in America*, ed. Alan Axelrod (New York: Norton, 1985), 15. Butler attributes this post-1876 New England dominance of Colonial architecture to two main factors; firstly, most architects thought that the earliest buildings erected on the north-eastern seaboard were the oldest in the country and therefore the most American, and secondly,

that portion of the nation had just established its supremacy in a bloody civil war.

51. The official reason for Sarah's cocktail party was to celebrate Tom Allenby's engagement to Jo-Anne Frisby, a beautiful Southern gold-digger. Unlike in Ron and Carey's relationship, the fact that Tom, a wealthy upper-class businessman, has decided to wed a much younger and poorer woman is not considered to be a violation of bourgeois etiquette. It is only when the gender roles are reversed, and an older, more affluent woman expresses a desire to marry a more youthful, less well-off man, that the Stoningham elite will decide that its standards have been breached. After Carey brings Ron as her escort to this semi-public event, the widow and her children are so relentlessly disparaged by the other members of their community that she will finally call off her marriage.
52. Butler, 24–5. 'Light yellow ochre, pale pearl grays and various shades of off-white' only became popular as part of the 'later neoclassical or federal aesthetic' around the beginning of the nineteenth century, according to Butler. He goes on to say, 'the stark white that is so familiar to us today was, in fact, first produced during the colonial revival' [p. 31].
53. Butler, 18–19.
54. Butler, 39. He notes that Litchfield had 'attracted worldwide recognition in 1913' when it became the first town in America to attempt to 'colonialize' its whole inventory of historic architecture and landscapes (p. 21).
55. Butler, 39–43.
56. Butler, 20.
57. Butler, 20.
58. Butler 20, 33, 36.
59. David Gebhard, 'The American Colonial Revival of the Mid 1930s', *Winterthur Portfolio* 22 nos 2/3 (Summer–Autumn 1987), pp. 120–34.
60. Robert Woods Kennedy, 101–4.
61. W. Lloyd Warner and Paul S. Lunt, *The Social Life of the Modern Community* (New Haven: Yale University Press, 1941), p. 107, quoted by Kennedy p. 100. The Chippendale chairs that are visible in Carey's entrance hall are also emblematic of upper-class status, according to Celia Betsky ['Inside the Past: The Interior and the Colonial Revival in American Art and Literature, 1860–1914' in ed. Alan Axelrod, *The Colonial Revival in America* (New York: Norton, 1985), 249]. By contrast, the Old Mill is furnished with the simple ladder back chairs that were associated with the Puritans, the Shakers and the Quakers, all of whom disdained displays of material wealth.
62. Warner and Lunt, 107, quoted by Kennedy, 100.
63. Kennedy, 99.
64. Celia Betsky has described this changing perception of the Colonial period as a 'shift from . . . "the goodwife spinning in the kitchen" to the "high-heeled aristocratic and wealthy woman" who was "accustomed to pedal the harpsichord, but who had slight acquaintance with the spinning wheel"' [p. 266].
65. Alan Gowans, *Images of American Living*, 164–8. Stoningham's country club,

the private institution that had replaced the public town hall as the preferred meeting place for Carey's select group of friends, also exhibits a number of Adams-Federal traits. For example, the combination of white panelled wainscoting and white painted trim around the arched doorway with the coloured walls that is visible in the first room we see is a residual trace of this style. In terms of its meaning, the juxtaposition of an exterior shot of a sign stating 'Stoningham Country Club – For Members Exclusively' with a shot of this interior immediately establishes an association between the insular prejudices revealed in this message and the Adams-Federal décor. Moreover, on page 171 of the above book Gowans went on to describe this style as 'an expression of a rising class of capitalists and merchants' intent upon becoming a 'new aristocracy'. Hence, in the context of *All That Heaven Allows* it discloses the sense of entitlement that many of the Stoningham country club's set seem to feel. Within this space, Howard will attempt to seduce Carey for the first time, despite the fact that he has a sick wife waiting for him at home.

66. Le Corbusier, *The Decorative Arts of Today*, 189. According to Robert Woods Kennedy, Modernists were still describing houses built in more traditional styles as 'mausoleums' in 1953. See his 'The Style of Life', 99.
67. Unlike the Old Mill, where neither Ron nor Carey ever appear to close the internal shutters for privacy, the windows in the widow's own home are covered by curtains to protect those inside from the relentless neighbourhood scrutiny. Paradoxically, these flimsy barriers also make the house's inhabitants seem much more walled in. In one crucial scene Carey draws the drapes across her bedroom window just as Kay launches into a speech about not believing in that 'old Egyptian custom' of burying widows alive with their dead husbands.
68. The spectator observes Carey's son through the mullions of the same window on the night Ron escorts her to Sarah's party. We see Ned loitering in the living room, waiting for his mother's return in order to express his low opinion of her fiancé. His disapproval of Carey's impending marriage is so strong that he threatens to never to visit her again if she actually goes through with the ceremony. The interposition of these wooden bars between the viewer and Ned throughout much of this scene implies that his judgement has been shackled by an upper-class prejudice against men who work with their hands.
69. Kenneth T. Jackson has noted that the development of the mowing machine in the mid-nineteenth century made possible the advent of the smooth suburban lawn, which replaced 'the rough meadow cut by scythe or sheep' [*Crabgrass Frontier*, p. 54]. Since 'the ideal house came to be viewed as resting in the middle ... of a picturesque garden' or park, houses in an American suburb were not generally enclosed by the fortified walls or iron gates that would have undermined this semi-rural aesthetic (pp. 55, 59).
70. Michel Foucault, 'The Eye of Power', in *Power/Knowledge: Selected Interviews and Other Writings, 1972–1977* (New York: Pantheon Books, 1980), 147.
71. Dr Joseph E. Howland, 'Good Living is NOT Public Living', *House Beautiful*, 92, No. 1 (January 1950), 30–1, 'Do Your Neighbours Know Your Business?',

same issue, 32–3, 'Is There a Picture in Your Picture Window?', same issue, 34–5.
72. William M. Dobriner, *Class in Suburbia* (Englewood Cliffs, NJ: Prentice-Hall, 1963), 9.
73. Jane Jacobs, *The Death and Life of Great American Cities* (New York: Vintage Books, 1961), 64–8.
74. Jacobs, 63.
75. Jacobs, 62.
76. Jacobs, 64–5. Jacobs contends that public space no longer exists in planned garden city communities such as 'Chatham Village in Pittsburgh'. Whatever activities take place in the shared 'interior lawns and play yards . . . [and the] residents' club which holds parties, dances and reunions . . . [t]here is no public life here in any city sense [just] differing degrees of extended private life' [p. 64].
77. Erwin Panofsky, '*Et in Arcadia Ego*: Poussin and the Elegiac Tradition' in *Meaning in the Visual Arts* (Garden City, NY: Doubleday Anchor Books, 1955), 300.
78. Panofsky, 300.
79. Geoffrey Scott, *The Architecture of Humanism: A Study in the History of Taste* (New York: Norton, 1999), 160–77.

Bibliography

'A Center of Living for the Whole Family'. *House Beautiful*, 98, No. 11 (November 1955), pp. 204–7, 260–2.

Adam, Peter. *The Arts of the Third Reich*. London: Thames & Hudson, 1992.

Adas, Michael. *Machines as the Measure of Man: Science, Technology and the Ideology of Western Domination*. Ithaca: Cornell University Press, 1989.

Adorno, Theodor. 'The Form of the Phonograph Record'. *October*, No. 55 (Winter 1990), pp. 56–66.

Adorno, Theodor. 'Functionalism Today'. *Oppositions*, No. 17 (Summer 1979), pp. 31–41.

'All That Heaven Allows – Campaign Ideas'. Ts. Box 434, File 12901, Universal-International Pictures Archives. University of Southern California, Los Angeles.

'All That Heaven Allows – Production Notes'. Ts. Box 451, File 12648, Universal-International Pictures Archives. University of Southern California, Los Angeles.

Allen, Frederick Lewis. 'The Big Change in Suburbia, Part I'. *Harper's Magazine*, 208, No. 1,249 (June 1954), pp. 21–8.

Ames, Kenneth. 'Introduction'. In *The Colonial Revival in America*, ed. Kenneth Ames. New York: Norton, 1985, 1–14.

Arnheim, Rudolf. *Film as Art*. Berkeley: University of California Press, 1957.

Banham, Reyner. '*Ateliers d'artistes*: Paris Studio Houses and the Modern Movement'. *Architectural Review*, 120 (August 1956), pp. 74–83.

Banham, Reyner. 'The Glass Paradise'. In *Design By Choice*. New York: Rizzoli, 1981, pp. 29–33.

Banham, Reyner. *Theory and Design in the First Machine Age*. 1960; repr. Cambridge, MA: MIT Press, 1980.

banker. 'Press release dated 9/12/58 [for *Imitation of Life*]'. Ts. Box 696, File 23704, Universal-International Pictures Archives. University of Southern California, Los Angeles.

Barry, Joseph A. 'The Architecture of Humanism'. *House Beautiful*, 95 (November 1953), pp. 224–7, 326, 329–31.

Barry, Joseph A. 'How Modern Architecture is Returning to the Middle West'. *House Beautiful*, 96, No. 11 (November 1954), pp. 232–9, 297, 299.

Barry, Joseph A. 'Report on the American Battle between Good and Bad Design'. *House Beautiful*, 95 (May 1953), pp. 172–3, 266, 270–3.

Barzun, Jacques. 'What Time the Good Life?' *The Atlantic Monthly*, 177, No. 2 (February 1946), 71–4.

Baxandall, Rosalyn and Elizabeth Ewen. *Picture Windows: How the Suburbs Happened*. New York: Basic Books, 2000.

Benjamin, Walter. 'On Some Motifs in Baudelaire'. In *Illuminations*. New York: Schocken Books, 1968, pp. 155–200.

Benjamin, Walter. 'One-Way Street (Selection)'. In *Reflections: Essays, Aphorisms, Autobiographical Writings*, ed Peter Demetz. New York: Schocken Books, 1986, pp. 61–94.
Benjamin, Walter. 'Theories of German Fascism'. *New German Critique*, No. 17 (Spring 1979), pp. 120–8.
Benjamin, Walter. 'The Work of Art in the Age of Mechanical Reproduction'. In *Illuminations*. New York: Schocken Books, 1969, pp. 217–51.
Benton, Charlotte and Tim. 'The Style and the Age'. In *Art Deco: 1910–1939*. London: V & A Publications, 2003, pp. 12–27.
Besant, Annie. *A Study in Consciousness*. 1904; repr. Adyar: Theosophical Publishing House, 1967.
Betsky, Celia. 'Inside the Past: The Interior and the Colonial Revival in American Art and Literature, 1860–1914'. In *The Colonial Revival in America*, ed. Alan Axelrod. New York: Norton, 1985, pp. 241–77.
Beyer, Torsten, and Sabine Danek. 'Beyond Cinema'. *Sight and Sound* (July 1994, Special Supplement entitled *Art into Film*), pp. 18–19.
Biddle, George. 'Modern Art and Muddled Thinking'. *Atlantic Monthly*, 180, No. 6 (1947), pp. 58–61.
Biddle, George. 'The Victory and Defeat of Modernism: Art in a New World'. *Harper's Magazine*, 187, No. 1,117 (1943), pp. 32–7.
Biette, Jean-Claude and Dominique Rabourdin. 'Entretien avec Douglas Sirk'. *Cinema*, No. 238 (1978), pp. 10–23.
Blavatsky, H. P. *Collected Writings 1888: The Secret Doctrine*. Volume II. Adyar: Theosophical Publishing House, 1979.
Bletter, Rosemarie Haag. 'Expressionism and the New Objectivity'. *Art Journal*, 43 (1983), pp. 108–20.
Bletter, Rosemarie Haag. 'The Interpretation of the Glass Dream – Expressionist Architecture and the History of the Crystal Metaphor'. *Journal of the Society of Architectural Historians*, 40 (1981), pp. 20–43.
Bloch, Ernst. 'II. Buildings on Hollow Space'. In *The Principle of Hope*. Volume II. Cambridge, MA: MIT Press, 1986, pp. 733–7.
Bloch, Ernst. 'C. Non-Contemporaneity and Contemporaneity, Philosophically'. In *Heritage of Our Times*. Cambridge: Polity Press, 1991, pp. 104–16.
Bloch, Ernst. 'Nonsynchronism and its Obligation to Its Dialectics'. *New German Critique*, No. 11 (Spring 1977), pp. 22–38.
Bloch, Ernst. *A Philosophy of the Future*. New York: Herder & Herder, 1970.
Bloch, Ernst. 'Transition: Berlin Functions in Hollow Space'. In *Heritage of Our Times*. Cambridge: Polity Press, 1991, pp. 195–208.
Bloch, Ernst. *The Utopian Function of Art and Literature*. Cambridge, MA: MIT Press, 1988.
Bourget, Jean-Loup. 'God is Dead, or Through a Glass Darkly'. *Bright Lights*, No. 6 (1977–8). <http://www.brightlightsfilm.com/48/sirkgodis.htm> (last accessed 17 October 2005).
Boyer, M. Christine. *Dreaming the Rational City: The Myth of American Planning*. Cambridge, MA: MIT Press, 1983.
Brecht, Bertolt. *Brecht on Theatre*. New York: Hill & Wang, 1964.
Brooks, Peter. *The Melodramatic Imagination: Balzac, Henry James, Melodrama and the Mode of Excess*. New Haven: Yale University Press, 1976.
Butler, William. 'Another City upon a Hill: Litchfield, Connecticut and the Colonial Revival Movement'. In *The Colonial Revival in America*, ed. Alan Axelrod. New York: Norton, 1985), pp. 15–51.

Campbell, Bruce F. *Ancient Wisdom Revived: A History of the Theosophy Movement*. Berkeley: University of California Press, 1980.

Camper, Fred. 'The Films of Douglas Sirk'. *Screen*, 12, No. 2 (Summer 1971), pp. 44–62.

'CIAM: La Sarraz Declaration'. In *Programmes and Manifestoes on 20th Century Architecture*, ed. Ulrich Conrads. London: Lund Humphreys, 1970, pp. 109–13.

Class, Heinrich, 'Americanism'. In *The Nazi Years: A Documentary History*, ed. Joachim Remak. Englewood Cliffs, NJ: Prentice-Hall, 1969, pp. 11–12.

Clelland, Doug. 'Berlin: An Architectural History'. *Architectural Design Profile*, No. 5 (1983), pp. 5–15.

Combined Showman's Manual [*Flower Drum Song* and *Imitation of Life*]. Universal-International Pictures Archives. University of Southern California, Los Angeles.

'Continuity Breakdown for *Written on the Wind*'. Ts. Box 175, File 05459, Universal-International Pictures Archives. University of Southern California, Los Angeles.

Cook, Nicholas. *Beethoven: Symphony Number Nine*. Cambridge: Cambridge University Press, 1993.

Crary, Jonathan. *Suspension of Perception: Attention, Spectacle and Modern Culture*. Cambridge, MA: MIT Press, 1999.

Crary, Jonathan. *Techniques of the Observer: On Vision and Modernity in the Nineteenth Century*. Cambridge, MA: MIT Press, 1991.

Curtis, William. *Modern Architecture Since 1900*. Oxford: Phaidon Press, 1987.

Dalle Vacche, Angela. *Cinema and Painting: How Art Is Used in Film*. Austin: University of Texas Press, 1996.

Daney, Serge and Jean-Louis Noames. 'Entretien avec Douglas Sirk'. *Cahiers du Cinéma*, 189 (1967), 19–20, 23–5, 67–70.

Davenport, Russell W. 'A *Life* Round Table on Modern Art: Fifteen Distinguished Critics and Connoisseurs Undertake to Clarify the Strange Art of Today'. *Life*, 25, No. 15 (11 October 1948), 56–68, 70, 75, 78–9.

Davis, Mike. *City of Quartz*. New York: Vintage, 1990.

Davis, Stuart. 'What About Modern Art and Democracy?' *Harper's Magazine*, 188, No. 1,123 (1943–4), pp. 16–23.

Deleuze, Gilles. *Cinema 2: The Time-Image*. Minneapolis: University of Minnesota Press, 1989.

Denton, Nancy A. and Douglas S. Massey. *American Apartheid: Segregation and the Making of the Urban Underclass*. Cambridge, MA: Harvard University Press, 1993.

Dimendberg, Edward. 'From Berlin to Bunker Hill: Urban Space, Late Modernity and Film Noir in Fritz Lang's and Joseph Losey's *M*'. *Wide Angle*, 19, No. 4 (October 1997), pp. 63–93.

Dobriner, William. *Class in Suburbia*. Englewood Cliffs, NJ: Prentice-Hall, 1963.

Donmoyer, Deidra and Tina M. Harris. 'Is Art Imitating Life?: Communicating Gender and Racial Identity in *Imitation of Life*'. *Women's Studies in Communication*, 23, No. 1 (Winter 2000), pp. 91–110.

'Do Your Neighbours Know Your Business?' *House Beautiful*, 92, No. 1 (January 1950), pp. 32–3.

Douglas, Lloyd C. *Magnificent Obsession*. 1936; repr. London: Allen & Unwin, 1952.

Drexler, Arthur and Henry-Russell Hitchcock. *Built in the U.S.A.: Post-War Architecture*. New York: Museum of Modern Art, 1952.

Duncan, Alistair. *Art Deco*. London: Thames & Hudson, 1988.

Durkheim, Émile. *Suicide: A Study in Sociology*. New York: Free Press, 1951.

Eisenstein, Sergei. 'Montage 1938'. In *Eisenstein, Volume 2: Towards a Theory of Montage*, ed. Michael Glenny and Richard Taylor. London: British Film Institute, 1991, pp. 297–326.

Eisenstein, Sergei. 'Unity in the Image'. In *Eisenstein, Volume 2: Towards a Theory of Montage*, ed. Michael Glenny and Richard Taylor. London: British Film Institute, 1991, pp. 268–80.

Eksteins, Modris. *Rites of Spring: The Great War and the Birth of the Modern Age*. London: Bantam Press, 1989.

Elsaesser, Thomas, trans. 'Documents on Sirk: With a Postscript by Thomas Elsaesser'. *Screen*, 12, No. 2 (1971), pp. 15–28.

Elsaesser, Thomas. 'Hollywood/Berlin'. *Sight and Sound*, 7, No. 11 (November 1997), pp. 14–17.

Elsaesser, Thomas. 'Tales of Sound and Fury: Observations on the Family Melodrama'. In *Imitations of Life: A Reader on Film, Television and Melodrama*, ed. Marcia Landry. Detroit: Wayne State University Press, 1991, pp. 68–90.

Elsaesser, Thomas. *Weimar Cinema and After: Germany's Historical Imaginary*. London: Routledge, 2000.

Evans, Bergen. 'Look Out, Here I Come!' *The Atlantic Monthly*, 178, No. 6 (December 1946), 119–21.

Farley, Reynolds et al. '"Chocolate City, Vanilla Suburbs": Will the Trend towards Racially Separate Communities Continue?' *Social Science Research*, 7 (1978), pp. 319–44.

Fassbinder, Rainer Werner. 'Six Films by Douglas Sirk'. In *The Marriage of Maria Braun*, ed. Joyce Rheuban. New Brunswick, NJ: Rutgers University Press, 1986, pp. 197–207.

Faulkner, William. *Pylon*. London: Chatto & Windus, 1955.

Fava, Sylvia Fleiss. 'Suburbanism as a Way of Life'. *American Sociological Review*, 21, No. 1 (February 1956), pp. 34–7.

Ferriss, Hugh. *The Metropolis of Tomorrow*. 1929; repr. Princeton: Princeton University Press, 1986.

Fineman, Mia. '*Ecce Homo Prostheticus*'. *New German Critique*, No. 76 (Winter 1999), 85–114.

Fischer, Lucy. 'Sirk and the Figure of the Actress: *All I Desire*'. *Film Criticism*, 23, No. 2/3 (Winter/Spring 1999), pp. 136–49.

Fischer, Lucy. 'Three-Way Mirror: Imitation of Life'. In *Imitation of Life*, ed. Lucy Fischer. New Brunswick, NJ: Rutgers University Press, 1991, pp. 2–28.

Fisher, Philip. 'Democratic Social Spaces: Whitman, Melville and the Promise of American Transparency'. In *The New American Studies: Essays from Representations*, ed. Philip Fisher. Berkeley: University of California Press, 1991, pp. 70–111.

Fishman, Robert. *Bourgeois Utopias: The Rise and Fall of Suburbia*. New York: Basic Books, 1987.

Fitch, James Marston. 'Frank Lloyd Wright's Contribution to Your Daily Life'. *House Beautiful*, 98, No. 11 (November 1955), 265–9, 367–71.

Foucault, Michel. 'The Eye of Power'. In *Power/Knowledge: Selected Interviews and Other Writings, 1972–1977*. New York: Pantheon, 1980, pp. 146–65.

Fred R. Kline Gallery, Sante Fe, New Mexico. 'George Biddle'. 15 November 2005 <http://www.klinegallery.com/Biddle01_Bio.html> (last accessed 15 November 2005).

Fried, Michael. *Absorption and Theatricality: Painting and Beholder in the Age of Diderot*. Berkeley: University of California Press, 1980.

Fried, Michael. *Courbet's Realism*. Chicago: University of Chicago Press, 1990.

Fritsche, Peter. 'Landscape of Danger, Landscape of Design: Crisis and Modernism in Weimar Germany'. In *Dancing on the Volcano: Essays in the Culture of the Weimar Republic*, ed. Thomas Kniesche and Stephen Brockmann. Columbia, SC: Camden House, 1994, pp. 29–46.

Fritsche, Peter. 'Machine Dreams: Airmindedness and the Reinvention of Germany'. *The American Historical Review*, 98, No. 3 (June 1993), pp. 685–709.

Fritsche, Peter. 'Nazi Modern'. *Modernism/Modernity*, 3, No. 1 (1996), pp. 1–22.

Gebhard, David. 'The American Colonial Revival of the Mid 1930s'. *Winterthur Portfolio*, 22, Nos 2/3 (Summer–Autumn 1987), pp. 109–48.

Giedion, Siegfried. 'Le Probleme du luxe dans l'architecture moderne'. *Cahiers des Arts*, Nos 5/6 (1928), 254–6.

Giedion, Siegfried. 'The New House'. In *Le Corbusier in Perspective*, ed. Peter Serenyi. Englewood Cliffs, NJ: Prentice-Hall, 1975, pp. 32–4.

Giovanni, Joseph. 'The Office of Charles Eames and Ray Kaiser: The Material Trail'. In *The Work of Charles and Ray Eames: A Legacy of Invention*, ed. Diana Murphy. New York: Harry Abrams, 1997, pp. 45–71.

Goldberger, Paul. *New York: The City Observed*. Harmondsworth: Penguin, 1979.

Goodnough, Robert. 'Pollock Paints a Picture'. *Art News*, 50 (May 1951), pp. 38–41, 58–9.

Gordon, Elizabeth. 'The Threat to the Next America'. *House Beautiful*, 95 (April 1953), pp. 126–31, 250–1.

Gowans, Alan. *The Comfortable House: North American Suburban Architecture 1890–1930*. Cambridge, MA: MIT Press, 1986.

Gowans, Alan. *Images of American Living: Four Centuries of Furniture and Architecture as Cultural Expression*. New York: Harper & Row, 1976.

Grosz, George. *The Autobiography of George Grosz: A Small Yes and a Big No*. London: Allison & Busby, 1982.

Hake, Sabine. 'The Melodramatic Imagination of Detlef Sierck: *Final Chord* and its Resonances'. *Screen*, 8, No. 2 (1997), pp. 129–48.

Hake, Sabine. *Popular Cinema of the Third Reich*. Austin: University of Texas Press, 2001.

Halliday, Jon. *Sirk on Sirk*. London: Faber & Faber, 1997, rev. edn.

Hansen, Miriam Bratu. 'The Mass Production of the Senses: Classical Cinema as Vernacular Modernism'. *Modernism/Modernity*, 6, No. 2 (1999), pp. 59–77.

Harlovitch, Mary Beth. 'All That Heaven Allows: Color, Narrative Space and Drama'. In *Close Viewings: An Anthology of New Film Criticism*, ed. Peter Lehman. Tallahassee: Florida State University Press, 1990, pp. 57–72.

Harvey, James. 'Interview with Douglas Sirk: Lugano, July 1977'. Ts. Douglas Sirk Clipping File, Museum of Modern Art, New York, pp. 1–24.

Harvey, James. 'Sirkumstantial Evidence'. *Film Comment*, 14, No. 4 (1978), pp. 52–9.

Hayward, Philip. 'Echoes and Reflections: The Representation of Representations'. In *Picture This: Media Representations of Visual Art and Artists*, ed. Philip Hayward. London: John Libbey, 1988, pp. 2–25.

Henry, Michael, and Yann Tobin. 'Entretien avec Douglas Sirk'. *Positif*, No. 259 (1982), pp. 23–31.

Herf, Jeffrey. *Reactionary Modernism: Technology, culture, and politics in Weimar and the Third Reich*. Cambridge: Cambridge University Press, 1984.

Henderson, Harry. 'Rugged American Collectivism: The Mass-Produced Suburbs, Part II'. *Harper's Magazine*, 207, No. 1,243 (December 1953), 80–6.

Heung, Marina. 'What's the Matter with Sarah Jane?: Daughters and Mothers in Sirk's *Imitation of Life*'. In *Imitation of Life*, ed. Lucy Fischer. New Brunswick, NJ: Rutgers University Press, 1991, pp. 302–24.

Heynen, Hilde. *Architecture and Modernity*. Cambridge, MA: MIT Press, 1999.

Hirsch, Foster. *Kurt Weill on Stage: From Berlin to Broadway*. New York: Knopf, 2002.

Hitler, Adolf. *Mein Kampf*. Boston: Houghton Mifflin, 1943.

Hitler, Adolf. *The Speeches of Adolf Hitler, April 1922–August 1939*, ed. Norman H. Baynes. Oxford: Oxford University Press, 1942.

Howland, Dr Joseph E. 'Good Living is NOT Public Living'. *House Beautiful*, 92, No. 1 (January 1950), pp. 30–1.

Huyssen, Andreas. *After the Great Divide: Modernism, Mass Culture, Postmodernism*. Bloomington: Indiana University Press, 1986.

Huyssen, Andreas. 'Fortifying the Heart: Ernst Jünger's Armoured Texts'. *New German Critique*, No. 39 (Spring–Summer 1993), pp. 3–23.

'Is There a Picture in Your Picture Window?' *House Beautiful*, 92, No. 1 (January 1950), pp. 33–5.

Iversen, Margaret. *Alois Riegl: Art History and Theory*. Cambridge, MA: MIT Press, 1993.

'Jackson Pollock'. *Arts and Architecture*, 61, No. 2 (February 1944), pp. 14–15.

Jackson, Kenneth T. *Crabgrass Frontier: The Suburbanization of the United States*. Oxford: Oxford University Press, 1985.

Jacobs, Jane. *The Death and Life of Great American Cities*. New York: Vintage, 1961.

Jameson, Fredric. 'The Constraints of Postmodernism (Extract)'. In *Rethinking Architecture: A Reader in Cultural Theory*, ed. Neil Leach. London: Routledge, 1997, pp. 247–55.

Jelavich, Peter. *Berlin Alexaderplatz: Radio, Film and the Death of the Weimar Republic*. Berkeley: University of California Press, 2006.

Johnson, Erkine. 'Excerpt from a 15 minute TV show called *Hollywood Spotlight* – 2nd Episode featuring *All I Desire*. Eskine Johnson interviews various members of the technical staff'. Ts. Box 391, File 04404, Universal-International Pictures Archives. University of Southern California, Los Angeles.

Jünger, Ernst. 'On Danger'. *New German Critique*, No. 59 (Spring–Summer 1993), pp. 27–32.

Jünger, Ernst. *Storm of Steel*. London: Allen Lane, 2003.

Jünger, Ernst. 'War and Photography'. *New German Critique*, No. 59 (Spring–Summer 1993), pp. 24–6.

Kallai, Ernst. 'Ten Years of the Bauhaus'. In *Form and Function: A Source Book for the History of Architecture and Design 1890–1939*, ed. Tim and Charlotte Benton. London: Open University Press, 1975, pp. 172–5.

Kandinsky, Wassily and Franz Marc, eds. *The Blaue Reiter Almanac*. 1914; repr. New York: Da Capo Press, 1974.

Kandinsky, Wassily and Franz Marc, eds. *Concerning the Spiritual in Art*. 1914; repr. New York: Dover, 1977.

Kandinsky, Wassily and Franz Marc, eds. 'Reminiscences/Three Pictures'. In *Kandinsky: Complete Writings on Art*. Volume I. London: Faber & Faber, pp. 355–91.

Kant, Immanuel. *Critique of Judgement*. New York: Hafner Press, 1951.

Kaufmann Jr., Edgar. 'Precedent and Progress in the Work of Frank Lloyd Wright'. In *Nine Commentaries on Frank Lloyd Wright*. Cambridge, MA: MIT Press, 1989, pp. 67–74.

Kellogg, Susan. *Domestic Revolutions: A Social History of American Life*. New York: Free Press, 1988.

Kennedy, Robert Woods. 'The Style of Life'. *Magazine of Art*, 46, No. 3 (March 1953), pp. 99–107.

Kirstein, Lincoln. 'The State of Modern Painting'. *Harper's Magazine*, 197, No. 1,181 (1948), pp. 47–53.

Klinger, Barbara. *Melodrama and Meaning: History, Culture and the Films of Douglas Sirk*. Bloomington: Indiana University Press, 1994.

Koepnick, Lutz. *The Dark Mirror: German Cinema between Hitler and Hollywood*. Berkeley: University of California Press, 2002.

Kracauer, Siegfried. 'The Mass Ornament'. In *The Mass Ornament: Weimar Essays*. Cambridge, MA: Harvard University Press, 1995, pp. 75–86.

Koch, Gertrud. 'From Detlef Sierck to Douglas Sirk'. *Film Criticism*, 23, No. 1 (Fall 1998), pp. 14–32.

Larrabee, Eric. 'The Six Thousand Houses that Levitt Built'. *Harper's Magazine*, 197, No. 1,180, pp. 79–88.

Lastra, James. 'From the Captured Moment to the Cinematic Image: A Transformation in Pictorial Order'. In *The Image in Dispute: Art and Cinema in the Age of Dispute*, ed. Dudley Andrew. Austin: University of Texas Press, 1997, pp. 263–91.

Le Corbusier. *The City of Tomorrow and Its Planning*. 1929; repr. New York: Dover, 1987.

Le Corbusier. *The Decorative Arts of Today*. 1925; trans. London: Architectural Press, 1987.

Le Corbusier and Françoise de Pierrefeu. *The Home of Man*. London: Architectural Press, 1948.

Le Corbusier and Françoise de Pierrefeu. *Precisions: On the Present State of Architecture and City Planning*. 1930; trans. Cambridge, MA: MIT Press, 1991.

Le Corbusier and Françoise de Pierrefeu. *The Radiant City*. 1933; repr. London: Faber & Faber, 1967.

Le Corbusier and Françoise de Pierrefeu. 'The Spirit of Truth'. In *French Film Theory and Criticism. Volume 2, 1929–1939*, ed. Richard Abel. Princeton: Princeton University Press, 1988, pp. 111–14.

Le Corbusier and Françoise de Pierrefeu. *Towards a New Architecture*. 1927; repr. London: Architectural Press, 1946.

Lehman, Peter. 'Thinking With The Heart: An Interview with Douglas Sirk'. *Wide Angle*, 3, No. 4 (1978), pp. 42–7.

Levin, Gail and Marianne Lorenz. *Theme and Improvisation: Kandinsky and the American Avant-garde 1912–1950*. Boston: Little, Brown, 1992.

Lipsitz, George. *The Possessive Investment in Whiteness: How White People Profit From Identity Politics*. Philadelphia: Temple University Press, 1998.

Lockwood, Charles. *Bricks and Brownstone: The New York Row House, 1783–1829*. New York: Abbeville Press, 1972.

Loos, Adolf. 'Ornament and Crime'. In *The Architecture of Adolf Loos*, ed. Yehude Safran and Wilfred Wang. London: Arts Council of Great Britain, 1985, pp. 100–3.

'"*Magnificent Obsession*" – *Campaign Ideas* – A. Movies are Growing Up'. Ts. Box 414, File 12352, Universal-International Pictures Archives. University of Southern California, Los Angeles.

Maier, Charles S. 'Between Taylorism and Technocracy: European Ideologies and the Vision of Industrial Productivity in the 1920s'. *Journal of Contemporary History*, 5, No. 2 (1970), pp. 27–61.

Marks, Laura U. *The Skin of Film: Intercultural Cinema, Embodiment and the Senses*. Durham, NC and London: Duke University Press, 2000.

Marx, Leo. *The Machine in the Garden: Technology and the Pastoral Ideal in America*. Oxford: Oxford University Press, 1964.

May, Elaine. *Homeward Bound: American Families in the Cold War Era*. New York: Basic Books, 1988.

McElhaney, Joe. 'Vincent Minnelli'. *Senses of the Cinema* 2004, 7 April 2005.<www.sensesofcinema.com/2004/great-directors/minnelli/> (last accessed 7 April 2005).

Mcleod, Mary. 'Undressing Architecture: Fashion, Gender and Modernity'. In *Architecture in Fashion*, ed. Deborah Fausch et al. Princeton: Princeton University Press, 1991, pp. 38–123.

Mock, Elizabeth, Ed. *Built in the U.S.A*. New York: Museum of Modern Art, 1944.

Moffitt, Jack. 'All That Heaven Allows Strong on Popular Appeal'. *The Hollywood Reporter*, 25

October 1955. Box 440, File 13494, Universal-International Pictures Archives. University of Southern California, Los Angeles.

Moholy-Nagy, Laslo. 'Constructivism and the Proletariat'. In *Moholy-Nagy*, ed. Richard Kostelanetz. London: Allen Lane/Penguin, 1970, pp. 185–6.

Morey, Anne. 'A Star Has Died: Affect and Stardom in Domestic Melodrama'. *Quarterly Review of Film and Video*, 21 (2004), pp. 95–105.

Morgan. 'Press release for *Imitation of Life*, 5/9/58'. Ts. Box 696, File 23704, Universal-International Pictures Archives. University of Southern California, Los Angeles.

Moussinac, Leon. 'Cinema: *Fièvre, L'Atlantide, El Dorado*'. In *French Film Theory and Criticism*. Volume 1, 1907–1939, ed. Richard Abel. Princeton: Princeton University Press, 1988, pp. 249–55.

Müller, Lothar. 'The Beauty of the Metropolis: Toward an Aesthetic Urbanism in Turn-of-the-Century Berlin'. In *Berlin: Culture and Metropolis*, ed. Charles Haxthausen and Heldrun Suhr. Minneapolis: University of Minnesota Press, 1990, pp. 37–57.

Mumford, Lewis. *City Development: Studies in Disintegration and Renewal*. London: Secker & Warburg, 1946.

Mumford, Lewis. *The City in History: Its Origins, Its Transformations, and Its Prospects*. London: Secker & Warburg, 1961.

Mumford, Lewis. 'Megalopolis as Anti-City'. *Architectural Record*, 132, No. 6 (December 1962), 101–8.

Mulvey, Laura. *Death 24x a Second: Stillness and the Moving Image*. London: Reaktion Books, 2006.

Nelson, George. 'Modern Furniture: An Attempt to Explore Its Nature, Its Sources and Its Probable Future'. *Interiors*, 108, No. 12 (July 1949), 76–117.

Nerdinger, Winfried. 'Bauhaus Architecture in the Third Reich'. In *Bauhaus Culture: From Weimar to the Cold War*, ed. Kathleen James-Chakraborty. Minneapolis: University of Minnesota Press, 2006, pp. 139–52.

Neumann, Dietrich. 'The Urbanistic Vision in Fritz Lang's *Metropolis*'. In *Dancing on the Volcano: Essays in the Culture of the Weimar Republic*, ed. Thomas Kniesche and Stephen Brockmann. Columbia, SC: Camden House, 1994, pp. 142–62.

nicholas. 'Universal-International Pictures Press release for *Tarnished Angels*, dated 12 December 1957'. Ts. Box 483, File 14195, Universal-International Pictures Archives. University of Southern California, Los Angeles.

Nolan, Mary. 'Imagining America, Modernizing Germany'. In *Dancing on the Volcano: Essays on the Culture of the Weimar Republic*, ed. Thomas W. Kiesche et al. Columbia, SC: Camden House, 1994, pp. 71–84.

O'Connor, Jim. '"Magnificent Obsession": Dramatic, Exalted Film'. *New York Journal-American*, 5 August 1954, p. 13. Douglas Sirk Clipping File, Museum of Modern Art, New York.

Oechslin, Werner. 'Light Architecture: A New Term's Genesis'. In *Architecture of the Night: The Illuminated Building*, ed. Dietrich Neumann. Munich: Prestel, 2002, pp. 28–35.

'Old House Made New: A Huge Glass Wall Helps to Convert an Ancient Connecticut Farmhouse into a Modern Dwelling'. *Life* (International Edition), 4, No. 5 (1 March 1948), pp. 32–3.

Packard, Vance. *The Status Seekers*. Harmondsworth: Penguin, 1959.

Panofsky, Erwin. '*Et in Arcadia Ego*: Poussin and the Elegiac Tradition'. In *Meaning in the Visual Arts*. New York: Doubleday Anchor Books, 1955, pp. 295–320.

Peucker, Brigitte. *Incorporating Images: Film and the Rival Arts*. Princeton: Princeton University Press, 1995.

Poling, Clark V. *Kandinsky: Russian and Bauhaus Years, 1915–1933*. New York: Solomon Guggenheim Museum, 1983.

Pommer, Richard and Christian F. Otto. *Weissenhof 1927 and the Modern Movement in Architecture*. Chicago: University of Chicago Press, 1991.

Porter, Philip W. and Fred E. Lukermann. 'The Geography of Utopia'. In *Geographies of the Mind*, ed. David Lowenthal and Martyn J. Bowden. New York: Oxford University Press, 1976, pp. 197–223.

'Preview Reaction Cards [*All That Heaven Allows*]'. Ts. Box 508, File 14513, Universal-International Pictures Archives. University of Southern California, Los Angeles.

'Production notes for *Imitation of Life*'. Ts. Box 696, File 23704, Universal-International Pictures Archives. University of Southern California, Los Angeles.

'Production notes for *Written on the Wind*'. Ts. Box 424, File 11977, Universal-International Pictures Archives. University of Southern California, Los Angeles.

'Public Opinion on: "The Threat to the Next America"'. *House Beautiful*, 95 (June 1953), pp. 28–9, 91–5.

Pundt, Hermann G. *Schinkel's Berlin: A Study in Environmental Planning*. Cambridge, MA: Harvard University Press, 1972.

Purdy, Ken W. 'Why all the Interest in Sport Cars?' *Better Homes and Gardens*, 35, No. 5 (May 1957), pp. 227–8, 230–1, 261.

Reid, Dennis. *Atma Buddhi Manas: The Later Works of Lawren S. Harris*. Toronto: Art Gallery of Ontario, 1985.

Rentschler, Eric. *The Ministry of Illusion: Nazi Cinema and Its Afterlife*. Cambridge, MA: Harvard University Press, 1996.

'Report on Preview comments "Pylon" [dated 11/9/57]'. Ts. Box 510, File 14985, Universal-International Pictures Archives. University of Southern California, Los Angeles.

'Reports picked up from the theatre after the first sneak preview [of *Magnificent Obsession*], held Monday, January 11, 1954 at the Encino Theatre, Encino California'. Ts. Box 690, File 22500, Universal-International Pictures Archives. University of Southern California, Los Angeles.

'Review of *Magnificent Obsession*'. *Boxoffice* (8 May 1954). Box 528, File 15979, Universal-International Pictures Archives. University of Southern California, Los Angeles.

'Review of *Magnificent Obsession*'. *Motion Picture Daily* (11 May 1954). Box 528, File 15979, Universal-International Pictures Archives. University of Southern California, Los Angeles.

'Review of *Magnificent Obsession*'. *Variety* (12 May 1954). Box 528, File 15979, Universal-International Pictures Archives. University of Southern California, Los Angeles.

Rich, Daniel Catton. 'Freedom of the Brush'. *The Atlantic Monthly*, 181, No. 2 (February 1948), pp. 47–51.

Riegl, Alois. *The Group Portraiture of Holland*. Los Angeles: Getty Research Institute, 1999).

Riesman, David. 'The Suburban Sadness'. In *The Suburban Community*, ed. William Dobriner. New York: Putnam, 1958, pp. 375–408.

Ringbom, Sixten. '"The Epoch of the Great Spiritual": Occult Elements in the Early Theory of Abstract Painting'. *Journal of the Warburg and Courtauld Institutes*, 29 (1966), pp. 386–418.

Rosenberg, Harold. 'The American Action Painters'. *Art News*, 51 (December 1952), pp. 22–3, 48–50.

'Royal Barry Wills: Boston Architect Designs the Kind of Houses Most Americans Want'. *Life*, 21, No. 9 (26 August 1946), pp. 67–74.

Rubin, William S. *Dada, Surrealism and their Heritage*. New York: Museum of Modern Art, 1968.

Rutsky, R. L. 'The Mediation of Technology and Gender: Metropolis, Nazism, Modernism'. In *Fritz Lang's Metropolis: Cinematic Visions of Technology and Fear*, ed. Michael Minden and Holger Bachmann. Rochester: Camden House, 2000, pp. 216–45.

Schäche, Wolfgang. 'Nazi Architecture and Its Approach to Antiquity: A Criticism of the "Neoclassical" Argument, with Reference to the Berlin Museum Plans'. *Architectural Design Profile*, No. 5 (1983), pp. 81–8.

Schatz, Thomas. *Hollywood Genres: Formulas, Filmmaking and the Studio System*. Boston: McGraw-Hill, 1981.

Scherman, Thomas K. and Louis Biancoli, eds. *The Beethoven Companion*. New York: Doubleday, 1972.

Schulte-Sasse, Linda. 'Douglas Sirk's *Schlussakkord* and the Question of Aesthetic Resistance'. *The Germanic Review*, 73, No. 1 (Winter 1998), pp. 2–31.

Scott, Geoffrey. *The Architecture of Humanism: A Study in the History of Taste*. 1914; repr. New York: Norton, 1999.

Seiberling, Dorothy. 'Jackson Pollock: Is he the Greatest Living Painter in the United States?' *Life*, 27 (8 August 1949), pp. 42–3, 45.

Selig, Michael E. 'Contradiction and Reading: Social Class and Sex Class in *Imitation of Life*'. *Wide Angle*, 10, No. 4 (1988), pp. 13–23.

Shapiro, David and Cecile. 'Abstract Expressionism: The Politics of Apolitical Painting'. In *Pollock and After: The Critical Debate*, ed. Francis Frascina. New York: Harper & Row, 1985, pp. 135–51.

Shi, David. *The Simple Life: Plain Living and High Thinking in American Culture*. New York: Oxford University Press, 1985.

Showman's Manual [*All That Heaven Allows*]. Box 667, File 20601, Universal-International Pictures Archives. University of Southern California, Los Angeles.

Shurlock, Geoffrey. 'Letter dated 8 November 1956 from the Motion Picture Association of America's office, describing the Production Code Violations of *Tarnished Angels*'. Ts. Box 188, File 0587, Universal-International Pictures Archives. University of Southern California, Los Angeles.

Singer, Ben. *Melodrama and Modernity*. New York: Columbia University Press, 2001.

Singer, Ben. 'Modernity, Hyperstimulus, and the Rise of Popular Sensationalism'. In *Cinema and the Invention of Modern Life*, ed. Leo Charney and Vanessa Schwartz. Berkeley: University of California Press, 1995, pp. 72–99.

Sirk, Douglas. Letter to Albert Zugsmith. 19 August 1956. Ts. Box 188, File 05787, Universal-International Pictures Archives. University of Southern California, Los Angeles.

Smith, Robert E. 'Love Affairs That Always Fade'. 'Sirk Speaks'. *Bright Lights*, No. 6 (1977–8). <http://www.brightlightsfilm.com/48/sirkloveaffairs.htm> (last accessed 17 October 2005).

Sonne, Wolfgang. *Representing the State: Capital City Planning in the Early Twentieth Century*. Munich: Prestel, 2003.

Spear, Ivan. '"Magnificent Obsession" Is Destined for Top Grosses'. *Boxoffice* (8 May 1954). Box 528, File 15979, Universal-International Pictures Archives. University of Southern California, Los Angeles.

Speer, Albert. *Inside the Third Reich*. London: Weidenfeld & Nicolson, 1970.

Spengler, Oswald. 'The Soul of the City'. In *Classic Essays on the Culture of Cities*, ed. Richard Sennett. New York: Meredith Corporation, 1969, pp. 61–88.

'Spring Ball Gowns'. *Vogue* (1 March 1951), pp. 156–9.

Stern, Michael Stern. 'Sirk Speaks'. *Bright Lights,* No. 6 (1977–8). <http://www.brightlights film.com/48/sirkinterview.htm> (last accessed 17 October 2005).
Stilgoe, John R. *Borderland: Origins of the American Suburb.* New Haven: Yale University Press, 1988.
Striner, Richard. 'Art Deco: Polemics and Synthesis'. *Winterthur Portfolio,* 25 (1990), pp. 21–34.
Sugrue, Thomas. 'Crabgrass-Roots Politics: Race, Rights, and the Reaction against Liberalism in the Urban North, 1940–1964'. *The Journal of American History,* 82, No. 2 (September 1995), pp. 551–78.
Sugrue, Thomas. 'Our Town: Race, Housing, and the Soul of Suburbia [review]'. *The Journal of American History,* 84, No. 1 (June 1997), pp. 315–16.
Taylor, Francis Henry. 'Modern Art and the Dignity of Man'. *Atlantic Monthly,* 182, No. 6 (1948), pp. 30–6.
Theweleit, Klaus. *Male Fantasies,* Vol. 1. Minneapolis: University of Minnesota Press, 1987.
Theweleit, Klaus. *Male Fantasies,* Vol. 2. Minneapolis: University of Minnesota Press, 1989.
Thoreau, Henry David. *Walden and Other Writings.* New York: Bantam Books, 1962.
Tönnies, Ferdinand. *Community and Association.* London: Routledge & Kegan Paul, 1955.
Troy, Nancy. *Modernism and the Decorative Arts in France: Art Nouveau to Le Corbusier.* New Haven: Yale University Press, 1991.
'Uncredited press release [for *Magnificent Obsession*] dated 7/4/54'. Ts. Box 547, File 17479, Universal-International Pictures Archives. University of Southern California, Los Angeles.
'Universal-International Offers Award for Best Angel'. *New York Journal-American,* 22 December 1957. Box 461, File 00275, Universal-International Pictures Archives. University of Southern California, Los Angeles.
Waldman, Diane. 'The Childish, the Insane, and the Ugly: Modern Art in Popular Film and Fiction of the Forties'. In *Picture This: Media Representations of Visual Art and Artists,* ed. Philip Hayward. London: John Libbey, 1988, pp. 127–49.
Warner, Benjamin. 'Berlin – the 'Nordic Homeland' and the Corruption of Urban Spectacle'. *Architectural Design Profile,* No. 50 (1983), pp. 73–80.
Warner, Marina. *Monuments and Maidens: The Allegory of the Female Form.* London: Picador, 1985.
'We Call it: "Hollywood Provincial"'. *House Beautiful,* 84 (July/August 1942), pp. 39–40.
Weiss, David. 'Magazine and Newspaper Ideas for *Magnificent Obsession*'. Ts. Box 414, File 12352, Universal-International Pictures Archives. University of Southern California, Los Angeles.
Whyte, Iain Boyd. 'Berlin 1870–1945: An Introduction Framed by Architecture'. In *The Divided Heritage: Themes and Problems in German Modernism,* ed. Irit Rogoff. Cambridge: Cambridge University Press, 1990, pp. 223–371.
'Why the Movies are Influencing American Taste'. *House Beautiful,* 84 (July/August 1942), pp. 36–8.
Willemen, Paul. 'Distanciation and Douglas Sirk'. In *Imitation of Life,* ed. Lucy Fischer. New Brunswick, NJ: Rutgers University Press, 1991, pp. 268–72.
Willemen, Paul. 'Towards an Analysis of the Sirkian System'. In *Imitation of Life,* ed. Lucy Fischer. New Brunswick, NJ: Rutgers University Press, 1991, 273–8.
Williams, Alan. *Republic of Images: A History of French Filmmaking.* Cambridge, MA: Harvard University Press, 1992.
Williams, Linda. 'Corporealized Observers: Visual Pornographies and the Carnal Density of Vision'. In *Fugitive Images: From Photography to Video,* ed. Patrice Petro. Bloomington: Indiana University Press, 1995, pp. 3–41.

Williams, Linda. 'Film Bodies: Gender, Genre and Excess'. *Film Quarterly*, 44, No. 4 (Summer 1991), pp. 2–13.
Williams, Linda. 'Melodrama Revised'. In *Refiguring American Film Genres*, ed. Nick Browne. Los Angeles: University of California Press, 1998, pp. 42–88.
Willis, Carol. 'Drawing Towards Metropolis'. In *The Metropolis of Tomorrow*. Princeton: Princeton University Press, 1986, pp. 148–87.
Winner, Langdon. *Autonomous Technology: Technics-Out-of-Control as a Theme in Political Thought*. Cambridge, MA: MIT Press, 1977.
Wright, Frank Lloyd. 'The Art and Craft of the Machine [1901]'. In *Frank Lloyd Wright: Collected Writings*. Vol. I, ed. Bruce Brooks Pffeiffer. New York: Rizzoli, 1991, pp. 58–69.
Wright, Frank Lloyd. 'For a Democratic Architecture: A Statement by the Greatest Architect of Today'. *House Beautiful*, 95 (October 1953), pp. 316–17.
Wright, Gwendolyn. *Building the Dream: A Social History of Housing in America*. Cambridge, MA: MIT Press, 1983.
Wright, Gwendolyn. *Moralism and the Model Home: Domestic Architecture and Cultural Conflict in Chicago 1893–1913*. Chicago: Chicago University Press, 1980.
Wright, William. 'An Interview with Jackson Pollock'. In *Pollock Painting: Photographs by Hans Namuth*, ed. Barbara Rose. New York: Agrinde, 1978, no pagination.
Zweig, Stefan. 'The Monotonization of the World'. In *The Weimar Republic Source Book*, ed. Anton Kaes, Martin Jay and Edward Dimendberg. Berkeley: University of California Press, 1994, pp. 397–400.
Zuckerman, George. 'George Zuckerman on Sirk'. *Bright Lights,* No. 6 (1977–8). <http://www.brightlightsfilm.com/48/sirkzuckzug.htm> (last accessed 17 October 2005).

Index

Page numbers in italics signify illustrations and those followed by 'n' signify notes

'absorption', 13–14
Abstract Expressionism, 53
Adams, Henry, 65
Adorno, Theodor, 134, 144n
Advisory Committee on Zoning 1922, 98
African-Americans
   colour line, 6, 93–9, 109n, 110n
   Imitation of Life, 23, 76, 89–90, 101–5
All I Desire (1953), 15–18, *16*, 21, 29n
All That Heaven Allows (1955)
   American society, 22, 91–3, 173n, 176n
   colour, 40, 50–1
   European Modernism, 170–1
   Le Corbusier, 6, 174n
   Modernist architecture, 147–78, 177n
   publicity, 26
   social problems, 20–1
   utopian ideal, 55, 61n, 81
'*All That Heaven Allows*: Color, Narrative Space and Melodrama', 51
An American in Paris (1951), 52–4
American Sociological Review, 150
Architectural Record, 88–9
'Art and the Obvious', 45–6
Art Deco, 115–16, 119, 132, *133*, 136, 137n, 145n, 146n
'attentiveness', 14–15, 17, 23–4
   selfless, 17–18
   sympathetic, 46
   willed, 23
Aufbruch, 115–46
automobiles, 6, 41, 70, 75, 76, 85n, 88
Avril, Jane, 24, 32n, 54

Banham, Reyner, 88
Barry, Joseph A., 149, 150
Bassett, Edward S., 98
Baudry, Jean-Louis, 19
Baumeister, Willi, 134, *135*

Baxandall, Rosalyn, 108n
Beckmann, Max, 50
Benjamin, Walter, 65, 74, 78–9, 134–6
Berlin, 6, 26, 115–46, 141n
Berliner Börsen-Courier, 121
Berliner Dom, 122–5
Besant, Annie, 39
Betsky, Celia, 176n
Better Homes and Gardens, 75
'Beyond Cinema', 1
Biddle, George, 43–4, 49, 58n
Biette, Jean-Claude, 15
Blavatsky, H. P., 36–7, 38
Bletter, Rosemarie Haag, 119
Bloch, Ernst, 117, 125–6, 137–8n, 137n, 142n
Bourget, Jean-Loup, 36, 38
Brechtian alienation effect, 13, 18–23, 83n
Bremen Schuspielhaus productions, 7n, 19, 26
Breton, André, 53–4, 60n
Breuer, Marcel, 148
Brooks, Peter, 24
Built in USA 1932–1944, 148
Butler, William, 163–4, 165, 175–6n, 176n

Cahiers du Cinéma, 52
California Arts and Architecture, 53
Carl-Otto (character in film), 134–6, 143n
Cathedral, 46
Chagall, Marc, 50
Chamberlain, Henry G., 148
'Chocolate City, Vanilla Suburbs', 94
cinema and painting, 51–5
Cinema and Painting: How Art is Used in Film, 52–3
City of Tomorrow and Its Planning, 148, 171n
Colonial Revival
   Alan Gowans, 110n

Colonial Revival (*cont.*)
   All That Heaven Allows, 15, 92–3, 151,
     157–8, 160, 163–7
   Imitation of Life, 96, 100
   William Butler, 175–6n
Color Advisory Service of the Technicolor
   Company, 51
colour
   blue, 40–2, 49, 50–1, 155
   German Expressionism, 27, 34
   Kandinsky, Wassily, 9n, 40–3
   white, 155, 161, 164
colour line, 6, 93–107
Concerning the Spiritual in Art, 28, 40, 43,
   51
Corbett, Harvey Wiley, 139n
*Crabgrass Frontier: The Suburbanization of the
   United States*, 108n
Crary, Jonathan, 18–19, 23–4

Dalle Vacche, Angela, 52–3
Davis, Stuart, 44–5
Death and Life of Great American Cities,
   169
The Decorative Art of Today, 133, 157
Le Déjeuner sur l'herbe, 14
Deleuze, Gilles, 17, 18, 52
Denton, Nancy, 93
Devlin, Burke (character in film), 66–8, 83n,
   84n
Diderot, Denis, 13–14
Dimendberg, Edward, 88
Dobriner, William, 169
Domkirche, 122–3, 124–5
Douglas, Lloyd C., 8n, 35–6, 37, 39, 56n
Dreamplay, 7n
Duncan, Alistair, 137n
Durkheim, Émile, 121
Dutch group portraits, 14–15, 16, 18
Duthoit, Charles, 46
The Dwelling (1927), *135*

Eames, Charles and Ray chairs, 1–2, *2*, 7–8n,
   81
'*échec*', 75–6
Eisenhower's America, 21, 35
Elsaesser, Thomas, 25
Et in Arcadia Ego, 170
European Modernist architecture, 81
Evans, Bergen, 85n
Ewen, Elizabeth, 108n
*Expositions des Arts Décoratifs et Industriels
   Modernes*, 133

Falling Water (1937–9), 152, *153*
Fascism, 43–4, 79
Fascist Berlin, 115–46
Fassbinder, Rainer Werner, 16–17, 29n
Faulkner, William, 67, 69, 83n
Federal Housing Administration (FHA),
   94–5, 96
female audience, 21–2
Ferris, Hugh, 119–20
Filmkurier, 118
Final Chord (1936), 75, 80, 89, 115–37,
   140–1n, 142n, 143n, 146n
Fischer, Lucy, 21, 110n
Fisher, Philip, 120–1
Fishman, Robert, 97
Ford, Henry, 76, 78, 79
formalist 'escapism', 43–4
Foucault, Michel, 169
Frankie (character in film), 103–6, *104*
French Classical painting, 45
French Modernism, 52–3
Fried, Michael, 13–14, 18
Fritsche, Peter, 84n, 140n
*From UFA to Hollywood: Douglas Sirk
   Remembers*, 31n

Garvenberg, Charlotte (character in film),
   75, 116, 127–30, 132, 134–6, 142n,
   143n, 146n
Garvenberg, Erich (character in film), 116,
   125, 127–30, 146n
German Expressionism, 4, 5, 7n, 9n, 25–8,
   32n, 34, 80
Germany, imperial, 121–6
Gesamtkunstwerk, 1, 7n
Giedion, Sigfried, 133, 146n
Giovanni, Joseph, 7–8n
Goldberger, Paul, 96
Golitzen, Alexander, 30n
Gordon, Elizabeth, 147–9, 171n
'Gothic romances', 43, 50
Gowans, Alan, 100–1, 110n, 167, 176–7n
Greenaway, Peter, 1
Greenberg, Clement, 46–7
Greene, Theodore, 46
Gropius, Walter, 148
Groves, Clifford (character in film), 24–5
Guernica, 43–4

Hadley, Jasper (character in film), 49
Hadley, Kyle (character in film), 27–8, 75
Hadley, Marylee (character in film), 27–8, 49
Hake, Sabine, 2, 137n

Index 193

Halliday, Jon, 7n, 19, 26, 75, 83n, 137n, 174n
Hansen, Miriam, 111–12n
haptic perception, 18–23
Haralovich, Mary Beth, 51
Harper's Magazine, 43–4, 47–8, 91, 108–9n
Harvey, James, 27, 103
Has Anybody Seen My Gal? (1952), 5, 47, 50, 53, 146n
Hayward, Philip, 51–2
Henderson, Harry, 108–9n
Heynen, Hilde, 86n
Hitchcock, Henry-Russell, 147, 171n
Hitler, Adolf, 121, 122, 124–5, 141n
The Hollywood Reporter, 20
Hollywood Spotlight, 30n
Home Owners Loan Corporation (HOLC), 94–5
House Beautiful, 147–9, *153*, 158–9, 162, 169, 172n, 173n
Hudson, Rock, 20–1, 34, 158–9
Hurst, Fanny, 6, 90
Huxley, Aldous, 45–6
Huyssen, Andreas, 80

'Imaginary Metropolis', 119–20
Imitation of Life (1959), 6, 21–3, 76–8, 86n, 88–112, *104*, 110–11n
Interiors, 49
International Style, 119, 147–9, 152, 171, 172n, 173n
  All That Heaven Allows, 55, 81
  Final Chord, 136
  Magnificent Obsession, 2, 55, 81
'Is There a Picture in Your Picture Window?', 108n
Italian painting, 15

Jackson, Kenneth T., 108n, 175n, 177n
Jacobs, Jane, 169–70, 178n
Jews, 94–5
Jim Crow laws, 102–3
Johnson, Annie (character in film), 21, 23, 89–90, 94, 97, 99–102
Johnson, Delilah (character in film), 96–7
Johnson, Peola (character in film), 96–7
Johnson, Philip, 147, 148, 171n
Johnson, Sarah Jane (character in film), 23, 76–8, 89–90, 94, 97, 100–6, *104*, 110–11n
Jünger, Ernst, 6, 66, 70–4, 85n

Kaiser, Georg, 7n
Kalmus, Natalie, 51

Kandinsky, Wassily, 7n, 8n
  All That Heaven Allows, 51, 155
  colour, 9n
  Magnificent Obsession, 5, 34, 39–43, 49
  There's Always Tomorrow, 32n
  Written on the Wind, 28
Kennedy, Robert Woods, 150, 166–7
Kettlehut, Eric, 120, 139–40n
Kirby, Ron (character in film), 6, 26, 61n, 81, 92–3, 147–71, 174n, 176n, 177n
Kirchner, Ernst Ludwig, 27
Kracauer, Siegfried, 65, 78
Kriegserlebnis (war experience), 66
Kuh, Katharine, 60n
Das Kunstblatt, 133

Lang, Fritz, 80, 92, 118, 139n
Lastra, James, 55
Le Corbusier, 8n, 147–8, 167
  against *Stadtkrone* city plan, 120
  All That Heaven Allows, 156–8
  Art Deco, 133
  camera-eye, 18–19
  City of Tomorrow and Its Planning, 138–9n, 171n
  Machine Age, 6, 117, 145n, 154
  Magnificent Obsession, 2–4
  Les Maison des hommes, 3
  New York, 138
  Plan Voisin, 119
  The Radiant City, 174n
  Towards a New Architecture, 32n, 143–4n, 174n
Le Prince, Jean-Baptiste, 14
Leadbeater, C. W., 39
Lehmann, Peter, 22, 82n
Levitt, Bill, 172n
Levittown, 95, 108–9n, 172n
Life magazine, 147
'A *Life* Round Table on Modern Art', 45, 47–8, 58n
Lipsitz, George, 109n
Loos, Adolph, 133, 144n
Lured (1947), 85n
Lust for Life (1956), 54

Machine Age, 133, 145n, 147, 151, 154, 157, 170–1
machine culture, 65–82, 88
Magazine of Art, 166
Magnificent Obsession (1954)
  audience reaction, 20–1, 111n
  European Modernism, 1–3, 8n, 34–63

Magnificent Obsession (1954) (*cont.*)
   modern technology, 74, 80–1
   photographers, 26, 56–7n
   reviews, 59n
   spirituality, 34–9, *38*
   utopian ideal, 61n
Les Maison des hommes, 3–4
Malone, Dorothy, 26
Man Visible and Invisible (1902), 39
Manet, Edouard, 14
Marks, Laura, 18
Marx, Leo, 81
Massey, Douglas, 93
Meet Me in St. Louis (1944), 52
Melodrama and Modernity, 5–6
Mendelsohn, Erich, 118, 138n
Meredith, Lora (character in film), 6, 21–2, 76, 89–90, 91, 97, 99–102, 110–11n
Merrick, Bob (character in film), 21, 34–7, 41–3, 57n, 81
Metropolis (1927), 80, 92, 120
The Metropolis of Tomorrow, 119, 139n
'metropolitanism', 88–9
Meyer, Hannes, 131, 137n, 140n
Minnelli, Vincent, 52–4, 55
Miró, Joan, 27
Mock, Elizabeth, 148–9
modern technology, 74–82
modernist architecture, 147–78
modernist art, 43–51
Moffitt, Jack, 20
'monumentalism', 115–37
Morey, Anne, 21–2
Morgan, Michele, 159–60
Morley Jr, Jay, 31–2n
'The Most Beautiful City in the World', 123
Moulet, Claude (character in film), 69–70
Müller, Christian (character in film), 127–30, 140–1n
Müller, Hanna (character in film), 116–17, 126–32, 133–4, 136–7, 140–1n, 143n
Mulvey, Laura, 1, 19
Mumford, Lewis, 88–9, 90–1, 107n, 152
Murdoch, Henry (character in film), 15–18
Murdoch, Naomi (character in film), 15–18, *16*, 29n
Museum of Modern Art, 44–5, 45–6

National Conference on Housing 1921, 110n
National Housing Act 1934, 94
National Socialism, 6, 117, 123–6, 140n, 142n
Nelson, George, 8n

Neue Sachlichkeit, 80
'*Die Neue Welt*', 6, 115–37, 137n, 140n, 145n
'Neues Bauen', 117, 121, 133, 136, 148–9
'New Architecture', 117, 121, 133, 136, 148–9
'New Englandness', 163–5
'The New House', 133–4
New Mexico, 2–3, 8n, 81
'New Objectivity', 80, 117, 119, 137–8n
'New World', 6, 115–37, 137n, 140n, 145n
New York, 6, 89, 91, 97–9, 110n, 115–37
New York Art Student's League, 26
New York Committee on the City Plan, 98
New York School, 46, 53
No Room for the Groom (1952), 59n
Nolde, Emil, 27
Northern paintings, 15, 17

Obereit, Professor (character in film), 116, 127, 136, 146n
O'Keeffe, Georgia, 8n
Old Mill, 6, 26, 81, 147–71, *155*, *160–1*, 173n, 174n, 177n
Olympia, 14
optic preception, 18–23
Ord, Matt (character in film), 67–9, 71, 83n

'Pace Setter of 1954', 149, 150
Packard, Vince, 107–8n
Panofsky, Erwin, 26, 170
Pastorale Russe, 14
Peter (character in film), 115–16, 127–8, 143n
Peucker, Brigitte, 55
Phillips, Helen (character in film), 1–3, 8n, 34, 37, 39, 42–3, 61n, 81
Phillips, Wayne (character in film), 35–6, 41–3, 50, 57n
Picasso, Pablo, 43–4, 48–9, *48*
Picture This: Media Representations of Visual Art and Artists, 51–2
Plan Voisin, 119
Playtime (1967), 93
Poindexter, Thomas, 111n
Pollock, Jackson, 46, 47–8, 53, 54, 60n
'poster style', 32n
Poussin, Nicolas, 45, 170
Principles of Scientific Management, 98
Public Works of Art scheme, 44
Pullman, Bea (character in film), 96–7, 99
Purdy, Ken W., 85n
Pylon, 67, 83n

Index

Rabourdin, Dominique, 15
race relations, 6, 93–107
The Radiant City, 174n
Randolph, Edward (character in film), 21, 34–9, *38*, 41–3
Raschdorff, Julius, 122–3, 124
Rathenau, Walter, 123
religion, 35–9, 57n
Renoir, Pierre-Auguste, 54
Riegl, Alois, 13–18, 23–4, 46
Ringbom, Sixten, 39, 40
Rivera, Diego, 44
The Robe (1953), 35
Rousseau, Henri, 54
Rutsky, R. L., 80

Schäche, Wolfgang, 123–4
Schatz, Thomas, 20, 22
Schinkel, Karl, 123
Schmidt, Eckhardt, 31n, 143n
School of Paris, 46
Schumann, Laverne (character in film), 66–8, *68*, 81, 82–3n, 84n
Schumann, Roger (character in film), 66–70, *68*, 71–3, 75–6, 83n, 84n
Schlussakkord see *Final Chord*
Scott, Carey (character in film), 6, 91–3, 102, 147, 150–8, 162–71, 173n, 176n, 177n
Scott, Geoffrey, 170
Selig, Michael E., 105–6
Seurat, Georges, 24
Shakespeare, William, 26, 37
The Silver Lake, 7n
Simmel, Georg, 65
Singer, Ben, 5–6, 65–6, 82n
Sirk, Douglas
   'cinema values', 19
   Expressionist period, 39–40, 49
   German period, 6, 115
   and pictorial reception, 13–33
   versus Stahl, 93–107
   and the visual arts, 12–61
Sirk on Sirk, 20
'Sirkian system', 21
Smedley, Dr (character in film), 131–2
Smith, Washington (character in film), 131, 133–4
Sonne, Wolfgang, 123
Spain, 43–4
Speer, Albert, 122, 124
'The Spirit of Truth', 8n
spirituality, 34–61, 56n
Spuren, 117

Stadtkrone city plan, 120
Stahl, John, 6, 35, 56n, 90, 93–107, 111n
'A Standard State Zoning Enabling Act', 98
Stanwyck, Barbara, 15–17, 31–2n
The Status Seekers, 107–8n
Steiner, Rudolf, 39
Stern, Michael, 8n, 17, 37
Sternberg, Josef von, 26
Stilgoe, John, 162–3
Stoningham, 91, 93, 162–70, 176–7n
Storm of Steel, 70
Strindberg, August, 7n
Stroheim, Erich von, 26
suburban space, 88–112, 168–70
Sugrue, Thomas, 96
Surrealism, 5, 27, 53–4, 60n
Susie (character in film), 97, 99–100
Sweeney, James J., 46, 49
Sweet, Frederick A., 60n

'Tarnished Angels', 26
The Tarnished Angels (1957), 6, 66–74, *68*, 75–6, 81, 82–3n, 83n, 84n
Tati, Jacques, 93
Taylor, Francis Henry, 46
Taylor, Frederick Winslow, 76, 98
Teichmüller, Joachim, 118
'theatricality', 13–14, 18
Theory and Design in the First Machine Age, 88
Theosophical Society, 36
There's Always Tomorrow (1955), 24–5, 32n
Theweleit, Klaus, 85n
Thoreau, Henry David, 149, 156, 172n
Thought-Forms (1901), 39
Toulouse-Lautrec, Henri, 24, 32n, 54
Towards a New Architecture, 32n, 138–9n, 143–4n, 174n
Transcendental Painting Group, 8n

Über das Geistige der Kunst, 40
UFA studios, 116, 120
'Universal Mind', 38–9
Universal-International Pictures, 21, 25–6, 151, 158
University of Hamburg, 26
The Utopian Function of Art and Literature, 117

Vale, Norma (character in film), 24–5, 32n
'The Victory and Defeat of Modernism', 43–4
'Visibility Principle', 169
Vogue, 48

Volkgeist, 122
Volkshalle (People's Hall), 122

Wadkins, J. F., 160
Walden, 156, 174n, 175n
Waldman, Diane, 43–4, 45, 49, 50–1
'War and Photography', 73
Warner, Benjamin, 125
Wayne, Mitch (character in film), 28, 32n
Weekend With Father (1951), 89
Weill, Kurt, 7n
Weiss, David, 35
Werkbund exhibition, Stuttgart 1927, 134, 145–6n
'What about Modern Art and Democracy?', 44
When Ladies Meet (1941), 159
Wilhelm II, Kaiser, 122, 124–5

Willemen, Paul, 20, 21, 22
Williams, Linda, 18–19, 22
Winner, Langford, 78
'The Work of Art in the Age of Mechanical Reproduction', 79
'world city', 88–9
World War I, 26, 65–74, 80, 84n, 122
World War II, 53, 82
Wright, Frank Lloyd, 147, 150, 152, *153*, 162, 172n, 173n
Written on the Wind (1956), 27–8, 32n, 49, 74–5, 82, 89, 107n
Wyman, Jane, 20–1, 34

zoning laws, 119, 139n
Zuckerman, George, 83n
Zugsmith, Albert, 69, 83n
Zweig, Stefan, 121

EU representative:
Easy Access System Europe
Mustamäe tee 50, 10621 Tallinn, Estonia
Gpsr.requests@easproject.com

www.ingramcontent.com/pod-product-compliance
Lightning Source LLC
Chambersburg PA
CBHW051059230426
43667CB00013B/2370